ROGER STEVENSON

NOV., 1994

Anthropology of Contemporary Issues

A SERIES EDITED BY

ROGER SANJEK

Lord I'm Coming Home

EVERYDAY AESTHETICS IN TIDEWATER NORTH CAROLINA

John Forrest

with illustrations by Deborah Blincoe

Cornell University Press

Ithaca and London

First published 1988 by Cornell University Press.

International Standard Book Number (cloth) 0–8014–2146–2
International Standard Book Number (paper) 0–8014–9483–4
Library of Congress Catalog Card Number 88–47728
Printed in the United States of America
Librarians: Library of Congress cataloging information
appears on the last page of the book.

The paper in this book is acid-free and meets the guidelines for
permanence and durability of the Committee on Production Guidelines
for Book Longevity of the Council on Library Resources.

To E.C.

Contents

Preface

The interest in aesthetics in anthropology is longstanding, although attempts to develop its study have been sporadic. For perhaps two reasons, anthropologists have been reluctant to examine this area. First, definition of the subject matter has proved problematic, even within the confines of Western culture. Philosophers have argued for centuries over what constitutes an "aesthetic experience," an "aesthetic form," and so on. The attempt to find terms that have some cross-cultural validity seems, as a result, hopeless. Second, responses to aesthetic forms are personal, interior states that are notoriously difficult to fathom by ethnographic means.

Anthropologists have resolved these problems by sidestepping them. Many fieldworkers have concentrated on a single genre or artisan and by so doing largely avoided the problem of definition. Hopi dance, pygmy music, Yoruba sculpture, and other such expressions fit our intuitive (Western) sense of what an aesthetic form is and so can be studied first and placed in an analytic framework afterward. Furthermore, many theorists have found it satisfying to explore and codify the formal features of aesthetic forms—preference for straight versus curved lines in painting, smooth versus staccato rhythms in music, horizontal versus vertical extension in dance. These preferences they could correlate with the formal features of other parts of the social system without making reference to the subjective states of the people involved.

Single-genre and formal studies currently dominate aesthetic anthropology and severely limit its enormous potential. This is not to say that such investigations have been wasted, for they have produced many richly complex analyses. But there is so much more that can be achieved. My aim in this book is to set a new agenda for aesthetic anthropology by broadening the field to encompass the total aesthetic experience of a people and to venture beyond the formal and external to the affective interior.

The most obvious reason for examining the total aesthetic experience of a community is that aesthetic forms exist in an *aesthetic* context. The music of a Southern Baptist church service, as I will show, is performed in a building whose furnishings and architecture are of aesthetic significance. The music is only one part of a larger performance whole that includes drama, poetry, and oratory, and these forms in turn have wider contexts. Church architecture may be like house architecture in certain respects and unlike it in others; music making may be frowned upon outside the church. To study Baptist church music in its *social* context, the commonest starting point for single-genre and formal investigations, is therefore to miss a vital step. First the music must be situated in its aesthetic context.

The natural result of investigating the entire aesthetic realm is a reduction in interest in particular forms. To tackle every aesthetic form the way an ethnomusicologist, say, would study the music might complicate matters so much as to obscure the general picture of aesthetics in action. What I have striven to present is a greater feeling for the aesthetic experience as an everyday experience and not some rarefied and pure behavior reserved to an artistic elite. I hope to show what a fisherman sees when he peers at sunset across still water, what he tastes when he eats greasy greens with vinegar and onions for supper, and how such sights and tastes complement one another in a coherent aesthetic sensibility.

To be a participant in, as well as an observer of, local aesthetic experiences, the anthropologist needs to employ special methods of ethnographic reportage. With the exception of Chapters 2 and 3, which deal in detail with theoretical and methodological issues, this book mirrors my own experience as an ethnographer. It begins with a fictionalized account of one fisherman's day in "Tidewater," the North Carolina fishing community studied. You, the reader, get to sit in the boat with Charlie, as I did, to follow his routine, to see how he makes decisions. From the outset you are immersed in the myriad social details that the ethnographer must somehow record and make sense of. From this vantage point you can sift out the aesthetic experiences, and, most important, you can begin to see them not as quantifiable social facts but as live, affecting, subjectively real entities. This chapter, then, is designed to provide what I so often miss in ethnographies, a feel for the general course of everyday life as it is lived by the people under study before every behavior is torn apart, microanalyzed, and categorized. Even though some artifice is involved in creating a composite, fictionalized picture, I hope to suggest here that daily life can be presented reasonably directly and that the aesthetic (and other) decisions people make can be seen in an operational context.

Once I had got my bearings in the community, I began documenting and sorting data into locally meaningful categories. Hence four chapters detail the aesthetic forms in four realms of life in Tidewater: home, work, church, and leisure. The material here is, for the most part, descriptive of what I saw, with only occasional attempts at analysis. I believe it is important to understand the many and varied aesthetic forms in their own terms before one dissects them. What analysis appears in these four chapters is of a preliminary nature, and I make no attempt to incorporate comparative materials. My goal is to see aesthetic forms in their local context.

In the years that followed my fieldwork I digested what I had recorded and worked it into a pattern that I am now satisfied is coherent and does justice to the community. This analysis concludes the ethnography and leads to some general theoretical speculations that continue to guide me in new fieldwork projects. The whole, therefore, has a circular (or perhaps helical) quality, starting with all of the aesthetic forms integrated, followed by the teasing out of individual elements, and leading to a new integration, this second time analytic and abstract where the first is personal and direct.

This work would not have seen the light of day were it not for the patient but insistent encouragement of my mentor and friend James Peacock. He was instrumental in my receiving grants from the Research Foundation and the Anthropology Department of the University of North Carolina at Chapel Hill to conduct the fieldwork, which support I also gratefully acknowledge. He has read and commented on every draft of the manuscript with great care. At times when I have set this project aside in favor of others, he has gently prodded me to return to it and provided me with opportunities to present segments of my research to interested scholars. In subtle and straightforward ways he has been a generous colleague and guide.

Likewise, Deborah Blincoe has given professional and technical assistance to the project at all stages. She has worked with the manuscript at every point in its development and used her deep understanding of the subject matter to create the illustrations. In so many cases these drawings epitomize the aesthetic forms of Tidewater in ways that not only enhance the text but express what it is often impossible to convey by words alone. She also devoted great energy to specific points of analysis, particularly of the tales, providing insights from her knowledge of the relevant literature. Finally, she added significantly to the style of the whole through patient and sensitive readings of the text.

I am fortunate to have had so many commentators at the manuscript stage and am mindful that this work has progressed in recent years because of the dialogue established with these readers. In this regard I owe a special debt to Roger Sanjek, Roger Haydon, Lee Schlesinger, and Simon Ottenberg.

All anthropologists know well the debt they owe to their hosts in the field and how inadequate a few words of acknowledgment are to express the depth of knowledge and affection freely shared. I too shoulder such a happy burden and hope this work duly expresses my gratitude for a year of bountiful gifts.

JOHN FORREST

Cuddebackville, New York

Lord I'm Coming Home

[1]

The Fishing Day

It is six A.M. Charlie wakes up to morning sun and rising heat. He'd like to roll over and go back to sleep, but last night's red sky and the radio weatherman told him today's going to be hot. If he doesn't get moving, he'll soon pay for it. He grabs a cigarette from a pack on his night table. A couple of drags, and he pitches out of bed. He reaches for the work clothes he shucked off last night in a heap by the door so the fish smell won't spread. Dungarees and hip boots are all he'll need today, but he puts on a T-shirt too.

Down in the kitchen his black Labrador, Bullitt, lies by the refrigerator. Charlie pours himself a glass of milk and dumps a little in the dog's dish. He grabs his water bottle from the refrigerator. Cramming down a doughnut in two bites and clamping a second one in his teeth, he takes his cap from a nail in the wall and kicks open the screen door. Bullitt tries to edge out after him, but he knees him back inside. He would love to take the dog along, but with Bullitt nosing among the crabs and getting pinched he knows it would take him twice as long to finish.

Outside a fine mist is quickly evaporating but clings to the swamp in shallow clouds. It is hot in the sun, cold in the shade, clammy everywhere. Charlie puts his water bottle under the front seat and starts his pickup. He backs up to his workshed door. A thick swarm of yellow flies and mosquitoes attacks him as he gets out of the truck. With the engine running, he loads up his bait baskets. This morning he has frozen fat backs, and they're a poor bait fish. He'd rather have fresh spots and croakers, but he was late getting to the bait dealer last night and had to take what was left. What's worse, he could get only four bushels, and that may not be enough. He'll have to get there earlier today. Poor bait means poor crabbing. He loads the rest of his equipment: crab boxes, poling oar, and spare crab pot. He reaches in the back for the gas can and shakes it a couple of times to be double sure it has enough in it for the day. Then he climbs back in the cab and starts off down the dirt track.

Charlie drives over high ground to the drainage ditch where he built his dock last summer—duckboards laid on marshy ground, and extended on pilings a little way into the ditch. His skiff is tied to one of the pilings. He hauls all of his gear off his truck and down to the water's edge. Last week he was in a hurry to get going and stepped off the boards carrying a full bait basket. Up to his thighs in the marsh, scrambling, he'd managed to get out before he sank. Today he walks down the middle of the boards.

Before loading up he quickly scoops with a cut bleach bottle at the half-inch of brownish-green water in the skiff's stern. Then he puts the empty crab boxes in the bows and the bait boxes toward the stern. A flat-bottomed skiff rides better under power if it is trimmed light in the bows. He hooks up the gas can to the motor, slings the spare crab pot on top of the bait, drops the poling oar down by the washboards, and makes one last trip back to the truck. He pulls open the hood, flips off the battery cables, which are loose, and eases the battery out of its cradle. He carries it to the skiff and connects it to the motor. It would be nice to have two different batteries, but you can't drive two things at once.

Charlie slips the bowline off the piling, stows it inboard, and grabs the poling oar. Here in the ditch by the dock the water is too shallow for the motor. Standing in the stern he digs the blade of the poling oar into the mud and gives a gentle shove. The trick is to push just hard enough to get going but not so hard that the pole sticks in the mud. The skiff glides softly, steadily forward ahead of his strokes.

A few hundred yards and the ditch runs into a small navigation canal. Charlie stops poling and drops the outboard propeller into the water. He squeezes the rubber bulb on the gas feed line a few times to prime the engine, adjusts the choke, and pulls the starter cord. There is no sign of life, but Charlie didn't seriously expect there to be on the first try. Still, after five or six tugs there's only a sputter. He gets impatient. He gives three hard, fast pulls. On the final go the engine catches and dies. He wrenches the cord once more. The engine roars. A plume of oily blue exhaust hangs over the water and mingles with the morning mist.

He lights a cigarette and settles down on the stern transom for the chug up the canal. He'd like to rip along at full throttle, but he can't afford the speeding fine. Instead he putters, mostly staring ahead, sometimes looking into the swamp if something catches his eye. There is no breeze. Wisps of mist curl over the swamp grasses growing thick to the horizon. At the canal's edge herons dabble in the waterlilies, stopping to peer into the water or up at Charlie as he cruises by, ripples from his bow slapping the banks.

Suddenly the canal widens and dumps out into a large, open, brackish sound. Immediately Charlie throws the throttle wide open. The bow rises out of the water, and the skiff bumps and crashes along at full speed. He makes straight for the point on the distant opposite shore which is his landmark for navigation. It is a little rise, about halfway between an abandoned coast guard station and a lighthouse. Somewhere between the canal's mouth and that point is his line of pots. Navigating out here is always a bit hit-or-miss, but as long as there isn't any fog around, there are enough shore points to get your bearings by. There is no wind, the water is flat, so he makes good time. In fifteen minutes he spots his first float almost dead ahead.

Charlie cuts the throttle. With the engine idling he glides up to the first pot. Now is his time to get all gear set for smooth fishing so he can be home for lunch. He lifts a crab box to the skiff's middle transom and opens a bait basket at his feet. Bad luck. The fish have not thawed overnight. He'll have a tough time eking them out. In hopes the sun will work on the frozen fish he opens all of the baskets and does what he can to pull apart the hunks of bait. The extra work makes him sweat. He strips off his T-shirt and stuffs it in a locker under his feet. He drags out a pair of thick rubber gloves to protect his hands from the combination of water, crab claws, pot netting, and frozen fish. He pulls the spare pot toward him and begins his routine.

A crab pot is a wire-mesh box with a hinged lid that fastens with a catch. Two of the sides have funnels leading in. At the bottom is the bait trap, a wire cage closed with a rubber plug. A waterproof line about five feet long hangs from the frame of the cage. The float attached to the line's free end is marked with the owner's name. Charlie likes to use bleach bottles for floats. They are strong and show up well from a distance. He marks them with a big C S, his initials, in waterproof marker. Because crabbers are always begging them, bleach bottles are not easy to come by, so a few of his floats are milk jugs. But these break easily and have to be replaced all the time.

Charlie flips the spare pot over, jerks the plug from the bait trap, reaches between his legs for a handful of bait, stuffs it into the basket, jams the plug back. With the pot in his right hand and the float in his left, he flings the whole contraption into the water. Then he stoops to grab the float line that will haul in his first pot of the day. Five or six blue crabs scuttle along the sides and bottom of the pot. Not good, not bad. The pots will have to average more than that for him to make money on the day. This end of the line is often thin, though, so Charlie is not too worried. He pulls the plug and lets the old bait drop over the side. He opens the pot and knocks the crabs out into the crab box, reaches in and pulls loose a crab that will not shake free. He sets the pot upside down in front of him, baits it, and gives a burst on the throttle to move the boat along to the next pot, several boat lengths ahead. As he gets near it, he tosses out the baited pot and hauls up the new one.

When the whole operation is running well Charlie can cast out, haul in, empty, bait, and move on in about two minutes. Today it may take him closer to three because of the frozen bait. Since he has a hundred pots to tend, he could be on the water an hour and a half longer than usual. That means he will be late to the bait dealer again. He thinks about rushing the job along to make up time but immediately decides against it. Changing your work pattern leads to mistakes, and mistakes out here can be fatal. Two of Charlie's uncles drowned in the sound, and he has had enough near-misses to respect the water. So he visits each pot at his normal pace.

Charlie doesn't pay much attention to the world around him when he is working his pots. The regularity of the task combined with the stillness of the day are relaxing and gently mesmerizing. Three hours into the job things have begun to pick up a little. The sun, which is now scorching hot, has softened the frozen fish, making it much easier to handle. It looks like the catch will be moderate to decent. He has filled two boxes and part of a third. If it holds up at this rate, he will at least come out ahead of his costs. But the bait situation is still not good. Because the frozen fish was hard to break up at the outset, he has used too much and may run out before the end of the job. He is part way into the third bushel with fifty pots to go.

At this point in the line Charlie sees a string of floats running beside his own. These are eel pots set by a neighbor. He does not mind having eel pots close by. They do no harm to the crabbing, some people even say they are good luck, and a few times a week he runs into his friend and stops to chat for five or ten minutes. Also, with two people working the area unwanted visitors can be kept out better. If they had been crab pots, there would be trouble. It is hard enough to make a living at crabbing without someone horning in on your territory. When that happens float lines get cut, pots are robbed, and men start carrying guns in their boats. No one has tried to move in lately, but the fishing has been generally good so far this season. Still, another month may bring short hauls, and everyone will have to look out.

Charlie starts baiting the pots light, but he is worried. The fat backs are poor bait to begin with and only do a halfway decent job if they are piled into the bait basket. Thin bait leads to poor crabbing: a lot of hard work and no money to show for it. But the choice is to bait regular until he runs out and leave the last string empty or bait thin and spread the losses. He thinks the catch will be about even whichever way he does it but chooses to bait thin because he cannot stand to throw out unbaited pots.

The rest of the work goes along pretty fast, partly because baiting takes less time than before and partly because the catch is poor in places. Several pots are empty. Even with careful measuring the bait looks as if it will give out toward the end. Charlie thins the bait out more and more until he has three fish left. He puts one in each of the next three pots and moves on down the line. When the bait gives out there are only two floats in front of him, so things are not so bad. He dumps the last baited pot and hauls in. There is a tiny bit of yesterday's bait in the basket; he leaves it in and dumps out the two crabs inside. He moves on to the last float, tosses out the partly baited pot, and hauls in the remaining one. It has no bait left in it and no crabs. Charlie takes this pot and rests it in the stern, then rearranges his gear for the ride home. He stacks the empty bait baskets inside one another and pushes them in the bow, wedging them in place with the spare crab pot. Then he lifts the filled crab boxes into the stern. He has just about filled four. He stacks them two on two and sticks the fifth, empty one in front of the pile. He pulls off his gloves, puts them in the locker. He takes out his water bottle and has a long drink. Next, he puts on his T-shirt, finds his cigarettes where they have been bunched up in the sleeve, lights up, and races the motor for the ride home.

At the beginning of the journey back Charlie stands up in the stern of the boat, slightly stooped because he is tall and the throttle is low. The filled crab boxes block the flow of air, and he wants the wind and spray to cool him off. The sun is directly overhead, but the breeze from the boat's headway is pleasant. After a few minutes he sits down

[5]

so he can go faster. It feels stuffy back there, but he resists the urge to keep standing up. It will slow him down too much, and he is already late.

Back at the dock it is hot and sticky. The flies swarm around as soon as the boat pulls in. Without getting out of the skiff Charlie piles his gear on the dock. Most of the crabs slowly jostle around in the boxes, but a few quicker ones have crawled out and flopped into the bottom of the boat. He scoops them up with his bailing jug and throws them back into the blue, clacking mass. He lumbers up the duckboards with the boxes, one at a time: they weigh maybe a hundred pounds apiece. He loads the boxes on the tailgate of his truck and piles everything else helter-skelter in the truck bed. He shuts off the gas valve to the outboard and disconnects the gas can, which he stores beside the spare tire behind the cab. Finally, he disconnects the battery and reinstalls it in the truck.

Charlie drives back to the house. Even at its slowest speed, the truck sways and lurches along the deeply rutted track. He backs up to his work table beside the shed, cuts the motor, and goes into the house. The kitchen clock says 1:30. He is over an hour later than usual. Bullitt leaps around him, butting him, so Charlie bends down and rubs his head fiercely. He searches in the cupboard for a can of potted meat and a package of Nabs crackers and takes the last can of beer from the refrigerator. It is too hot to eat inside, and anyway he hates to be cooped up indoors. So he walks down to the pecan tree in the side yard with Bullitt running beside him and sits down to eat in an old battered aluminum folding chair. He flips up the ring pull top of the lunch meat, rips open the Nabs packet with his teeth, and uses the crackers to shovel the meat out of the can. Ten minutes later he is finished. He tosses the last bite of cracker to Bullitt and then pops the top on his beer and takes a sip. He lights a cigarette, picks up the beer can, and walks over to the work table where he pitches the trash into a bucket. From the shed he collects a pile of bushel baskets and lids, and brings them to the table.

The work table is about five foot square with plywood sides rising eight inches above its surface to form a wide, shallow trough. In the center are two pairs of work gloves, one canvas, the other rubber. Charlie puts on the canvas gloves first, and over them the rubber ones. Then, protected against pincers, he dumps the crabs from the boxes onto the table. They cascade in a blue/white shower and settle in a scuttling, tumbling mass. Flies whiz and swirl over them, some landing on Charlie's arms. He slaps at them sporadically as he starts to grade the crabs.

He spreads two bushel baskets at his feet, one on the left for females and the other on the right for "jimmys," with a spare crab box at the side for those that are too small for sale. Charlie sorts mostly by eye. He pulls out one or two at a time and pitches them right or left according to sex. Every tenth one or so is too close to call, so he fits its body between slots he has cut in the plywood sides of the table. There are two slots: five inches wide for females and six inches for males. If the points on the body slip into the slots the crabs are too small and wind up in the crab box.

Today he checks some he usually would toss down unmeasured. The fish dealer has been giving him a hard time lately about making up baskets with undersize crabs. Charlie knows there haven't been any small crabs in his loads. The dealer is probably just using that as an excuse to stop buying from him for the season or cut the price. The crabbing has opened up in Maryland, and Northern buyers are not coming South as often. That means only the local trade is left, and there is not enough of that to keep everyone in business. The eeling season lasts longer, but Charlie can't bring himself to fish for eels— nasty, slimy things that remind him of snakes. Also, he would have to deal direct with Yankee buyers, and he doesn't want to do that if he can help it. Anyway, who would want to eat eels except some damn Yankee? He has heard somewhere that they are shipped to Europe, and Charlie believes it. They eat all kinds of crazy things over there.

The grading takes ninety minutes. He has just about seven bushel baskets full and half a box of smalls. He wires the basket lids down tight. Then he takes off his two pairs of gloves and spreads them out in the middle of the empty table. He rummages above the dashboard of his truck for a black felt-tip to mark the basket lids with a big F or J and his own initials underneath. He loads the crabs on his truck and stores his empty boxes along with his poling oar in the shed. He opens the passenger door and Bullitt, who has been grubbing around in the bushes after chipmunks, races to jump in. Charlie climbs in beside him and turns the engine over. They make off down the swamp road toward Tidewater; Charlie lights a cigarette, and Bullitt sits up straight as he can, staring ahead through the windshield.

The five-mile swamp road is absolutely straight to the horizon, and on either side are drainage ditches formed when they threw up mounds of mud in the center to build the road on. The road is about

[7]

forty years old. Charlie remembers when coming this way meant taking the corduroy road—a floating road of lashed logs, built before they had equipment to dig the swamps. Now the road is smooth and fast. On either side swamp grasses sway as the truck passes. Otherwise all is still in every direction.

Instead of turning left down to Tate's Point where the fish dealer is, Charlie turns right and swings onto a dirt drive. He stops at the house at the end and honks the horn. After a few minutes he honks again, and his nephew Gerry walks slowly out and gets in beside Bullitt. Charlie has promised his younger sister he will help her son get started crabbing. Today he wants him along to look at some equipment for sale down at Martin's Point. Gerry has one or two pots he has fished since he was fourteen, and his father has given him a few old ones he used to use before he took a factory job. Now that Gerry has finished high school and can begin a full day's work, these are not enough. He has been guiding for bass fishermen in the sound for most of the spring and early summer, so he has a little saved to buy pots. Charlie may end up lending him the rest if the price is too high.

Next stop is a big green house back on the main road. A friend of Charlie's mother lives here, and he has been meaning for several days to stop by and see if she wants some crabs. Charlie leaves the engine running and goes to the back screen door and hollers. He hears a shout from the inside and walks in. Florence is sitting at the kitchen table peeling potatoes. The aluminum pots bubbling on the stove fill the air with thick steamy smells: a blend of greens, cornmeal, and pork fat. She is a widow and lives alone, but she always cooks the evening meal for her two daughters and their families. She is known as a good cook, never turns anyone away at mealtimes, and always has plenty to go around, with some to spare for a quick lunch the next day.

Charlie stands just inside the door shuffling his feet. "Hello, Miss Florence, how're you making out today?"

"Oh, hello, Charlie. All right, I guess. Can't complain."

"Well, I've got some small crabs on the truck I can let you have if you want 'em. I'll be glad to give you however many you want."

She grins wide. "Thank you kindly. A half a bushel'll do me just fine, and if you don't mind, could you just leave 'em outside in the shade 'til I can get to 'em." She gives him a big steamer pot to put them in and thanks him again.

Just before he leaves, Charlie hesitates. "Miss Florence, would you happen to have any spare bleach bottles around?"

[8]

"Well, I'm about finished with one, so if you care to come around next Monday, I can let you have it then."

He says he'll do that. Out in the yard he tips a bunch of crabs from the box into the steamer. He leaves the pot under a mimosa tree by the kitchen door and climbs into the truck.

Back on the main road to Tate's Point, Charlie explains to Gerry about the equipment they are going to see. Charlie doesn't know the man very well. He heard from the fish dealer he's about ready to quit fishing and take a factory job. His sons don't want to take up the business. Rather than watch good equipment rot, he'll let it go. Charlie is sure it is all decent gear. Mostly it is a question of what he wants for it and how much he is willing to bargain.

It is twenty miles from Tidewater to Tate's Point, through small towns and open farmland. The fields are several feet below the road and are cut into large squares by deep drainage ditches. The soil is a rich, loamy brown. Most of the fields have soybeans in them, already looking green and bushy, and the rest are planted in corn. Every once in a while the neatly drilled rows are interrupted by clusters of grave-stones on land rises. Each of the towns they pass through is little more than a clump of a dozen houses or so, a church, and a general store. One has a bank, another has a diner, and a third has a garage. New businesses are dotted in isolation among the farm lands: a super-market, a realtor, an ice-cream stand. As they get nearer to Tate's Point the land to the left gets swampy. Through breaks in the trees the sound appears. Before long the road is hugged up against the shore of the sound. Charlie stops at a small dirt turn-around by the sound and goes to the back of the truck to get what is left of the box of smalls. He takes them down to the water's edge and pitches them in.

Smith's Fish Market is a long, narrow, whitewashed cement block building on the edge of town. Charlie backs the truck up to a door in the back, at one end. He makes Bullitt wait in the cab while he and Gerry unload and weigh the crabs. Charlie pulls on the long sprung door handle, and the heavy, foot-thick door swings open. Inside it is chill and very dark. Charlie flips on the sixty-watt naked bulb hanging from the middle of the ceiling. He wheels a large balance-beam scale out from the wall to near the door, and he and Gerry stack four bushel baskets on the metal weighing stand. Charlie slides the counterweight on the balance beam along to the 200-lb. marker. It does not move. He edges it several notches, but still it does not move. Several more, and it falls down with a clang. He pushes it back one notch, then,

[9]

another. The beam hangs poised for a second, then falls softly down: 216 lbs. Charlie and Gerry stack the baskets against the wall. The remaining three baskets balance out at 148 lbs. They stack the three baskets by the other four and return the scale to its place. Charlie pulls a clip board from a nail by the door and on the top sheet at the bottom of a list of names writes his own name, calculates the total in the margin, doublechecks his figuring, and then writes down 364 lbs. beside his name.

Charlie and Gerry walk around the side of the building to a small storefront and walk in. A bell tinkles from the top of the door and Sam Smith, who is arranging fish filets in a refrigerated cabinet lined with shaved ice, looks up to see who has come in. He finishes stacking the fish and wipes his hands on a towel. Charlie tells Sam he has brought in 364 lbs. of crabs. Sam pulls a calculating machine toward him and punches a few buttons, then takes an invoice pad from the counter and draws up a receipt. He gives the carbon copy to Charlie, and as he hands it to him says he hopes they are all good-sized ones. Charlie says nothing and jams the receipt in his T-shirt pocket. Before leaving he introduces Gerry to Sam and tells him he is planning to take up crabbing soon. Sam nods and tells him to come by when he has some crabs to sell.

Back in the truck Charlie starts the engine and pulls the receipt from his pocket. It says: "364 lbs. crabs @ 25c. TOTAL $91." Things could be worse. The price is holding at about its best, and seven bushels is a moderate catch. But he can't expect the price to hold for too much longer. Before July is out Sam will probably be paying twenty cents, and by mid-August he could be down to fifteen. At that price it doesn't pay to go out, so the more he can make now while the price holds, the better. Still, it is hard to save much out of ninety-one dollars. Charlie clips the receipt to a wad of others fastened to a clip on the back of his sun visor, on the left-hand side, and throws the truck in gear. He will settle up with Sam at the end of the week.

Charlie turns left on the main road back to Tidewater but almost immediately pulls off at a house to the right. Charlie and Gerry get out, and this time Bullitt jumps out too and follows them down a rutted dirt track leading to a dock on the sound. At the dock two men are stacking eel and crab pots. Charlie recognizes Jo Midgett, the one who is selling the pots, but does not know the man with him.

"Hi, how're you doing?" says Charlie.

Jo spits into the water. "All right," he says. "How're you?"

"I hear you've got some pots for sale. Mind if we take a look?"

[10]

Jo shows him around several stacks of gear: a haul seine net, ten gill nets, eighty crab pots, and thirty eel pots. Charlie looks at each piece but doesn't say much. Gerry follows after him turning some of the nets over, looking at the pots. All of the equipment is in good shape. The nets don't have holes in them, and the float lines are almost new. Most of the pots look like they haven't even been used two seasons—they are not battered and have no patches in their netting.

"I made these crab pots a couple of winters ago to build things up a little bit. I was just eeling before that, but I thought I'd try crabbing to spread out some. I was using the gill nets to catch shad for bait, but I only did a little better last season than before, and this year was worse. July, bass boats ran over three of my gill nets and cut the float lines. Plus I was having to make two trips out a day—one for the pots, and one for the nets—so my gas bill was double and my motor's about done."

Charlie smokes a cigarette as he listens to Jo's story. He has heard similar tales from many people over the years, but he nods sympathetically all the same. He stamps out his cigarette stub. "What do you want for the pots?"

"I'll take three dollars apiece for the crab pots and two dollars and a half for the eel pots."

Charlie looks the pots over. "All right," he says. "I'll think about it."

Gerry has been tossing a stick in the water for Bullitt to fetch, so now the dog is streaming with water and panting hard, his tongue flapping out. Charlie makes Bullitt ride in the truck bed on the way back to Tidewater. Riding with a wet dog is all right when it is just the two of them, but three up front makes it uncomfortable. As they ride along, Charlie asks Gerry what he thinks of the equipment. Gerry allows it looked pretty good to him, and Charlie agrees. They both decide the price is too high, but if Jo will come down to two-fifty that would be reasonable. They figure they'll stop by again in a week and offer him two dollars. Charlie doesn't expect there will be many buyers this late into the season. There is no rush.

Charlie drops Gerry off at his house and then stops at the bait dealer, several hundred yards down the main road. Bill Casey has lived in Tidewater for only four years. He moved from a big city in Virginia because he likes the water and because the cost of living is low out in the swamp country. He had always come down to Tidewater to hunt and fish, so when he saw a parcel of land suitable for a trailer he leased it, moved down, and rented out his house in Virginia. For most of the day he works as a home handyman, while his wife,

Libby, takes care of the bait business. She makes no secret of her dislike for Tidewater and escapes to her old friends in Virginia on most weekends. She was active in the Ladies Auxiliary and the Women's Missionary Society back home but cannot seem to make the same kind of friends in the church in Tidewater. She went to church regularly when she first moved down. Now she has rejoined her former church and rarely attends the Tidewater church.

Bill Casey runs his bait business out of a refrigerated tractor trailer behind his house trailer. Charlie drives his truck up beside the tractor trailer and sees Bill sitting in a folding chair there in the shade. Most days when Charlie comes by there are three or four crabbers buying bait, but today he is late again and he is the only one there. "Running a little late again, ain't you, Charlie?" remarks Bill.

"Yeah. Frozen bait slowed me down."

Bill raises his eyebrows. "If I were you I'd keep it where it could thaw out better."

"Yeah, I guess I ought to. What you got left?"

Bill has three baskets of spots and croakers, and the rest are frozen fat backs. Charlie takes the three and makes it up with two baskets of fat backs. At least if they are still frozen tomorrow, he can start with the spots and croakers, and he won't have to worry about running out of bait.

As Charlie loads up the bait Bullitt sniffs at the baskets. Charlie whistles him down from the truck bed and opens the passenger door for him. Bill comes out of the trailer with the pink carbon copy of the bait invoice. Charlie gets into the cab and puts the invoice in a clip on the right-hand side of the sun visor without reading it. He knows what it says—"5 Bushels Bait @ $4. TOTAL $20." He will settle up with Bill when Sam pays him off at the end of the week.

There is not much time before supper, but Charlie decides he has a few minutes to spare and heads off down the swamp road. As soon as he has left town, he pulls off the road and takes his fly rod from the gun rack in the back of the cab, warning Bullitt to stay inside. He stands on the brink of the drainage ditch and makes a long, high arcing cast at a diagonal to the bank. Just before the spinner reaches the far bank he releases the thumb lock on the reel, and the bailer snaps in place, ending the cast and causing the spinner to plop down in the water. Charlie reels in slowly with his rod held horizontally forward. When the spinner is just about to the near bank, he lifts the tip of the rod, jerking the spinner out of the water, and casts again.

After fifteen casts he decides he will cast five more times. After five more, he casts once more for luck and then once again. He puts the rod back in the gun rack and lets Bullitt out. He finds a stick and throws it as far as he can into the ditch. Bullitt splashes into the water and swims after the stick. He mouths it gently, swims to the bank, and runs back to where Charlie is standing. He drops the stick at Charlie's feet and sits, waiting for him to throw it again. Charlie keeps the game up for ten minutes or so. Bullitt is a good retriever and likes the water. Charlie tries to keep him in shape all through the year. In the winter he earns his keep retrieving ducks, but he has to have some exercise in the summer too. Some dogs get lazy and won't retrieve at all if they are not kept in practice.

Charlie sits down on the bank to smoke a cigarette, and Bullitt runs up and down the bank snuffling in the weeds. The sun lies low over the swamp grasses and is beginning to turn blinding red. Occasional puffs of air rustle the grasses and then die out. The cigarette smoke keeps some of the insects at bay, but soon they are brave enough to withstand it and they swarm around Charlie's head and arms. When he gets tired of swatting them he calls Bullitt, and they head back to Tidewater, to Charlie's mother's house.

Charlie's mother lives in a house on the main road near the center of town. It was built in 1868 by her grandfather, Cull Kinsey, and added onto, up and out, by him and later generations. Charlie enters the house by the front door and turns right, toward the kitchen, with Bullitt close behind. On his way he checks the mail on the telephone stand. He uses his mother's post office box for convenience. He cannot always check the post office during the day, and anyway he doesn't get much mail. Today there is nothing addressed to him. Charlie's mother sits at the kitchen table, her arms folded on her bosom, staring out the window. Whenever she is working or taking a rest, she sits at one of the front windows, watching the road. She was born in this house and has lived in it all her life. Everything that has happened to her, almost, has come down that road.

Charlie's sister Jean Anne is working in the kitchen, finishing up supper under her mother's supervision. She sets the table with a knife, fork, shallow bowl, and plate at each of six places and tears off paper towels from a roll for napkins. Charlie grabs a can of dog food from the pantry at the back of the kitchen, opens it and dumps it out into one of two plastic bowls by the back door, then fills the other bowl with water. Bullitt chews down the meaty mush and then laps his water bowl dry. Charlie refills it. Jean Anne is standing at the stove keeping an eye on the pots when her husband, Frank, comes in. Charlie and Frank sit down at the table, their backs to the stove, facing the front window. Jean Anne mixes a jug of instant iced tea and

[13]

carries it to the table. Then she goes back to the stove to begin dishing up.

She spoons cornmeal dumplings from the top of the greens pot, where they have been steaming for the last hour, and arranges them on a large flat plate. Then she ladles the boiled greens into a deep, round dish, making sure that a good quantity of the pot liquor comes with them. She makes a wreath of boiled potatoes around the edge of the bowl and then fishes down into the green water in the pot for the lump of salt pork, which she places on top of it all. Adding a few more spoons of pot liquor for good measure, she places the dish of greens and dumplings in the center of the table. At this point Gerry and his younger brother, Willie, come in and sit opposite the men with their backs to the window. Mary explains to the table in general, and Charlie in particular, that Marvin Hayman, the superintendent of the Sunday School, had brought the greens over this morning. He had said he might have some work for Charlie if he wanted it, and she had told him he could probably catch him at the store tonight. She tells him she expects it has something to do with the foundation of the new preacher's house, and Charlie nods. He knows exactly what it is.

Jean Anne scoops the last three bluefish fillets out of the grease in a castiron skillet on the stove on to a plate of already cooked fish that have been keeping warm in the oven. They are nubbly and brown with a cornmeal breading. She hands the plate to her mother. She is about to sit down at her place at the foot of the table when she asks her mother if there is anything else to do. Mary says her friend Margaret across the street is doing more and more poorly, and it would probably be good to send her a bowl of greens. Jean Anne gets out a clean bowl and makes up another mess of greens and potatoes, this time without the salt pork. She covers the dish with a tea towel and carries it out the back door.

Mary takes a piece of fish and passes the dish on to Charlie, who does the same. She spoons two potatoes on to her plate and a pile of greens into her dish. She reaches down beside her for a bag that contains white onions and pulls out a large one. With a paring knife from the counter behind her she peels the onion, crosshatches it a third of the way through, and slices the dice on top of her greens. She passes the onion and knife to Charlie and reaches for the vinegar bottle to pour over the onions. Charlie dresses his greens in the same way and places onion and knife between himself and his mother. He knows the others at the table will not take raw onions, but he may have more.

Jean Anne gets to the table just as all plates are filled. Mary asks her to say grace, and she quickly recites "For these and all blessings, Lord, let us be thankful, Amen." The men pass all of the food dishes down to Jean Anne, and everyone sets to eating in silence. Charlie and Frank eat quickly and soon take second helpings of everything. The women and boys eat slower, the women taking small extra helpings of greens and fish. Mary offers Charlie and Frank more of all the dishes in turn. Frank refuses, Charlie takes a very small spoonful of greens.

As they are finishing, Jean Anne gets up and puts a full kettle of water on the stove to boil. The boys ask to be excused, and the men slide their chairs back from the table. Jean Anne clears the plates from the table, scraping the scraps into a basket under the sink. Bullitt bustles around her. Sometimes he gets the table scraps, but today there may be fish bones in them. To make up, she scoops a small piece of fish from the table and throws it at his muzzle. Meanwhile the kettle whistles, and she pours out four cups of instant coffee.

Over coffee, Jean Anne asks Charlie, "Did you all get to see them crab pots?"

"Yeah, they seemed all right. If he'll come down on the price some, Gerry ought to go ahead and get 'em."

Frank has been listening as he drinks the hot coffee. "What's he asking for 'em?" he asks now.

"Three dollars apiece. But he'd probably take two dollars and a half."

The men lapse into silence. Mary asks Jean Anne, "How's Miss Margaret making out?"

"She says she's been in bed all day. She looked poorly to me."

"Well, she sure has suffered," says Mary.

"Yes, she sure has," Jean Anne agrees. "It's real hard on the family when the cook is sick."

Coffee over, Jean Anne gets up to wash dishes. Frank moves into the living room, sits down on the couch, and looks over the evening paper. Charlie calls Bullitt, who has slumped on the floor, and leaves by the front door.

It's a short ride to the general store. Charlie pulls into the parking lot—paved with gravel and crushed bottle caps. On a bench by the door two men sit looking straight ahead. One of them is short and lean. He is V. B. Griggs, the store owner and a good friend of Charlie's: they go hunting together in the winter and fish when they can in the summer. The other man is stout with grey whiskers. He is Roy Midyett, an old-time fisherman who still looks after his nets every day. He plays Santa Claus at the annual church Christmas party, and he still reminds Charlie of Santa without the costume—even more so tonight because he is wearing red pants and a red checkered shirt. Roy hardly ever misses a night at the store, and Charlie is always glad to see him. He can tell stories nonstop that make you laugh and laugh.

V. B. stands up when he sees Charlie, insisting that Charlie take his own seat since he has to be up and down anyway to pump gas. Charlie sits down beside Roy, and Bullitt sniffs around the side of the buildings where the garbage cans are. V. B. walks off to pump gas for a blue sedan that has just pulled in. When he comes back, he leans against a freezer containing bags of ice and folds his arms. The left side of his face is lumpy and distorted: he has an enormous plug of tobacco in his cheek. No one likes to chew more than V. B. He takes his plug out only to eat and sleep, and Charlie has even caught him napping with it in his mouth.

The three men drift into a conversation about the heat and the yellow flies, and they all have a good laugh at V. B.'s story about the Zuzu flies and the state trooper. V. B. leaves again to pump gas and ends up taking care of three in a row. Meanwhile, three more men join the group at the bench: Mike Branch the barber, "Bub" Saunders and Bob Fulcher, fishermen. Roy is beginning to warm up, and soon everyone is hooting over his story about the troubles a friend of his had with a cottonmouth that wanted to get into his skiff. It reminds Charlie of the day last deer season when he was poling V. B. from one stand to another along a drainage ditch and killed eleven cottonmouths in the water with his pole.

As Roy starts in on the story of a friend who was bitten by a cottonmouth, Charlie sees Marvin Hayman, the Sunday School superintendent, drive up. Marvin is a farmer and almost never comes down to the store at night. Charlie knows Marvin has come especially to see him, so he eases himself away from the group of storytellers and goes over to greet him. The two men go inside the store. Each pulls a bottle of cola from the drink cooler, and they sit down on a bench by the store window.

Marvin explains they've had a hard time keeping the building of the new preacher's house going. They were hoping to do most of the construction using volunteer labor, but they've had trouble with some of the skilled jobs. They've dug and poured the footings but haven't found anyone yet to lay the block foundation. He knows Charlie doesn't have the time to volunteer. Marvin will pay him if he wants the job.

What he doesn't say is that getting the money to pay skilled workers has caused a crisis in the church. It had taken years of bake sales, chicken suppers, October sales, and special collections to save the money to buy the materials for the house. Inflation kept eating away the buying power of their savings each time they thought they were ready to build. A few younger members had suggested floating a loan to get things started, but this idea was quickly squashed. In its hundred-year history the church had never once been in debt, and many of the older members of the church had never held loans. The church had been built with donated materials and volunteer labor, and the old preacher's house had been bought through fund raisers. Borrowing seemed an admission of defeat. But volunteer labor was scarce and county building codes required expert interpretation, so some people had to be hired. The building fund was dry. Marvin realized they would have to take out a loan, like it or not. He had spent nights visiting executive officers and church leaders, bringing them around. Last Sunday after worship service he called an extraordinary business meeting and put the matter up for vote. Before the decision he had several key members testify their support. The motion passed unanimously, and Marvin was sent out to hire workers.

Charlie had learned the trade of mason not long after he was married. He had fished with one of his uncles since he left high school, but married life wasn't easy when a man couldn't count on his profits from one day to the next. He had apprenticed with a mason in a city forty miles away. Once he'd learned his trade, he was working jobs in towns over a wide radius. Sometimes he had to stay over on week nights, only coming home weekends. He had been married fifteen years when his wife died suddenly. He kept up masonry for two years after her death and then little by little began to take up fishing again. At first he just helped out with the winter haul seining and set a few gill nets. The break came the following spring, when he set a line of crab pots. Tending crab pots cuts out other occupations. He still takes out his masonry tools to do odd jobs around Tidewater when he is desperate for cash.

He tells Marvin he will think about the job. Charlie will have to give this matter some serious thought. He can't give up crabbing now for fear of losing good money while the prices are holding. And if he quits now for a week, Sam Smith probably won't take him back. All dealers want regular workers. On the other hand he has a personal obligation to the church. His great grandfather donated the land on which the church is built and was a charter member. His mother is president of the women's Bible class, his sister is church secretary, and her husband is a deacon. If the church could hold off on the construction a few more weeks, he might be able to take care of both commitments.

Charlie goes back outside to find that Roy is in the middle of a story

[17]

about a wildcat. He sits down to catch the end of it. Bub and Mike have gone home, and a group of boys, including Charlie's two nephews, are lounging by the ice freezer, half taking in the stories. Tales continue as the dark thickens. Finally the strong light from the store front draws too many bugs and forces the men inside.

Charlies uses the move as an excuse to get going. He pulls a can of two-stroke oil from the shelf, goes out, and drives his truck up to the pumps. He pumps the gas himself. While his truck fills, he empties the can of oil into the gas can in back. Then he fills his can, screwing the truck's gas cap on at the same time. Inside the store V. B.'s daughter, Lisa, is at the register. He flips her a quarter for the cola and tells her he has bought a can of two-stroke oil and ten dollars' worth of gas. She pulls a box of invoice books toward her and finds the one marked with Charlie's name. Charlie pulls a pack of cigarettes from the rack beside her and puts it on the counter. She writes up the invoice. He signs it, pockets the cigarettes, turns to the knot of men in the corner, says goodnight, and walks to his truck. Bullitt is sniffing the tires, waiting for him, and Charlie holds open the door for him to jump in.

The swamp road is pitch dark on the way home. The truck headlights light the column of road between the fields of swamp grasses. Once he sees a pair of dull orange points of light close to the road: a possum, probably. Frogs hop and glitter across his path. About a mile from home the music on the radio ends, the DJ announces it is 9:30, and gives the bottom-of-the-hour weather forecast. Overnight lows in the seventies, clear, mild, and humid. Tomorrow hazy, hot, and humid, highs in the low nineties, zero percent chance of rain. Extended forecast: more of the same.

Charlie pulls into his driveway and backs up to his shed. He puts the bait baskets away, then drives the truck to his back door. He takes his water bottle with him as he gets out of the cab. He pushes open the screen door and goes into the house, Bullitt right behind him. In the kitchen he turns on the cold tap, lets it run until the water is good and cold, fills up the bottle, puts it in the refrigerator. It's too hot to go to bed right away. He'll sit outside on the back step for one last cigarette. The stars are shining clear and hard. There is no breeze. Katydids argue endlessly; cicadas, spring peepers, and bullfrogs add to the din. Charlie thinks back over the day; uneventful. That suits him fine.

[2]

The Aesthetic Realm

The everyday world is filled with aesthetic experiences, yet anthropology has barely scratched the surface of this most significant area of human behavior. Part of the problem is that the philosophical basis of aesthetics is so shaky. Although philosophical investigations in aesthetics have their origins in antiquity, J. O. Urmson could write not too long ago: "Philosophers have hoed over the plot of aesthetics often enough, but the plants that they have raised thereby are pitifully weak and straggling objects. The time has therefore not yet come for tidying up some corner of the plot; it needs digging over afresh in the hope that some sturdier and more durable produce may arise, even if its health be rather rude" (1957:75). Nor is Urmson alone in his seemingly radical opinion (see, for example, Weitz 1956, 1977; Passmore 1951; Kennick 1958; Aschenbrenner 1959; and Ziff 1984). If after nearly three millennia theory and method in aesthetics are still in the starting blocks, then rational inquiry seems doomed. But these modern dissenters provide the anthropologist with an important lead. Many are inclined to abandon as unanswerable, absurd, meaningless, or trivial the ageold question of what an aesthetic form *is* and instead inquire into what an aesthetic form *does* (see Tejera 1965).

I have two relatively modest goals for this book. The first is to document the entire aesthetic sphere of a community in all of its myriad details. The second is to give some account of what the people in the community do with their aesthetic forms. The larger aim is to see how the aesthetics of everyday life works as a system, how aesthetic forms work in harness, and how people manipulate the aesthetic sphere to achieve desired outcomes.

Almost inevitably the first question is the definition of "aesthetic."

[19]

If the first ethnographic task is to document aesthetic forms or experiences, then presumably the fieldworker should be able to delineate the field. But this is precisely the mess the philosophers got themselves into. To attempt a definition of "aesthetic" at the beginning of the investigation is to embark on theory prematurely and inappropriately. Instead of rigorous definitions, all we need at this stage is a set of signposts to point us in the right direction.

Attempts by aestheticians to give rigid definitions of *aesthetic form, aesthetic experience, aesthetic genre, art*, and so forth have repeatedly failed. (See Maquet 1986, Merriam 1964:259–76, and D'Azevedo 1958 for useful discussions of the philosophical problems as they relate specifically to anthropology. Dickie 1971 and Redfern 1983 provide concise reviews of the philosophical literature.) One half of the problem lies within the very nature of aesthetics: as it is a creative sphere, new forms repeatedly arise to challenge old notions. In technical terms, *aesthetic form* is not a closed concept—that which may be rigorously delineated by definition or enumeration or both (Weitz 1956). "The sonnets of Shakespeare," for example, is a closed concept bounded either by a set of necessary and sufficient conditions (sonnet form, written by William Shakespeare, and so on) or by simple enumeration (numbers 1–154). *Aesthetic form* is inherently an open concept and cannot be defined in terms of necessary and sufficient conditions.

The other half of the problem is that definitions generate theory prior to investigation of objects and behaviors. They tend to define aesthetic forms and experiences in terms of emotion, symbolism, referential meaning, expression, creativity, or formal relationships so as firmly to lodge all conclusions of subsequent investigations in the definitions. The charge of circularity is often and accurately aimed at aestheticians.

Morris Weitz has recommended a new program that avoids definition and theory as the first steps (Weitz 1956:176). He follows a line of reasoning proposed by Ludwig Wittgenstein in *Philosophical Investigations* (1953, pt. 1, secs. 65–77). Wittgenstein argues that the term *game* (like *art*) cannot be rigorously defined. When we begin to list all of the games we know, we find it increasingly difficult to find a feature or group of features common to them all which can be used as definitive. Instead:

We see a complicated network of similarities overlapping and criss-crossing: sometimes overall similarities of detail (# 65).

I can think of no better expression to characterize these similarities than "family resemblances"; for the various resemblances between members of a family: build, features, colour of eyes, gait, temperament, etc., etc. overlap and criss-cross in the same way.—And I shall say: "games" form a family (# 67).

Similarly Weitz argues that instead of trying to define *art* one should attempt to characterize it by first enumerating examples of objects people generally agree are art and then extrapolating from them to those objects about which some doubt exists. From these enumerations may arise empirical generalizations, that is, characteristics that make up the family resemblances in the "art family." These are not universal generalizations, nor are they necessary and sufficient conditions. It is not necessary for an object to have all of them to be designated *art*.

This book provides an enumeration of aesthetic forms in a community, so to begin the listing here is unwarranted. It is possible, however, to provide a few preliminary, empirical generalizations concerning aesthetic forms to act as orienting concepts. Aesthetic forms are:

1. Capable of sensory perception.
2. Open to judgments based on taste.
3. Capable of affecting the perceiver.
4. Capable of disinterested appreciation.

At this stage of the investigation these generalizations are rough aids in orientation and may or may not provide the basis of family resemblances later. They are useful because they preserve some of the essential characteristics of aesthetic inquiry from the past three thousand years and therefore conform to relatively common understandings of the meaning of *aesthetic*. But they do not constitute a rigid definition for determining what is and is not aesthetic. Nor are they complete descriptions of aesthetic forms. Aesthetic forms may have many more features, but these few are sufficient for initial orientation.

Why are these generalizations appropriate starting points? After all, one of the most serious criticisms of the "family resemblances" method asks why one set of resemblances should be preferred to any other (Mandelbaum 1965). What follows is not meant as a review of the history of aesthetics, nor as a full-scale review of the generalizations, which is outside the scope of this work. (Redfern 1983 provides a good general overview of the key issues. For recent critiques of the Wittgensteinian method see Carroll 1986 and Eldridge 1987.)

The word *aesthetic* is derived from the Greek adjective *aisthetikos,* "capable of sensory perception." In Platonic philosophy the distinction between the *aestheta,* entities perceptible to the senses, and the *noeta,* entities knowable through the mind, is of paramount importance. In the well-known similes of the Cave, the Sun, and the Divided Line in Books 6 and 7 of the *Republic,* Plato sharply distinguishes between the physical world and the intelligible world, the former appreciated by the senses and subject to error, the latter appreciated by the mind and free from error. Although since classical times the term *aesthetic* has been more narrowly defined, "being open to sensory appreciation" is still one of its fundamental semantic components.

In his *Primitive Art,* Franz Boas includes under the rubric *aesthetic* forms that appeal to all the senses (1927:9–10). At the outset he claims that "forms that appeal to the eye, sequences of tones and forms of speech which please the ear, [and] impressions that appeal to the senses of smell, taste and touch" may all have aesthetic value.

The word *aesthetic* took on an additional meaning when Alexander Baumgarten suggested in *Reflections on Poetry* that "aesthetics" serve as a synonym for "the philosophy of taste" (1735). When added to the old Greek word, this new meaning considerably refined the definition and established a program of inquiry that is alive today. Are aesthetic tastes universal? cultural? idiosyncratic? Are they based on rational principles? Are they quantifiable? Are they reducible to formal properties of aesthetic objects? These questions have been of prime importance in aesthetics since Baumgarten's day.

In this context *taste* does not refer to idiosyncratic likes and dislikes of individuals alone. It is a complex term. *Taste* may involve deep critical appraisal that can be shared or may be superficial and personal. The former is closer to the eighteenth-century notion, so that it is appropriate to say that aesthetic forms are open to criticism in all senses of the term.

The debate concerning the nature of aesthetic taste prompted some philosophers to consider aesthetic experiences as based on feelings, or affect, even though these scholars often fundamentally disagreed as to what this assertion implied for the possibility of developing a rational theory of taste (compare, for example, Hutcheson 1725 and Kant 1790). These speculations were taken up by the nineteenth-century Romantics and recast into a familiar theory of aesthetics in which affect is of primary significance (e.g., Arnold 1865, Carlyle 1828, Wordsworth 1800). The view of aesthetic forms as affecting is found very commonly in anthropology (e.g., Boas 1927, Armstrong 1971, Mills 1957) and frequently used as the starting point of analysis.

Finally, the debate concerning aesthetic tastes also spawned the notion that there is a way of experiencing forms which is uniquely aesthetic and is marked by an attitude of disinterested contemplation. In essence the form is appreciated for its own sake alone and not because of any utility or instrumentality it may have. This approach is commonplace and stands behind such catchphrases as "art for art's sake." One could, for example, view the smooth, hard curve of a well-crafted chef's knife with enjoyment purely for its own sake and not with respect to its capacity to chop onions efficiently. Such an experience is commonly considered to be aesthetic by philosophers and anthropologists alike (see Maquet 1986, Osborne 1970, Dickie 1971).

This very brief discursus is not meant to assert that my generalizations concerning the term *aesthetic* have some kind of magical, a priori validity because of historical precedents. My intention is simply to show that they point in the right direction and do not in the process apply some arcane, obscure, or narrowly technical meaning to the concept *aesthetic*. As I have already argued, it is pointless to begin an analysis of aesthetics by defining the subject matter in an idiosyncratic manner.

These generalizations help us distinguish the aesthetic and the non-aesthetic, and a few examples will be instructive, provided it is borne in mind that this process cannot be conducted mechanically: the generalizations are not necessary and sufficient conditions. New cases may arise that require us to add further generalizations or admit of exceptions. This is the strength of a family resemblances approach.

The taste of raw onions is aesthetic. It is perceptible to the senses, some people like it and others do not, it can arouse pleasurable feelings, and it can be savored without concern for the good or harm the onions are doing the eater. The look of a sunset is aesthetic. It is visible, one may or may not like any or all sunsets, it can be moving, and it can be viewed without concern for meteorological portents and the like. Similarly, the way a garden is laid out, the way a house is painted, the look of a duck decoy, the smell of fried chicken, all are aesthetic.

On the other hand, certain things are clearly not aesthetic. The color of the studs that frame a house is not an aesthetic aspect of the house. The studs are not visible, the color is hardly a matter of taste, and it is difficult to conceive of the chosen color arousing feelings through contemplation.

So far the discussion has been rather more philosophical than anthropological and has been cast in terms of the abstract potential of things as opposed to concrete behavior that can be studied ethnographically. This is so because the generalizations are signposts for the ethnographer, indicating possible starting points for observation. As soon as the ethnographer observes people going about their daily lives, however, a new dimension is added. In this context the aesthetic potential of an object may or may not be realized. The look of a sunset can be aesthetic, but farmers in a particular town may never look at a sunset without concerning themselves with what they believe it predicts for the next day's weather. So the ethnographer starts to document what has the potential to be aesthetic experiences but must then decide whether particular experiences are aesthetic or not. This decision necessitates getting to know the subjective states of individuals, which is notoriously difficult (some would say impossible) and is perhaps the single most important reason why aesthetic anthropology has not attracted consistent interest.

A truly anthropological investigation of aesthetics, then, must concern itself both with the range of entities that have the potential to be contemplated aesthetically and with the reasons why some are and some are not. These are natural steps in explaining what the aesthetic experience does for individuals or communities. To take an example from my own fieldwork, fishermen in the community of Tidewater never view their boats in a disinterested fashion. The look of a boat is potentially aesthetic, but that potential is never realized. An understanding of why fishermen choose not to view their boats aesthetically is vital for comprehending their general worldview and gives us a context for those objects, such as duck decoys, which they do view aesthetically. Because of these observed behaviors the ethnographer is justified in concluding that *for this community* decoys are aesthetic forms whereas boats are not.

It may seem tempting to simplify matters by dispensing with the notion of *aesthetic form* and concentrating exclusively on *aesthetic behavior,* because the study seems to depend on the ways in which people relate to entities rather than on qualities inherent in the entities themselves. It is certainly true that entities are not by definition aesthetic and that the generalizations regarding the aesthetic status of entities concern how people may relate to these entities. But aesthetic

[24]

forms are still aesthetic forms when they are not being viewed aesthetically, and people manipulate them for a variety of ends (aesthetic and nonaesthetic) knowing they are aesthetic forms even though the act of manipulation is not an aesthetic experience. Hanging a painting in a room may involve functional considerations such that in the process of hanging, the painting is not viewed aesthetically at all. But it is being hung with the full knowledge it is an aesthetic object that will be viewed aesthetically at some later date. The person hanging the painting is responding to its potential as an aesthetic object and not directly experiencing it in aesthetic terms. Thus an exclusive focus on aesthetic experiences confines ethnographic investigation too narrowly. To discover when people have the opportunity for aesthetic experiences but decline to take it can be enlightening and enrich our understanding of aesthetic choices. Such analysis is possible only if we begin by asserting that some forms have the potential to be viewed aesthetically, that is, they are aesthetic forms.

I have deliberately chosen to work in aesthetics rather than art for several reasons. The terms are often confused in anthropological, philosophical, and popular writing, but they can be distinguished, thereby clarifying discussion considerably. *Art work* is a subset of the category *aesthetic form:* all art works are aesthetic forms but not all aesthetic forms are art works. An art work is an object or form whose primary (or sole) purpose is to be contemplated aesthetically (see Carroll 1986 for a discussion of the philosophical issues involved). Some works—a sculpture, painting, sonata, play—are art because they were consciously created as such, and they may be called "art by destination" (Malraux 1967). Other works are art even though they were not expressly created as such because they have been placed in a context that forces or encourages a viewer or audience to overlook their original purpose and instead contemplate them aesthetically. Such works may be called "art by metamorphosis" (Malraux 1967). A typewriter in a glass case in a museum is art by metamorphosis. Although the machine may type perfectly well, the museumgoer must ignore that function and derive pleasure by dispassionately observing line, form, color, and so forth. Whether a work is art by destination or art by metamorphosis, we in the West recognize it as art by a number of means, including the way in which it is presented or framed. A sculpture may be framed by a glass case, a classical sonata is framed by stylized behaviors such as tuning, bows, and applause. Museums and concert halls are not everyday fare for most Westerners, however, so that to define aesthetic anthropology in terms of art is to narrow the scope of investigation to the point of excluding the majority of aesthetic experiences.

A considerable number of anthropological investigations into aesthetics, like their philosophical counterparts, have tended to focus on *art* and have concerned themselves with questions of framing, presentation, criticism, and the like (see, for example, Boas 1927, Fischer 1961, Otten 1971, Jopling 1971). The problem with this approach, as many anthropologists have noted, is that the category *art* meaning "work whose primary purpose is to be contemplated aesthetically" seems to be a predominantly Western concept (see Maquet 1986, D'Azevedo 1973). What is called "primitive art" or "non-Western art" in the anthropological literature are forms that do not function exclusively or even primarily as aesthetic entities. A Balinese mask may owe its form as much to ritual, religious, or magical considerations as to aesthetic concerns. Are we justified in calling the mask "art"? Jacques Maquet (1986) has explored this problem at length, and he concludes that the term "art" is justified because it is possible to identify in many non-Western cultures behaviors that are analogous to what we in the West consider important for defining an art work, namely, appropriate framing, criticism based on good form, disinterested contemplation, and so on. I am nonetheless concerned that a focus on *art* limits the sphere of study and discourse.

Even in the West, art works are a very small subset of what I call aesthetic forms. To limit analysis to art is to claim that in some way one kind of aesthetic experience is special. This potentially elitist argument has brought some anthropologists to argue for the expansion of the term *art* to include a much wider variety of aesthetic forms. Boas, for example, states that a "composition of scents, a gastronomical repast may be called works of art provided they excite pleasurable sensations" (1927:10), although he adds the following to expand his definition: "When the technical treatment has attained a certain standard of excellence, when the control of the processes involved is such that certain typical forms are produced, we call the process an art, and however simple the forms may be, they may be judged from the point of view of formal perfection; industrial pursuits such as cutting, carving, moulding, weaving; as well as singing, dancing and cooking are capable of attaining technical excellence and fixed forms" (1927:10). Such a broadening of the definition of *art* has a clear appeal for those troubled by the potentially elitist connotations of the term. After all, the word carries with it notions of approval, so that to call a work "art" is to give it value in a prestigious sphere. Quilts, duck decoys, dance masks, decorated pots can be called "folk art" or "primitive art" and thereby, at least nominally, accorded the rights and privileges of a Matisse (that is, laying aside the condescension inherent in the terms "primitive" and "folk"). Though I am sympathetic to this social cause, I believe the confusion that results from redefining *art* seriously impedes analysis of aesthetics.

A pot used for carrying water may be highly decorated, but no amount of aesthetic elaboration can alter the fact that the pot is an object with a utilitarian purpose. As such it is fundamentally different from a ceramic sculpture that has no utilitarian purpose. In the interest of accurate ethnographic reportage, if for no other reason, we ought to keep the categories distinct. This distinction does not summarily exclude quilts and duck decoys from the category *art*. It is quite conceivable (see Forrest 1983) that duck decoys are made and used almost exclusively as objects of aesthetic appreciation and deserve to be called "art" in the conventional sense. Their supposed utility may screen their basic aesthetic purpose, but only careful ethnographic observation will reveal the fact.

Beyond the need to report one's fieldwork experiences precisely is a more obvious reason for not expanding the term *art* endlessly. Although few if any scholars would recommend the notion, the term *art* could hypothetically be expanded to include all aesthetic forms, certainly solving the problem of elitism but making two terms serve the same function and leaving unmarked the category of art for art's sake. This redefinition also entails the inclusion under the rubric *art* of sunsets, storms at sea, bird songs, the smell of a rose; most analysts for a variety of theoretical reasons want to exclude natural phenomena from consideration as art (not least because *art* and *artifact* are closely related semantically and etymologically). By omitting natural phenomena from the definition, however, the observer either ignores an important set of aesthetic experiences or else documents all aesthetic experiences but arbitrarily distinguishes between those which are art and those which are not. In the first case important data are lost, and in the second the observer ends up sorting field data into two piles because of preconceived categories that may or may not have any local meaning. Any other expansion or contraction of the term *art* runs the same risk.

The simple solution, which I have adopted, is not to think in terms of art at all. Freed from categorical assumptions, I claim the widest possible observation of aesthetic forms and experiences. Such an approach might well be adopted throughout aesthetic anthropology. Af-

[27]

ter all, many ethnographers are interested in aesthetics rather than art and waste a good deal of theoretical energy justifying their subject matter as art when what they really want to discuss are good form, critical perspectives, disinterested contemplation, technical complexity, creativity—all of which can be discussed adequately without reference to art.

Another problem is the tendency to think in terms of conventional Western art genres, such as music, dance, drama, sculpture, and poetry, and to specialize in the analysis of one only. Such specialization entails an unfortunate limitation. To undertake a cross-cultural analysis of music, for instance, requires considerable technical sophistication. The fieldworker must have comprehensive ear training, a thorough grounding in general music theory, and a deep understanding of and sensitivity to musical forms unusual in Western music, such as microtones, polyrhythms, and gapped scales. In addition, recording and documentation require special training, all of this to be absorbed on top of general anthropological theory and method. Given such stringent requirements, ethnomusicology has produced many penetrating insights into aesthetic behavior (for an overview see Merriam 1964). However, these insights come at a cost.

There is no reason to suppose that the aesthetics of music is an isolated cultural category. Even in the West music is inextricably linked to language (in song) and movement (in dance), and it may serve as a frame or background for a variety of aesthetic and non-aesthetic activities. A focus on music alone may miss important associations between aesthetic forms (see Brenneis 1987). Similar problems arise in any single-genre analysis.

A partial solution can be found in a multigenre approach, as Boas proposed in *Primitive Art* (1927). Such studies are rare but have been attempted periodically (Armstrong 1971, Price and Price 1980, Price 1984). Even multigenre approaches, no matter how catholic, miss some of the aesthetic forms and experiences in the community under study. I know of none that deals with the aesthetics of the natural environment, for example. Yet how carvers view living plants may be of fundamental importance to how they carve plants. In short, I believe that nothing less than a survey of the entire aesthetic realm of a community can provide an aesthetic context comprehensive enough for the situating of individual aesthetic experiences.

No one has attempted an ethnography of the entire aesthetic realm of a community, although many may have contemplated it. The task is made immensely difficult by compounding problems. First, the aesthetic realm has resisted attempts to delimit and conceptualize it adequately. Second, the range of aesthetic experiences in even a small community is potentially enormous. The sheer size of the aesthetic realm presents the fieldworker with a hard task even without other theoretical or methodological complications. The diversity of the materials requires the fieldworker to master a whole battery of notation and documentation techniques and to be sensitive to nuances in the forms of entities as different as fried fish and the tango. Yet it is precisely because the aesthetic realm is so vast and omnipresent that it ought to be a major concern in anthropology.

Warren D'Azevedo gives a summary history of aesthetic anthropology in *The Traditional Artist in African Societies* (1973:1–14). Here I want to point out two approaches that have received wide attention and that bear on the methods I employed: quantitative investigations and "symbolic" studies.

Quantitative investigations into aesthetic phenomena were for a time very popular and promised significant insights into the relationships between aesthetic value and social structure. Much of the impetus for this research came from the culture and personality school—anthropologists concerned with the interplay between individual psychology and the culture the individuals were raised in.

Herbert Barry (1957) sought statistically rigorous relationships between the formal characteristics of "works of graphic art" from thirty societies and the severity of socialization of children in those societies as measured on a scale developed by John Whiting and Irvin Child (1953). Barry took eleven "art variables" such as "presence of sharp figures," "presence of curved lines," and "representativeness of design" and graded ten objects from each society on a seven-point scale for each variable. He formally compared these results with the Whiting and Child scale and tested for statistically significant correlations using standard methods. His main finding was a strong positive correlation between complexity of design and severity of socialization. Other studies followed Barry's lead (Fischer 1961, Lomax 1968), finding a variety of correlations in many media. Fischer, for example, tested a host of social variables, such as degree of egalitarianism, male solidarity in residence, marriage types, against a list of design variables similar to Barry's. By broadening the social variables he was able to find many more correlations. Lomax and his coworkers have done the same for music and dance.

These studies are suggestive, providing fieldworkers with new avenues to explore. However, their results do not appear to serve the primary needs of inquiry into the nature of aesthetics, because the methodology used to develop codable variables ends up eliminating from study what is aesthetic about aesthetic forms. The variables must of necessity deal with quantifiable, scalable data, which means choosing objectifiable, formal aspects of objects for analysis. Two cultures will be assessed as similar if selected objects from both show roughly the same number of straight lines. The affective states created by these lines, their local interpretation and criticism, and their relationship to other design elements are not considered. Thus, fundamental aesthetic qualities of the lines are ignored. What is more, the investigators tend to use museum objects, commercial recordings, and the like to build a database without concern for the status of the entities as aesthetic forms in their local environment. A mask is "art" because it is treated as such by a museum, whatever its function in the culture of origin.

The basic problem with these approaches is that aesthetic forms are by nature subject to lack of agreement. This lack of agreement is the very heart of criticism that is fundamental to aesthetic forms. Quantitative studies either study those aspects of aesthetic forms which are indisputable, "this line is straight"—in which case they are not studying aesthetics because the matter is not open to judgment—or else they *are* studying aspects upon which people disagree—in which case they have no business quantifying them.

Lack of agreement in different cultures (rather than elements of design) has received very little attention in quantitative studies. Irvin Child and Leon Siroto (1965) opened this field by asking members of BaKwele society and art experts in New Haven to rate thirty-nine BaKwele masks. The results were not fully conclusive but indicated that although the general ratings of the two cultures did not agree, the ratings of experts did. Previous psychological studies had failed to show such agreement because they had not isolated the responses of expert critics (Lawlor 1955, McElroy 1952).

This procedure may prove useful in directing the attention of fieldworkers, but I am concerned about the general validity of its elicitation methods. If an informant is looking at an aesthetic form for the purposes of a survey (and perhaps being paid for services rendered), can it be said that he or she is viewing the form in a disinterested manner? Such experiments may prevent the informant from engaging in aesthetic behavior or may elicit responses according to predefined notions of aesthetic criticism. I take this issue up again when dealing with my own fieldwork procedures.

[30]

The second set of approaches to aesthetic materials can be styled "symbolic," although no single rubric can encompass the range of studies involved without oversimplifying. Both James Peacock (1975: 129–153) and Hugh Duncan (1969:47–98) provide penetrating insights into the use of symbolic theory in the anthropological analysis of aesthetics.

It is commonplace to hear aesthetic forms referred to as "forms of expression" or "modes of communication" and to leap from these (controversial) assumptions to think of aesthetic forms as symbolic. By this analysis, aesthetic forms are a language that requires only the appropriate dictionaries and grammar books for adequate translation.

One line of action begins by identifying the units of the aesthetic language under consideration and then examines the structures into which they fit. It follows a well-established mode of linguistic analysis which begins by establishing units of sound (phonemes) and meaning (morphemes) through some form of contrastive opposition and then examines the structures that can be built from them (see Hockett 1958). Alan Dundes (1964), for example, breaks folktales into minimal narrative units (motifemes) and shows how these units are built up into logical narrative structures. Similar methods may be found in the investigation of dance (Kaeppler 1967), artifacts (Deetz 1967), and architecture (Glassie 1975, Preziosi 1979). General systems of signs or symbols have been explored at great length by Claude Lévi-Strauss (1963, 1966, 1969), Roland Barthes (1967, 1972), Edmund Leach (1976), and Dan Sperber (1975), and these works frequently allude to aesthetic forms. The theoretical power and shortcomings of these models are well-known. Indeed, in the final chapter of this book I provide a structural analysis that superficially shares features with the works of these scholars. The points of divergence are of fundamental importance, however, though at this stage I simply give some general guidelines to mark my position.

There is no question aesthetic forms may act as symbols, and when they do so the perspectives of the semiotician and semiologist can provide many insights (see Maquet 1986:93–117 for an outline of the semiotic position on aesthetics). But treating aesthetic forms as signs, icons, or symbols exclusively may limit interpretation in several ways.

A symbol, by definition, stands for something else. Conventionally a symbol is called a *signifier* and what it stands for, the *signified* (see Leach 1976 on terminology). Clearly, however, an aesthetic form need not have a signified. As Merriam (1964:229–58) points out, it is difficult to see how most music in the Western tradition can be said to signify anything. Music may evoke various affective states without signifying them (which would not necessarily evoke them, anyway) and without signifying other objects that would evoke them. Also, some categories of aesthetic forms, natural objects for example, are not symbols until deliberately cast as such. And even if an aesthetic form does have symbolic aspects or as a whole may be treated as a symbol, the recognition of assorted signifieds does not provide an exhaustive understanding of the form because the form can still be appreciated without consideration of the signifieds. The Statue of Liberty is burdened with multilayered symbolism, but it can still be viewed in isolation from all these symbols.

Treating aesthetic forms as symbols, and especially treating them as languagelike, presupposes that they stand as intermediaries between two communicators. As Armstrong (1971) has amply demonstrated, however, we have no reason to think of aesthetic forms as conveyors of meaning from one person to another: we may respond directly to them and need not try to understand what they communicate from someone else. It is possible to establish a relationship directly with an aesthetic form without wondering what another person is saying through the form. Again, this point is obvious in the case of natural phenomena, and one can extend one's experience from these to other aesthetic forms.

Those who take a symbolic approach to aesthetic forms find it hard to break away from a content analysis because symbolic interpretation often entails looking for signified or referential meaning—that is, content. But aesthetic forms have form, and their form is of vital importance (see Alland 1977, 1983). Some scholars, notably Lévi-Strauss, overlook form when convenient: his analysis of the Oedipus story is a classic example (1963:206–231). Even when symbolic form is given some attention, it may still be treated as a vehicle for communication and not as an aspect of an object worthy of discussion without respect to signification. Rather than conveying meaning, however, aesthetic form may be identical with its meaning. The harmonious juxtaposition of shapes in a painting does not simply *represent* order, it *is* order.

The basic idea in philosophy that a work can be divided into its form (relationships of elements in the medium employed) and content (what it represents) can be traced to Plato and found detailed expression in the aesthetic treatises of Kant (1790). Thus a painting, by this analysis, may have aspects of form (use of color, arrangements of shapes, surface texture) and content (the Crucifixion, the Birth of Venus).

Formalists took the form/content distinction to be vital in understanding a work aesthetically, arguing that aesthetic judgments appropriately lay in the appraisal of form alone; content was not relevant. Roger Fry (1920), for example, speaks of "mediumistic" values as those suitable for discussion in aesthetic terms. This position (see, for example, Bell 1914, Parker 1926, Eichenbaum 1926) was responsible in large measure for the later development of several schools of structuralism.

Many philosophers have nonetheless been uncomfortable with the form/content distinction (see, for example, Weitz 1950, Ransom 1941, Brooks 1947, Blackmur 1952, Tate 1968, Kaplan 1954, and Vivas and Krieger 1953). First, the distinction is not applicable to all works. It makes some sense when applied to figurative painting, literature, and the like but has little or no value when discussing music or smells. Second, there is no analytic need to divide aspects of a work in this fashion, and to do so often involves wrangling over strict definitions. It is much simpler to talk of various aspects, such as shape, size, feel, color, loudness, hardness, physical composition, referential meaning, and iconic references. (It is still occasionally convenient to refer to manipulation of the medium in terms of "formal" qualities, but the reference is now simply shorthand and not a strictly defined analytic term.)

The fact that the form/content distinction does not work in aesthetics is an important reason for keeping aesthetic and symbolic analysis distinct. A symbol has, by definition, a form and a content. Without content it is not a symbol, and much symbolic analysis rests on preserving the form/content distinction (for an informative debate see Morris 1939 and Price 1953).

I advocate, therefore, that we treat aesthetic forms as aesthetic forms. Quantitative and symbolic methods have been extremely powerful, but their use can direct attention away from aesthetics as such. My aim here is primarily to serve the needs of aesthetic forms and to search for bridges to other methods of analysis only when necessary to deepen the understanding of aesthetics.

[3]

The Field Site

To my knowledge no one has attempted an ethnography of *all* of the aesthetics of a community. Although the task may appear formidable, it seems an obvious exercise from which to begin building genuinely anthropological theories of aesthetics. But to be truly valuable such a study must at least attempt to be exhaustive, to document the profound and the trivial, the rare and the commonplace. It must not be limited by conventional notions of art and beauty or by traditional fieldwork practices. It must cast its net as widely and as dispassionately as possible. These aspirations made the selection of a field site a particularly demanding first exercise.

For a new kind of fieldwork, it is tempting to argue, one place is as good as another. In a general sense this is true, and I hope this study is the first of many such ethnographies. However, for an initial field trial I wished to limit obvious difficulties in order to make the task manageable. To this end I sought a community that was small, well-established, relatively isolated, and newly undergoing change through an influx of outsiders.

I looked for a small community so that I could get to know most, if not all, of the people in it and have a reasonable chance of documenting all of their aesthetic forms and activities. In the course of a year I hoped to participate in the full gamut of the activities of young and old, men and women, and to record and photograph aesthetic forms in as much detail as possible. A community of three hundred to five hundred inhabitants seemed ideal for these purposes.

It was also important to me that the community had been settled long enough for a range of social, political, religious, and economic networks to have established themselves. In such a community aesthetic forms could be observed in a variety of settings and circumstances, ensuring that the question of what aesthetic forms do would not be unduly limited by the absence of particular social institutions. At the other extreme, however, I did not wish to investigate a community too rigorously defined by a limited set of externally imposed criteria, such as political or postal districts, lest these boundaries and the agents that had created them obscure the aesthetic. Ideally, then, the community would be old and defined in terms of local categories.

Relative isolation was important to control to some extent the factors influencing aesthetics and aesthetic choices. The perfect world of the controlled laboratory experiment is not replicable in the ethnographic realm, and any attempt to emulate it is likely to fail. No community is immune from outside influences or so isolated that external forces are trivial in comparison with internal ones. But relative isolation does give the fieldworker a fighting chance of separating the two and estimating their separate effects.

The final consideration, a new influx of outsiders, was predicated on an assumption, to be tested fully in the field, that such a transition might bring traditional values into sharp focus as one of the community's defenses. Social networks and relationships that might otherwise be only latent would become more easily accessible, and such hypothetical functions of aesthetics as markers for group and individual identity, facilitators and inhibitors of social interactions, cues for appropriate behavior, and so forth, would be more easily recognizable. The nature and functions of community bonds, in sum, may be examined more easily when they are in use. Should aesthetic forms play a role here, as one might reasonably expect without necessarily comprehending the mechanisms involved, the role may be readily analyzed.

Preliminary research indicated that the coastal region of North Carolina was a suitable area in which to find a field site. Most of this region has been settled since the colonial era, it is made up primarily of small, white, rural townships, and until recently many populations were isolated by sea, swamps, and sounds. In latter years, however, a modern road system was constructed, and tourists now flood the area from spring to fall.

After two tours of the area, I chose central "Marsh County" in North Carolina as the best site. Nucleated settlements here are small yet have a variety of social networks, and there are few if any rigid town boundaries. Tidewater, the focal community in this study, is bureaucratically divided in different ways—postal, voting, school districts—

each division running athwart the others with none of the boundaries even closely coterminous with social or geographic ones.

The county was granted a charter at the end of the seventeenth century and, while this date does not provide a firm index of Tidewater's settlement, it is well documented that there has been a relatively large, stable population in the general neighborhood of the town for at least one hundred and fifty years. Until the 1930s the area was accessible by boat only, because it is surrounded by water and swamp. Since then bigger and better roads have established permanent links with outside towns and cities, and in the last two decades tourists have begun to invade the area in search of sun and sport. There is also a steady flow of migrants from Virginia seeking the area's lower cost of living while still commuting to the industrial parts of Virginia.

I believe, in retrospect, that the circumstances of my settling into the community were vital to the success of my fieldwork. Some consideration of those circumstances helps explain my choice of field techniques and my confidence in the general validity of my data.

It was important for me and the people of Tidewater that I am not an American—I was raised in Australia by parents of British birth and went to college in England. Thus I did not come to the community with the common American stereotypes concerning the rural South and in many ways was able to see and experience my surroundings with a fresh eye. Also, the people of Tidewater did not treat me as they would a slicker, a Yankee, or some other stereotyped American visitor but quite correctly assumed that how they lived was to me unusual but of interest and should be explained in detail. That is, they did not suspect me of harboring prejudices about their way of living, as American visitors often do, and against which they shield themselves in various ways.

I settled into what had once been a well-known boarding house but now was scarcely used as such because the widowed owner (whom I here call Florence) was becoming increasingly infirm. I was told I could stay for two weeks; then a decision as to my long-range accommodations would be made. Thus the community and I had a probationary period to adjust to each other, with an escape clause for both parties.

The day after my arrival was a Sunday, so I attended morning services at the local Baptist church. As I had scarcely been in the community twelve hours, it was something of a shock to hear the preacher mention my name during morning announcements and give a brief account of my mission. He, and a good number of the congregation, had been apprised by Florence of my coming during Sunday school in the previous hour. On Monday morning Florence sent me off with a list of names of people it would be useful to know, people who had either been in church on Sunday or been called on the telephone to be put in the picture.

I did not make a deliberate effort during the first weeks of my stay in Tidewater to be "accepted," but the events of that time coupled with aspects of my own personality made the two-week deadline pass without notice or comment. Perhaps because of a Protestant upbringing I take pleasure in helping other people with household tasks, and I found it quite natural to assist with yardwork and the like around the house where I was living. In the first week of my stay, for example, I came home in the early afternoon to discover Florence and her daughter sizing up a limb that had sheared from a tree in a recent storm. Without demur they accepted my offer to cut it down. Also, since I spent a good deal of time going from house to house, it was easy for me to run errands or take messages in the process. It was not long before I was integrated into the daily workings of the house, treated more as a family member than as a lodger. I ate with the family, worked on projects with them, discussed personal affairs with them, and in the end formed lasting friendships with them.

Florence and her daughter were more responsible for my establishment in the community than I was through my own efforts. She made many decisions on whom I was to meet and when, and on how I should comport myself. When I arrived in the community, for example, I did not know how to drive a car. Florence considered this state of affairs intolerable, gave me a manual for the written test, and advised me that in a week we were going down to the county courthouse to get me a learner's permit. Thereafter she regularly took me out for lessons, which we sometimes combined with shopping expeditions or opportunities for visiting.

Whenever it was within her power Florence ingratiated me into social groups that it would have been inconceivable for me to get involved with on my own. She belonged to a bridge club of eight women who met in one another's houses in turn. When it came her turn to host them, she asked me to take her seat for her, claiming she was not up to playing. From that day on I was a member of the club.

A great deal of my fieldwork methodology I had to invent as the study progressed, although participant observation was the essential ingredient. I attempted a blanket photographic documentation of all visual aesthetics, ranging through house interiors and exteriors, clothing, automobiles, decoys, quilts, and so on. I participated in work, religious, and leisure activities such as fishing, farming, guiding, hymn singing, storytelling, hunting, card playing, and television watching, using a camera and portable tape recorder whenever they were unobtrusive.

I considered formal methods of elicitation but rejected most of them because of the nature of my relationships to the community and the particular needs of my investigation. I rejected out of hand formal questionnaires and formal experimental testing as essentially destructive to the relationships I had established and as unlikely to reveal the kind of information I was seeking. During my first tours of the area I had watched an anthropologist use a questionnaire as part of a government survey. Although the responses of the local people were obviously meant to be sincere, the questionnaire created a clear barrier: before and after the question period relations were relaxed and cordial, but during it they were strained and artificial. I saw no value in creating uncomfortable situations, particularly as I had little reason to suppose the results would be of any significance for what I sought. My goal was to understand the aesthetic realm in normal life, not to create unnatural situations.

Perhaps the most important reason for eschewing formal methods concerned the community's posture toward outsiders. Tidewater has had to come to terms in recent years with a flood of newcomers whose full effects will be made explicit in later chapters. From the standpoint of methodology certain points should be stressed. For dealing with newcomers and tourists, long-term residents have developed postures that tend to be polite but distant. These postures help bring the aesthetic realm into focus; I could observe them easily but, for obvious reasons, did not want to be on the receiving end, which was likely if I behaved too much like a "foreigner" or a "scientist."

Several discussions with men convinced me that scientists were not held in high regard. When I told one man that a friend of mine, an oceanographer, was studying the causes of the meandering of the Gulf Stream along the North Carolina coast, he replied that he already knew the cause: "God made it that way." Another pointed with disdain to a working party from a local university documenting the growing habits of milfoil in Chesapeake Sound with a view to eradicating it. "It'll be here when you and I are long gone" was his main comment. Use of formal methodologies would almost certainly have cast me as a scientist for such people.

Under any circumstances aesthetic contemplation is fragile and can be destroyed by questioning of any sort, formal or informal (imagine trying to listen to a favorite piece of music while a stranger fires questions at you about it). Yet once an aesthetic experience is over, it can be difficult to recapture and articulate subjective states. To overcome this dilemma I tried to participate in everyday life as fully as possible without being too obtrusive. I learned the aesthetic components of activities by engaging in them, observing local responses, and asking questions when appropriate. Sometimes I was taught correct aesthetic behavior directly when I was struggling with unfamiliar occupations, such as duck hunting. At other times I noted the aesthetic import of conversations and activities. I tried to tie my questions to current activities and not talk in abstractions and generalizations when away from the relevant activity. Thus I talked about cooking with women as they cooked and about the placement of duck decoys with hunters during hunting sessions.

In the normal course of events clear linguistic cues or other behaviors gave me strong indications of aesthetic experiences. For example, the common local expression "It's all according to what you like" was a signal that what was being discussed was a matter of taste. On one occasion I was quail hunting with a man who knew I had a camera in my pocket. When his dogs froze on point at a covey, he took a long look and said to me, "That's just beautiful, take a picture of it for me." In regular conversation I was never able to elicit from this same man any statements about what he considered beautiful.

A few coincidences of mental states between me and those around me prompted a deep rapport on aesthetic issues. Several of the women in the community occasionally expressed concern about my eating habits, a concern brought on by two distinct factors. First, I have by local standards a slight build (5'10", 120 lbs.) and a spare appetite. Second, it took me some time to adjust to the local food. But not eating heartily can be cause for concern on the part of local cooks, who take it as a sign both of sickness and of indifference to their offerings, in which they take great pride. One raw November day, however, a cook prepared haslet stew for me—a watery concoction of pig's heart, liver, and other offal with wheat flour yeast dumplings floating on top. As it happens, my mother had made a similar dish when I was a small boy and I was quite partial to it, but she stopped making it when I was ten years old or so and never made it again despite my occasional nudgings. When the great bowl of stew was put in front of me, I immediately made up a big plateful and wolfed it down, did the same to a second, and made a strong attack on a third,

[39]

to the complete and overt delight of the cook. The incident led to a long discussion about the aesthetics of food and its associations.

Despite my conscious effort to stay away from formal methods, it was convenient, from time to time, to conduct directed interviews on topics that would normally be discussed in conversation. Most of these interviews took place toward the end of my study year, when my position in the community was firmly established and not likely to be jeopardized by such behavior. I also carried out limited experiments that began with requests from people in the community. On two separate occasions people who knew my general project asked me to give slide shows. One woman had me set up my projector in her house and invited a few of her friends over, and a general store owner set up a screen in the store after hours and let it be known to the men who hung around the store that they were welcome to participate. In both cases I selected slides of a variety of objects and events and noted responses. These experiments were useful in that they confirmed my general suspicions, but they were not essential to my general explorations.

What I hope to convey in ensuing chapters, therefore, is a sense of the aesthetic realm of Tidewater in action, as I saw it and participated in it rather than as it was related to me. Although I make no absolute claims as an insider, I have good reason to suppose that my vantage point was generally privileged.

Before launching into data concerning aesthetics, however, I note some basic information about Tidewater and especially about the natural environment (I consider the aesthetic judgments associated with the natural landscape in later chapters). The natural environment is a major component in the lives of all the people who live in Tidewater and a significant factor in generating aesthetic forms. I follow this outline of the natural world with some observations on the relationship between the environment and a few key social facts, in particular the ongoing movement of people in and out of Tidewater.

Tidewater is located on a wide peninsula that runs out into Tidewater Sound. The center of the peninsula is about fifteen feet above sea level and slopes gently down on either side through marsh and swamp to the water. A narrow, sluggish river runs through the town, draining toward the sound in the east. Otherwise the physical landscape is featureless.

There are four broad classes of soil on the peninsula. The central ridge is characterized by high-quality loams. Sloping gradually away from these prime lands, which are very narrow, are broader bands of poorer yet cultivable loamy sands and sandy loams. Together these soils form a strip approximately three thousand feet wide. They are moderately to poorly drained, though occasional stretches in the higher elevations are well-drained. The water table is on average fifteen inches below the surface, so that flooding is an intermittent problem. Beyond the cultivable soils lie wide bands of deep, poorly drained, alluvial sediments. Beside them stretching to the water are broad, flat expanses of swamp land soils, typically wet on the surface with a poor topsoil layer.

These soils support five plant communities, roughly divisible into dryland and wetland: agricultural/settled, old field, and mixed mesic forest in the former, cypress swamp and sawgrass marsh in the latter. These communities, like the soils that support them, run in bands of increasing width from the ridge down to the water.

The central corridor of good soils has been cleared of its natural covering and is planted in commercial crops or built on. However, the margins of these cleared areas support remnants of the original mixed mesic covering, such as button bush, sweetgum, blackberry, and honeysuckle, and weedy species such as dandelion, bedstraw, and a variety of grasses. Interspersed in these cleared lands are old fields, used at one time for agriculture but recently allowed to go more or less wild. They are mostly covered with broomsedge, with loblolly pines dotted about. Like the agricultural lands, these cleared fields show remnants of the original mixed mesic growth, particularly on the margins.

On either side of the cleared lands the mixed mesic forest forms a high, dense wall, so that standing on the peninsular ridge one has the impression of being enclosed on both sides by wilderness. Deciduous trees such as oaks, willow, sweetgum, and red maple form the primary tree covering and make a thick canopy in spring and summer. Beneath them grow smaller trees and shrubs—American holly, sweet bay, sourwood, cane, and wax myrtle. The floor is sparely covered by different grasses.

The mixed forest gives way to cypress swamp as the ground gets lower and less well-drained. Between the mesic growth and the cypress swamp proper are narrow strips of swampy lands dominated by red bay, black gum, and pond pine. As the ground water becomes deeper, toward the margin of the sound, the bald cypress becomes the dominant species. The bases of these trees are host to several shrubs, including swamp rose, sweet pepperbush, Virginia tea, and winterberry. Between the river and the swamp are small pockets of sawgrass

[41]

marsh mostly covered in sawgrass, but drier spots support a few mesic shrubs. The river itself supports a small plant community of open-water species: milfoil and Lilaeopsis.

The fauna of the region is rich and diverse. The agricultural land corridor supports the smallest number of species. Crop lands are picked over by white-tailed deer, snow geese, meadowlarks, and mourning doves. Margins, drainage ditches, and brambly hedgerows house small rodents. Old fields have a similar population, with scattered colonies of rabbits and quail and a proportionately higher number of predator species, including the red-tailed hawk and black ratsnake.

The mesic forest lands are inhabited by a great variety of perching and predator birds and a host of land mammals and land reptiles. Small rodents occupy the forest floor, along with lizards, snakes, and toads. White-tailed deer forage and browse, while overhead passerine birds and raptors perch, nest, and feed.

The wetlands teem with wildlife. True amphibians (frogs, toads, and salamanders) share the habitat with amphibious mammals (mink, nutria, and marsh rabbit) and amphibious reptiles (watersnakes and turtles). These lands are also important breeding grounds for such waterfowl as green heron and wood duck, and wintering territory for many species of ducks and geese. Black bear and bobcat are occasionally though rarely sighted, the latter being more often heard than seen.

Beyond the wetlands the open waters of the sound provide spawning ground and territory for both freshwater fish, such as alewife, largemouth bass, perch, shad, carp, and catfish and saltwater types that spend portions of their life cycle in brackish waters, such as spots and croakers. These in turn support fish-eating birds: ducks, gulls, and osprey.

The climate is oceanic, with mild winters and temperate summers. The average temperature in January is 45°F. and in July is 80°F. The average rainfall is fifty inches per annum, half of which falls between April and August. The first frost of the year generally comes in mid-November, the last at the beginning of April, giving an average frost-free period of 235 days. Tropical storms and hurricanes are not frequent but create serious flooding problems when they occur. Severe storms generally come out of the northeast and push water back up rivers and creeks flowing toward Chesapeake Sound.

The natural environment of Marsh County has severely restricted housing in Tidewater. Because the whole region is a peninsula, with well-drained soils only along its spine, the potential for growth has

Figure 1. Kindred, showing patterns of migration

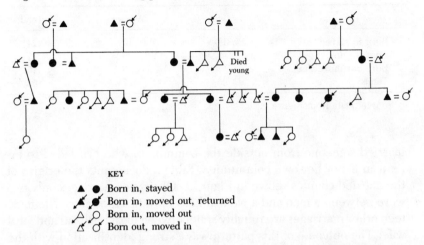

KEY

▲ ● Born in, stayed
◢ ◓ Born in, moved out, returned
△ ○ Born in, moved out
◿ ♂ Born out, moved in

always been limited. From the earliest days a road has run down the spine for access between local communities, but until the 1930s the road did not lead out of the peninsula because deep swamp blocked the way. The oldest houses in Tidewater were built on the road and spaced evenly along it with farmlands beside and behind them; each house commanded ten to twenty acres of prime land. These apparently small plots were primarily for food and supplementary income, because families earned their living at freshwater fishing and market hunting. Even so, the farms were a vital part of the family economy, and a waterman could not live without a smallholding. Once the land had been carved into these small family farm plots, there was little prospect of expansion. New houses could not be built without reducing the area of farmland, and new land for farming was not available because of physical limits set by the marshes.

These chronic limitations on land established a pattern of in- and out-migration to be seen clearly in the movements of a kin group over several generations. Figure 1 shows the movements in and out of all of the members of four generations of related families.

Patterns of movement are roughly similar for men and women, with the numbers moving out slightly higher than those moving in (see Table 1). The net effect was to stabilize the numbers of each family living in the community, the net loss to other communities balancing fertility. In simple terms, one child inherited the "home place" and the rest married outside the community. The child who inherited

[43]

Table 1. Movements of Tidewater men and women

	Men	Women	Total
Born in/stayed in	11	10	21
Born in/moved out	8	9	17
Born out/moved in	7	8	15
Totals	26	27	53

Source: Data from Figure 1.

married someone from outside the community who had failed to inherit in his or her own community. Table 2 documents the origins of the married couples shown in Figure 1. Of sixteen marriages only two were between a man and a woman both born in Tidewater. The fourteen other marriages are roughly split between local husband and local wife. The outcome of this pattern was a strong identification with the family land and the homestead on it.

In the 1930s, with the development of the technology to build roads through swampland, the local road was linked to the mainland of North Carolina and residence patterns changed significantly. Men who in the past had moved away because family lands could not support them now could commute to jobs in larger towns outside the county. The road also solved the problem of where they would live. Two men who owned substantial farms by the river took outside employment and carved up their lands into building plots. The community became nucleated where these two farms had been, and there was a flurry of building in the 1930s and 1940s.

The new road also brought outsiders into the town. In the 1960s families began moving in from Virginia and from other parts of North Carolina for a variety of reasons. The general cost of living is low, state and local taxes are reasonable, and there are opportunities for water sports of all kinds. The arrival of these outsiders was made possible as

Table 2. Marriages and movements of Tidewater men and women

Man	Woman	Number
Born in = Born in		2
Born in = Born out		8
Born out = Born in		6
Total		16

Source: Data from Figure 1.

[44]

more local families sold building plots or turned farmland into mobile home parks. They did so for a number of reasons, including a general decline in the profitability of small farms and fishing. This pattern of in-migration is fundamentally different from the old one. In the days before the new road system the men and women who moved into the community were from other parts of the county and shared their cultural values with the people of Tidewater. Furthermore they did not simply move in, they *married* into the community. Modern newcomers are real outsiders. They come from different cultural backgrounds, and they move in as entire family units. The tensions that now exist between newcomers and old families have brought some social structures—the aesthetic in particular—into sharp focus.

For the sake of convenience I have divided my field data on aesthetics into four categories: home, work, church, and leisure. These categories have no special theoretical import and are not entirely discrete entities. In many ways, however, the data fall naturally into these domains, which local people recognize as socially significant. I have tried to present the data from the local perspective as much as possible, though I am mindful of the problems inherent in making such a claim (see Clifford and Marcus 1986). Whenever my own feelings or viewpoint are expressly given, they are clearly marked as such. In general such statements involve preliminary classification and comparison of the data on a very limited scale in order to create a series of analytic threads. For example, I indicate from time to time when aesthetic forms are conspicuously present or absent, when they are natural versus artifactual, when they are highly embellished in contrast to others that are unadorned, when aesthetic values are those of men or of women or both, and so on. I pick up these threads and use them in a more extensive analysis in the concluding chapter.

[4]

Aesthetics at Home

The main aesthetic forms that I consider in this chapter on the homes of Tidewater are architecture and architectural space, internal decor and furnishings, food, gardens and landscaping, and leisure activities.

The history of settlement in Tidewater has had a clear effect on local architecture and its aesthetics. Houses can be divided into those built (1) between 1860 and 1929, before the road to the mainland was constructed, (2) between 1930 and 1950, the first period of expansion after the road came through, and (3) after 1950, the later expansion. Although the land was owned and settled earlier, no house survives that was built before 1860. Houses from period 1 are typically two rooms wide, two stories high, and one room deep. Period 2 houses are predominantly small, cabinlike structures. The houses of period 3 are either mobile homes situated in block lots planned for that purpose or brick-veneer frame houses with a great variety of floor plans.

The vocabulary of this typology and the chronology associated with it are my own, but these groupings have broad local currency. "Old house" in local language, for example, invariably means a period 1 house, and "brick house" or "mobile home" is used to identify period 3 houses. Period 2 houses form a residual category identified in various ways, mostly referring to their smallness or cheapness of construction: "small place," "a nothing house," or "a cheap old place." I use my chronological typology rather than local terms because the time spans are important to an understanding of the building practices involved and related aesthetic decisions.

The houses of period 1, the homesteads of the oldest families in the community, are spaced evenly along the road, sometimes with newer houses between or behind them where owners have sold off building plots. Although many of these houses were built as central-hallway houses, with two rooms on each of two floors, a substantial proportion started out as humbler dwellings, and all have been structurally altered since they were erected. Schematically the downstairs rooms in the original houses were arranged as in Figure 2. The two upstairs rooms were identical in size and position to those downstairs. Kitchen, dining room, and toilet were separate buildings located close to the rear of the house. Characteristically the house was built with an open front porch.

Many of the basic features of this house serve utilitarian ends. The central hall with opposite front and back doors provided a breezeway in summer, and the separate kitchen kept the heat from cooking away from the main living space. In the winter the doors of the living and sitting rooms could be closed to provide small heatable units, avoiding the expenditure of energy to heat unused or rarely used space. These aspects of the house appear purely functional, but they also have aesthetic and psychological dimensions.

A central hallway and closed-off rooms reflect, Henry Glassie (1975:190) suggests, a desire for privacy. A visitor admitted to the hallway is still in limbo between the outside and the main living area. Aspects of the house other than the basic room plan are also important. The front porch was (and still is) a major part of the house; there

Figure 2. Downstairs floor plan for basic period 1 house

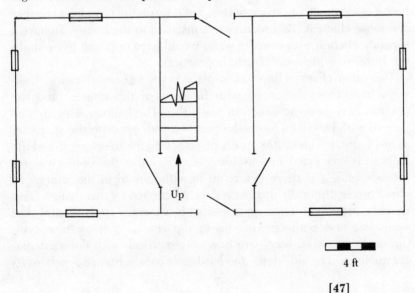

4 ft

residents sat in the afternoons to catch a cooling breeze and kept an eye on passersby. Far from withdrawing from the world, they relaxed in the most open part of the house. Admittedly the house provided a retreat should it be needed, but clearly the psychological needs of the occupants were complex. Adequate provision was made both for exposure and for seclusion, so that this type of house gives the occupants a fundamental choice between confinement and openness. However, the basic house plan does not supply the analyst with sufficient firm clues regarding the psychological advantages and disadvantages of particular features. One must see the house in use to understand how space is used and what it means to its occupants. This information in turn helps interpret the aesthetics of architectural space and its relationship to other aesthetic forms, such as decor. Also, patterned changes in the basic house indicate changes in usage and desires and so affect aesthetic decisions.

The first change in these older houses came in the 1930s, when the kitchen and dining-room units were butted up against the main house and roofed continuously with it to form an ell. In some cases a second story was added to the ell and divided into two bedrooms. Some of the older people in Tidewater, indicative of times before this change, still refer to going from the kitchen to the living room as "going into the house." The main incentive for this structural change was the advent of indoor plumbing; electric lines were run along the new highway in the 1930s and the electricity was used to power water pumps. Indoor plumbing demanded a compromise. Moving the kitchen closer to the house made the living space hotter, but it made the plumbing cheaper and more efficient. Bathrooms were installed in the house. To have a separate kitchen with running water would have required two plumbing systems, which was clearly impractical.

Two other changes have taken place in the last few decades. Hallways have been dispensed with in many of the houses, and the porches have been screened or walled in. The hallway is easily dispensed with by taking down the partition wall opposite the staircase, as in Figure 3. The visitor enters directly into the living area, and the hallway is converted into usable space. Even so the breezeway remains useful, and there is a room to withdraw to in the winter. In effect two aesthetically distinct spaces are created by this change. Two roughly equivalent living spaces—that is, spaces of approximately the same size and both opening on to the central hallway in a symmetrically balanced way—are now asymmetrical, with different spatial qualities. The old "den," the left-hand room in Figure 3, retains its former characteristics. It is fully enclosed and confined, providing an intimate space. By contrast, the other room, the "living room," is opened up in several ways. It is, of course, bigger, but the general feeling created by the space is even more expansive because doors from this room now open directly on the front and back yards and the staircase at the end leads up to the second floor. The breezeway continues to function, but it helps circulate air through the entire room, and the open front and back doors provide additional light. I consider how these spaces function later in this chapter. For now I simply note that the new room configuration gives the occupant a choice between a more closed and a more open space for a range of tasks. This choice was cited by all the people who had made the structural change as their prime motivation.

Screening in porches might have occurred sooner had it been technologically or financially possible, for obvious reasons. The swamp is a breeding ground for all manner of stinging and biting insects, and a hot day in July is pure torment for anyone out in the open. Yet this structural change also involved a compromise. The very openness of the porch was dramatically reduced, and those sitting on the porch became largely hidden from view. Screened-in porches are like two-way mirrors in that those inside can look out easily but those outside

Figure 3. Downstairs floor plan for basic period 1 house after modification

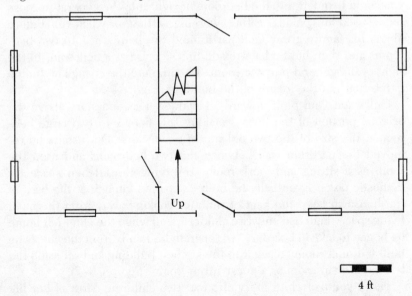

4 ft

[49]

cannot look in unless they are very close. It is thus impossible for people on the porch to make contact with people outside without shouting out, and even then someone on the road must turn aside and enter the porch to make two-way contact. Part of the virtue of an open porch is that one can exchange a wave or a brief greeting with some-one on the road without making any special effort. Most people who have screened their porches lament the loss of openness, and a few of them, men in particular, now sit out in the yard in order to recapture the old feeling of openness.

Because the family histories and fortunes of the occupants are so intimately linked to a house's architecture and its structural changes, I rehearse the development of one old home place. This narrative should make it abundantly clear that a period 1 house is a living, changing structure and not a static object. The large house of today may have started life as a one-room cabin, and in no case is what one sees today the result of a single period of building. My main aesthetic point is that the people of Tidewater do not treat architectural space as a fixed quality of an old house. They feel free to manipulate it as they wish or as technological advances create new choices.

The house I consider in this exercise was built in 1868 by Cull Kinsey and added on to, up and out, by him and by later generations. Cull started by building two rooms side by side with a breezeway down the center. As you entered the house through the breezeway, you could turn left into the bedroom or right into the general-purpose room, used for cooking, eating, working, sitting, or whatever (Figure 4). As his family grew, Cull partitioned the bedroom into two bed-rooms and then built a lean-to addition, for use as a bedroom, to the right of the general-purpose room. To complete the change he built a porch that ran the length of the building (Figure 5).

Cull's son Paul built upward. He added a second story above the original portion of the house, making this floor into two large bed-rooms, the size of the two old rooms downstairs. Downstairs he re-moved the partition wall between the two bedrooms and used the room as a sitting and work room, reserving the kitchen space for domestic tasks. Eventually he built a separate kitchen at the back of the house to keep the heat of summer cooking away from the main living space. Paul had only two children, and when the elder left home he began to take in boarders. To separate his family from the guests he built a dining room adjacent to the kitchen building and set aside the left-hand main room as a guest sitting room (Figures 6–7).

Paul's younger child Mary also had two children. Most of her life

Figure 4. Kinsey house original plan

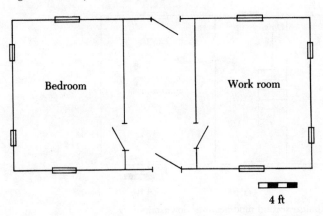

Bedroom

Work room

4 ft

Figure 5. Kinsey house first modification

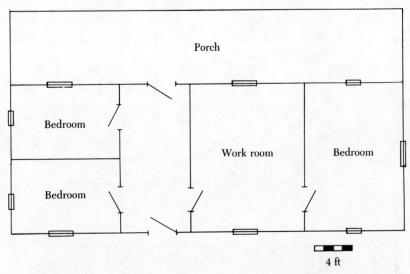

Porch

Bedroom

Bedroom

Work room

Bedroom

4 ft

she had looked after the guests with her mother, so she simply continued existing practice when she inherited the house. In the 1930s, when electricity and running water became available in the county, Mary could not take immediate advantage of the opportunity because it necessitated major structural changes. Before long, however, she

[51]

Figure 6. Kinsey house second modification, upstairs

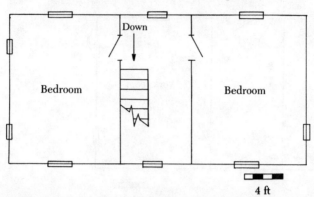

4 ft

Figure 7. Kinsey house second modification, downstairs

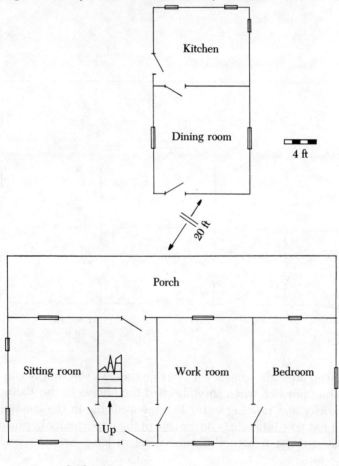

[52]

Figure 8. Kinsey house third modification, downstairs

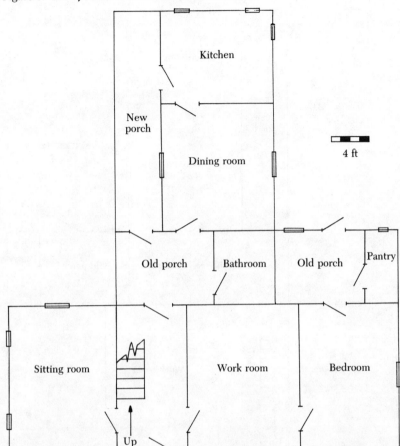

had saved enough money to have the kitchen and dining room moved, forming a tee at the back of the house butted up against the old porch. She had the whole extension, including the porch, roofed continuously. The old porch, which was shortened somewhat, became a bathroom and washhouse, and the adjacent kitchen and dining room extension now had electricity and running water. The outbuildings had to be moved beside the house to limit plumbing and wiring for kitchen and bathroom facilities. To make up for the lost porch she had a new one built on the kitchen and dining room tee, forming a walkway into the main house (Figure 8).

In the 1950s Mary grew tired of the arrangement of the downstairs

[53]

Figure 9. Kinsey house fourth modification, downstairs

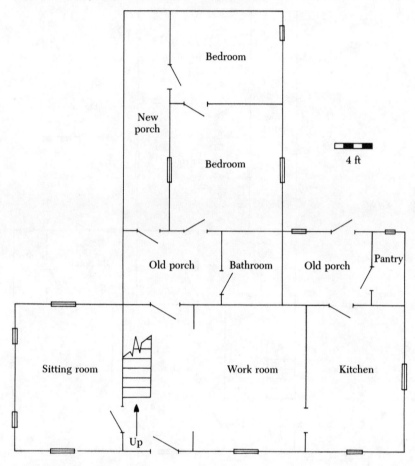

and determined on a complete overhaul. She converted the lean-to bedroom into the kitchen and made guest bedrooms of the dining room and the old kitchen. She took out the righthand breezeway wall to enlarge the center room, which served as a spacious congregating place for dining, bridge parties, dancing, and so on. Now people entering from the road walked directly into the main room instead of a narrow passage. She also screened in the new back porch (Figure 9). Since then the house has remained the same. Her husband died not long after the changes were made, and she has now lost interest in home alterations.

This continual reshaping of the architectural space is a characteristic

Figure 10. Period 2 house

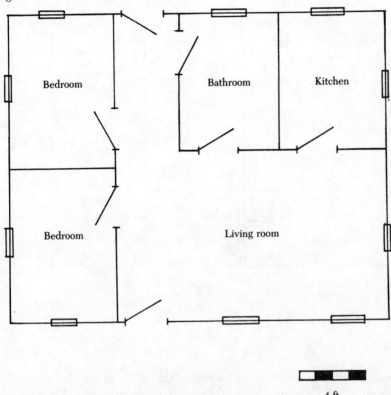

4 ft

of period 1 houses only. As a result, inheriting the old home place brings with it aesthetic possibilities and responsibilities. Whoever lives in such a house takes over a never-ending task of molding and modifying space.

The houses of period 2 are generally one-story frame houses. The floor plans differ so widely from one another that few generalizations can be made. Some are classic hall-and-parlor type, others are arranged like shotgun houses; some have ell or tee appendages, others do not; some have front porches, others do not (see Figures 10 and 11). Two general points can be made. First, this beginning of structural diversity is a symptom of increasing concourse with the larger world. Most of these houses were built from architect's plans, whereas most period 1 houses were not. Second, all of these houses were cheap to build and are smaller than period 1 houses. Few have been structurally altered since they were constructed. Although they vary in

Figure 11. Period 2 house

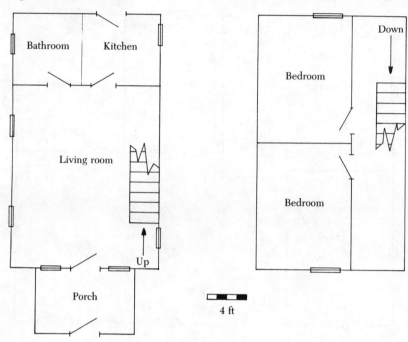

plan, they were built at a time when the order of the day was maximum utility for minimum cost. Present occupants agree that little can be done structurally to use internal space better. Also, owners are reluctant to pay for changes to a house that does not have a high market value. Most of the houses of period 2 were built to accommodate the offspring of large families who could not all inherit the family house but did not wish to move away. By the 1930s a road system gave easy access to a wide area; it was feasible to live in Tidewater and work elsewhere.

After this somewhat mixed period two trends emerged. Long-term residents and old families of Tidewater began building large brick dwellings, whereas newer residents moved into mobile homes. The floor plans of the brick houses, show great variation, and all of these houses are architect-designed. They are basically frame houses on a concrete foundation with a brick-veneered exterior. Most of them are much larger than anything previously built in town; not only do they have more rooms than the older houses, but the rooms themselves are bigger. All are built on one level or are split-level, so that they present

Figure 12. Period 3 brick house

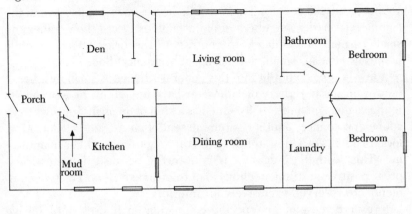

4 ft

Figure 13. Period 3 split-level brick house

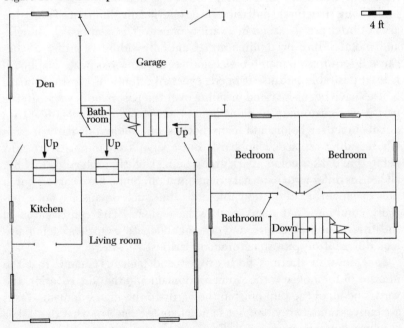

4 ft

a much broader profile than any of the older houses (see Figures 12 and 13).

The second trend is diametrically opposed to the first. In the last few decades some members of older families have turned farmland into commercial trailer parks. For the most part newcomers and younger married couples live in mobile homes. Newcomers live in the commercial parks, members of older families locate their trailers on small corners of farmland. In contrast to the brick houses, mobile homes are cheap, small, and have a stereotypical floor plan.

A few houses do not fit into this general schema. A small number of houses on the periphery of Tidewater have been built by newcomers to the region since the 1950s. One has a kind of Spanish/Southwestern adobe appearance, another is reminiscent of an A-frame chalet. Most local residents of Tidewater describe these houses as odd or unappealing. This aesthetic judgment is noteworthy because they never express positive aesthetic feelings about house exteriors. Positive comments are reserved exclusively for interiors.

I reserve most of my specific comments on houses until I have examined decor, but one point should be borne in mind. Classification by house type tends to simplify and to smooth out diversity. Few houses in Tidewater look similar, however, and even those that have underlying structural similarities are superficially different. Those that are not brick are sheathed in a variety of materials, clapboard, shingle, and metal siding predominating. Generally siding is preferred because it requires no maintenance and yet always looks neat. Clapboard is least desirable because it needs constant attention. Most clapboard houses have been sheathed in siding over the past twenty years. In the past it was customary to paint houses white and pick out a few trim details in a dark color, and many houses still follow this pattern even where siding replaces clapboard. But a significant minority are now painted in darker colors, dark green being slightly preferred. Finally, all houses differ as to external ornamentation. Some have carved porch rails or gingerbread in the gable ends, but such details are not especially common, and many houses have none. The combination of sheathing material, colors, and ornamental features makes each house look different despite structural similarities.

In Tidewater there is both explicit and tacit agreement that the interior of the house is the woman's domain and that the exterior, the yard, and all of the buildings in the yard are the man's domain. Tasks are conventionally divided not so much on the basis of what the task is as where it will be performed. For example, women paint the interiors of houses, men paint the exteriors; women cook inside, men outside; and so on. Of course it is easy to find exceptions: men repair faulty plumbing indoors, and women hang the washing outside to dry. Perhaps the domains should be seen as somewhat overlapping or shading into one another.

This conscious split in domains is manifested in daily behavior. Women spend most of their time inside the house, and men outside. The men of Tidewater have social and traditional reasons for spending their days outside the house, but there are definite disadvantages as far as personal comfort is concerned. For example, one waterman, a great ox of a man who is generally admired for his staunch adherence to traditional values, is almost always to be found, when not working or sleeping, in his backyard. Even though his house is fully aircondi-tioned and centrally heated, he will not seek refuge from the elements indoors. On a hot humid day in August he can be found sitting under a shade tree, swatting flies and chewing tobacco. On one occasion his wife held an afternoon party for one of his female relatives, and he was obliged to attend out of kin loyalty. Even though it was close to one hundred degrees in the shade outside and airconditioned inside, he complained throughout the party that he was hot and left periodically to sit outside. As soon as he felt his loyalty to kin had been served, he left permanently.

When sex roles are reversed, there is inevitable comment. Women hunters, though very uncommon, do exist and are considered either mannish, if they are good, or a nuisance, if they are not good. Inter-estingly, women who are bad hunters evoke far less comment than good ones. A married man who helps in the family cooking may also evoke adverse criticism or become the butt of jokes. On several occa-sions I helped an infirm woman by transferring prepared foods from her work table to pots on the stove, which produced considerable joking among her friends. Furthermore, men who become tied to the house, as in the case of disability, lose influence in the men's world. The home is not without prestige and influence; quite the opposite, as this chapter demonstrates. But it is the woman's influence that resides in the house, not the man's.

Very few houses in Tidewater have a room especially furnished as a formal sitting room (as distinct from a family room). This absence is unusual for the South. In Tidewater one room serves as both formal sitting room and family room, with the degree of formality of the decor varying according to the desires of the woman of the house. These rooms run the gamut from spotless, elaborately planned spaces set with antiques to random assortments of styles of furniture in various stages of disarray. Most, however, lie somewhere in a middle range, that is, neat, comfortable, and generally organized without too many appointments of high monetary value. In appropriate weather, and at appropriate times of day, all guests—whether old family friends or strangers, whether of high or low status—are welcomed in the family

[59]

room. This style of living is found in all house types and therefore serves as a general indication of the needs and cares of modern residents. Tidewater people represent themselves to outsiders as friendly. A sign on the highway at the edge of town advises motorists that the local church is "a friendly church in a friendly town." By the same token a visitor should not be held at bay in the prim formality of a sitting room but accepted into the heart of family activity. Also, Tidewater women cannot abide devoting a major portion of the house to a highly specialized function such as formal entertaining.

Aesthetic judgments about house interiors were easy to elicit from women, who couched them in terms readily identifiable as aesthetic. Samples include "the most beautiful house in Tidewater," "pretty, but hard to keep clean," and "very attractive." Those houses generally considered attractive or beautiful differ from one another both structurally and decoratively. Admittedly, most of these houses are the newer brick ones, and one might be tempted to think their very newness predisposes people to view them favorably. But in Tidewater "new" does not signify "good" as it does in many subcultures in the United States. The expression "new-fangled" is used for a wide variety of modern inventions and is derogatory. Newness by itself is not sufficient for the brick houses to be called "attractive."

Attractive houses have in common what might be called a thematic unity of decor. In each the rooms open to general inspection are decorated in an identifiable style. One is entirely furnished with flawless antiques, another with furniture that was in vogue in the 1940s, a third with modern reproductions of older pieces, and so on. Each room in these houses looks deliberately planned and laid out, whereas rooms in other houses are more of a mixture of accumulated pieces in different styles.

Whatever notions might be held of beauty in house decor, there is often a correlation between aspects of the occupants' lifestyle or pleasures and decor. Both the man's and the woman's concerns are represented, even though the interior is primarily the woman's domain. Thus, for example, the houses of keen hunters are often adorned with working guns, old guns, decoys, pictures of wildfowling, and the like. But the relationship between furnishings and personal concerns, particularly in older families, goes deeper. Many pieces evoke strong memories, have a story attached to them, or are stylistically similar to pieces from a cherished era.

One well-known raconteur and his wife have their house furnished in turn-of-the-century style, with a great number of marble-topped pieces. The few new pieces in the house are reproductions of this same style. Many of the lamps in the house are made from oil lamps salvaged from shipwrecks, and scattered about the house are objects from and mementos of old boats and water activities. The husband prides himself on the stories he can tell concerning events at the end of the nineteenth and beginning of the twentieth centuries, of shipwrecks, the Wright brothers, market hunting, and so on. His strong associations with this time are reinforced by the overall decor.

Another home, originally a plantation house and still owned and occupied by a female member of the family that built it, is furnished with inherited pieces of the same vintage as the house. Pictures of family members past and present adorn walls and table tops, and a few items associated with the legal profession are prominently displayed in remembrance of the current owner's late husband, a county judge for many years.

Generally speaking the houses occupied by the eldest scions of the oldest families, that is, period 1 houses, are filled with furnishings and decorations that have been accumulated over several generations. Each one has a kind of family style reflecting the common interests of many members of the family. The houses of the younger generations do not contain many inherited items, and if they are unified at all it is around modern furnishings. Most have only one or two older items inherited from a family member and cherished as a token.

The thematic unity of the furniture is often accented by items on display on walls and in cabinets. Some men and women are collectors and are proud to display their collections. One farmer collects projectile points that his plough turns up, another mounts the breast bones of birds. One woman collects flowers carved from ivory, a second has a cabinet filled with china replicas of swans. Also to be found are collections of guns, decoys, fishing lures, deer antlers, and all of the paraphernalia associated with water sports. It is common to find small pieces of handiwork such as cutwork, needlepoint, embroidery, and cross stitch on table and chest surfaces. These are more likely to be heirlooms than produced by the woman of the house, since needlework is declining in popularity.

There is also one common taboo in interior decorations: it is considered the height of bad taste to display things from the wild unless they have been fundamentally transformed. No one displays stuffed ducks or fish, even though the area is known for hunting and fishing and some guides practice taxidermy for the tourists. Taxidermy is deemed a "foreign" habit that violates a basic local premise of sporting: fish and game are for eating. One local hunter was given a stuffed wood duck as a birthday present by a tourist, and the gift left him in a quandary. He could not throw it out (which is what he and his wife wanted to do) because it was a present, but he did not want to display it. However, the tourist might arrive unexpectedly and ask where the duck was, so he could not bury it in the attic. His solution was to shift it around constantly, sometimes daily, trying to find a spot where it was "on display but out of sight," that is, where it could be seen if you cared to look for it but where it was not in regular view.

It is, however, appropriate to display artifactual treatments of the wild or objects that are employed in the struggle with the wild. China ducks or paintings of birds in flight are perfectly acceptable and relatively common. Photographs of hunters and fishermen with their spoils are rarer but not uncommon. Guns and other hunting paraphernalia frequently form prominently placed displays. In general, however, the outside world does not belong inside, and whatever comes from the outside must be transformed. Wildfowl and fish for cooking are not brought into a house until they have been prepared. Fowl are plucked, gutted, and feet and head are removed. Fish are at least gutted, scaled, and the head is removed, and they may also be fileted. These tasks are performed in the yard.

The clear distinction between inside and outside may be manifested in a clash of styles of decor. The exterior may give no evidence of the thematic unity of the interior. For example, several of the new brick houses are furnished with antiques. The owners delight in the surprise of newcomers when they enter these houses. Furthermore, it is virtually impossible to elicit aesthetic judgments about house exteriors from either men or women. The woman's lack of interest is understandable; as the exterior is neither her domain nor her concern (hence her delight when newcomers find the interior, her work, appealing after they have seen an exterior that is not her work). When a woman compliments another by saying she has a nice or pretty or attractive house, she is invariably referring to the interior and will qualify her remarks by mentioning some aspect of the decor or the furnishings. A man's reluctance to talk about the exterior, his realm, in aesthetic terms may simply reflect a general anti-aesthetic posture assumed by males. Basically, a house exterior "looks good" to man if it is trim and functional. Well-painted boards will not rot, and a well-placed tree gives shade.

Details of the use of internal space and furnishings are examined below, but here it is instructive to show the layout and furniture plan of one house and give a general sense of how the woman who owns it uses the space. Figure 14 shows the furniture plan of the ground floor of the period 1 house whose building and additions were described above. Mary arises at about 7:00 A.M., dresses, and goes to the kitchen to make breakfast for herself and her daughter Libby, who is married and lives in a separate house that she and her husband had built on old family land soon after they were married. Her daughter arrives at about 7:30, and they eat breakfast together at the kitchen table. This meal usually consists of fried eggs and bacon or sausage with coffee, and it is quick to make and eat. Libby leaves to begin her own household chores at about 8:00.

Mary usually lingers over a second cup of coffee after her daughter

Figure 14. Furniture plan

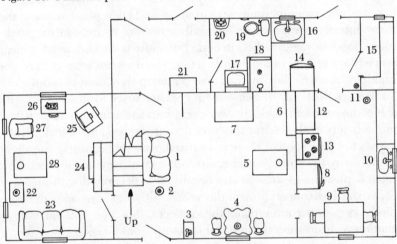

1. Sofa
2. Floor lamp
3. Telephone table
4. Marble-topped table and chairs (lamp on table)
5. Oil-burning stove
6. Shelves
7. Gate leg table (folded)
8. Refrigerator
9. Table and chairs
10. Sink and cabinets with counter top
11. Dog and cat dishes
12. Table
13. Electric stove
14. Freezer

15. Shelves
16. Utility sink
17. Washer
18. Shower stall
19. Commode
20. Basin
21. Quilt and blanket chest
22. Table with lamp
23. Sofa
24. Piano and bench
25. Two televisions
26. Sewing table and chair
27. Recliner
28. Oil-burning stove

[63]

has left and plans her day's itinerary. Although she has a pretty regular weekly routine (washing on Monday, grocery shopping on Thursday . . .), things can crop up to throw her schedule off, such as a neighbor's illness or a change in the weather. By the early morning, though, she knows what she has to contend with and can plan accordingly. At this point she decides on the major chore of the day and plans the evening meal (so she can check supplies to see if she needs to run out to the general store for odds and ends before she begins preparations in mid-afternoon). Also, if she knows what she is to prepare, she can decide what to do with gifts of food when they show up, that is, whether to use them immediately in some way or to prepare them for saving.

Once she has made these decisions, Mary clears away the breakfast dishes and sets to work on the day's big chore. This may be vacuuming, washing, ironing, canning, and so on, and takes place in one of the many interior work spaces. Naturally, washing is done in the washroom, food storage in the kitchen. But most tasks that need a clear space Mary sets up in the middle room. She does her ironing here, for example, dries clothes by the stove on damp days, and cuts out cloth for dresses. Not only does the room give her space to spread out, with a big dining-room table to work on, but she can also see visitors immediately as they enter the front door (friends do not knock). If she wishes to take a spell or there is a natural pause in her work, she sits at the table by the window that commands a good view of the road. This room is pleasing to work in also because it is decorated with pieces of china she has collected over the years. Although she does not routinely stop and contemplate these pieces, her eye falls on one or another as from time to time she looks up from a task.

At midday she stops to prepare a quick lunch, usually consisting of leftovers from the previous night's meal. Often this preparation entails little more than setting dishes from the refrigerator on the kitchen table and selecting a plateful from them. After lunch she finishes her chore from the morning and then retires to her easy chair in the sitting room. Often she is working on a number of needlework projects, and she may work on these until around 3 P.M. when it is time to start the evening meal. Throughout this time people may stop by, always with a specific purpose but also willing to chat for a while. Mary entertains her visitors wherever she is and does not usually stop what she is doing to talk. Nor does the status of the visitor matter. If the preacher calls while she is peeling potatoes, she asks him to sit at the kitchen table with her and lets him conduct his business while she continues her job. Every downstairs room is equally appropriate for guests.

[64]

Mary plans the evening meal for 6 P.M. to coincide with her son-in-law's return from work. She begins preparations at about three o'clock, and soon her daughter shows up to assist. They both sit at the table to get the raw ingredients ready, with Mary supervising all operations and doing the actual cooking. When Libby's husband finishes work he goes straight to Mary's house for dinner, and all three sit down at the kitchen table together. After dinner Libby clears away the dishes and then goes home with her husband. Mary spends the remainder of the evening in the sitting room, continuing her needlework or watching the television, or both. In the past she would not have watched television or listened to the radio without doing some handcraft at the same time, but here eyesight is failing and she now finds it hard to do both.

Architectural space and furnishings, it is clear, work together to create different internal environments, each with its own feeling. Partly because of custom and usage, partly because of general layout, Mary feels differently about each of the spaces in her house and chooses the space appropriate to her needs or her mood. These feelings can be augmented by the different ways that rooms confine the air and the resultant aesthetic effects. The central room has the breezeway in it, and so air is constantly cycled through, whereas the sitting room and kitchen have relatively still air. The air in the central room is clean-smelling and invigorating, and rather cooler than in the other two rooms.

The air in the kitchen is always hot and humid. Most meals involve the long, slow boiling of one or more green vegetables, creating a steamy atmosphere in which the general smells of cooking linger. Over time kitchens can take on the permanent smell of cooked greens because the cooking steam clings to walls and surfaces, imparting a kind of seasoning to them. Older houses are particularly susceptible to this effect. The air in the sitting room is also still, and warmer than in the middle room, creating a mildly soporific mood (enhanced by the darkness relative to the middle room). All of the seats in the sitting room are soft whereas most in the middle room are hard, and so Mary's general pace is slower in the former than in the latter.

The internal spaces of the houses of Tidewater are organized by constellations of aesthetic forms. The dimensions of the space itself, decor and furniture, the texture of surfaces to sit on, the air quality and associated aromas—all combine to create units of space that affect the occupant differently.

The gardens and immediate environs of Tidewater houses are not ornate, and the town has few avid ornamental gardeners. This is not to

[65]

say the residents tolerate unkempt surrounds to their houses, but they do prefer plainer landscapes. Because of the uniform flatness of the land no gardens have any contour, and most of the deliberate planting does little to alleviate this flatness. Generally houses are surrounded by lawn, with foundation plantings of evergreens or perennial flowering shrubs. Few houses are shrouded in trees, but most have a few trees strategically placed to provide shade. Most are ornamental, fruit, or nut trees. All of the yards of Tidewater require a minimum of care to keep them looking neat. Few people plant annuals or any kind of flower that takes more than the most perfunctory tending, so that yards are not highlighted by flower beds (see Figures 15 and 16).

Care of the yard is primarily the responsibility of the males in the households. For them, as far as the garden is concerned, the pragmatic outweighs the aesthetic. They frown upon spending too much time and money on a decorative aspect of the house's exterior, yet they do not wish their yards to appear uncultivated or untidy. They compromise with plantings that are easy to keep well-groomed without much effort. Only one man showed overt satisfaction in collecting and planting varieties of flowers, and he was considered an oddity, his behavior only partially excused because he had married into an old, local family from an equally respectable but slightly eccentric one from an adjacent county. His garden stands in absolute contrast to all of the others in town and is the source as much of amusement and bewilderment as of aesthetic pleasure. Even his wife tells stories of times he would ride to Virginia for a particular item but return with flower plants instead of what he had gone out for. In this and many other domestic matters he was considered unusual.

Those men who spend time in their gardens mostly tend vegetable patches. Yet even this activity is declining in popularity somewhat and now concerns perhaps a dozen older men. Their vegetable gardens are large, some over an acre, and the gardeners usually grow enough to take care of their own annual needs with a surplus for distribution to relatives and friends. Wives pickle or can much of the summer surplus, particularly tomatoes, beans, corn, and cucumber, for winter use.

In the very center of Tidewater the gardens of adjacent houses are contiguous. A scant quarter-mile from the center the farmland begins, sometimes behind the houses but mostly between them. Where farms are situated between houses, lawns and foundation plantings mark the homesites as clearly separate. The majority of the older houses have family burying plots on the grounds beyond the boundaries of the

Figure 15. Yard plan, period 2 house

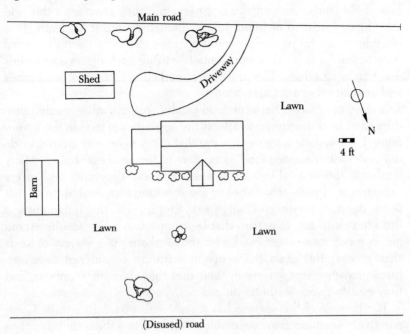

Figure 16. Yard plan, period 3 house

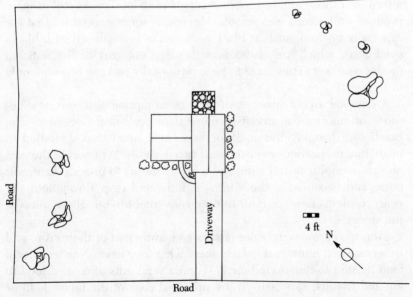

lawns. Dead forebears are located away from the innermost sphere of household lands, the cultivated garden, but they remain on the land they owned instead of being totally alienated from it in death. It is considered a vital part of annual gardening chores to keep the burial plots "cleaned up." This work entails cutting back briers and weeds and trimming edges. The graves are marked with simple headstones and are not otherwise decorated.

A close association between food production, including garden produce, and food consumption affects the aesthetics of food in the home. Some local women suggested to me that many people in Tidewater do not ordinarily consider food to be part of the aesthetic realm. Many locals ate the same things from week to week, they said, and rarely experimented with new dishes or ate at restaurants, except those that serve standard Southern family food. Empirically, this judgment is a little too clear-cut. It is true that by comparison a few families stand out as much more concerned with the aesthetics of a variety of foods than others. But even those people who are considered unadventurous have greater variety in their diet than might first appear, and they clearly make aesthetic judgments.

The passage of the seasons has a great effect on daily meals. Comparatively few men grow vegetables, but between them they supply a large number of households. Also, many nearby roadside produce stands sell locally grown vegetables. These vegetables are always preferred over those sold in supermarkets, and so local cooks still prepare produce as it comes into season. Moreover, some vegetables that are especially savored, such as black peas (not to be confused with black-eyed peas, which are also a favorite), are not part of the national produce market. They have to be grown locally and can be eaten only in season.

A seasonal aspect survives in meat consumption also, but now because of cultural conservatism more than ecological necessity. The practice of keeping livestock for household needs has dwindled to negligible proportions over the past two decades. Whereas in the past most households raised a pig and a few chickens to provide ham, salt pork, and bacon over the winter months and eggs throughout the year, residents now consider it more convenient to buy these items at the stores.

Men who grow vegetables always give away part of their crop, and fisherman and hunters regularly share what they have. Nor are gifts of food limited to raw ingredients. Women send gifts of cooked food to kin and friends, especially if the principal cook of the house is ill or indisposed. Gifts may vary from a full meal to a mess of greens. When a member of the community dies, friends prepare a meal at the deceased's house on the day of the funeral. The meal centers around a boiled ham bought by contribution. The presentation of food for the sick or bereaved from a friend's kitchen is considered "neighborly" and is perceived as an important act on the part of every established member of the community. Food gifts will most often be forthcoming even when rivalries exist between households, because "neighborliness" transcends most social dissension.

It is also considered neighborly to invite people to eat at one's table if they are visiting near mealtime and do not obviously have a meal to go to elsewhere. Many older cooks prepare meals that can be stretched to accommodate an extra person or two, and some cooks, considered miserly in other respects, are unfailingly generous with their hospitality at the meal table. Such generosity may derive in part from the fact that Tidewater has always been a food-producing community, and so food is a direct product of one's labor and not something bought with money. As the following stories attest, it is possible to be "poor," that is, have little ready money, but eat very well:

> For Sunday dinner a lot of times we'd have about fifteen, twenty come to dinner, and we'd have to put two tables together, and all that. And in those days I thought, "Oh my Lord, I've never seen so many dishes in my life." My mamma would have a great big roast of beef, like the old rump roast, and cut up. And then fried chicken, and corn pudding, and stewed tomatoes, and all that stuff. We were poor but always had something good to eat.

> My granddaddy ran a country store, and when it came lunch time he closed the store. The store was sitting out by the road and the house was set back. And whoever was in there, he invited them to lunch. And so they never knew how many they were cooking for. It was sorta like a hotel. It was in the thirties when we were growing up. We were poor but so was everybody else. We lived in the country and grew just about everything we ate.

Although Tidewater households are nuclear families, a family meal is not cooked in each home every night. Rather, one family cook, usually the eldest woman, cooks for the extended family. The core of this family grouping is matrilineal: men and children eat at the houses of their wives' mothers or wives' aunts. Many older women told me they did not learn how to cook until after their mothers had died. Such behavior not only maintains intergenerational ties among women but also relieves the financial burden and workload of young married couples.

A woman's mother's way of cooking tends to form the aesthetic standard by which the woman judges or describes her own:

> You cook rabbit just about like you do squirrel. Salt and pepper it, and flour it, or not flour it. Now really and truly my mamma was the only one around here that didn't flour. She never cooked much with milk and it would be good. Most of us have to cook with milk to make it good. She could just use water, and her eggbread and all would be better than mine. But I'd have to put milk in mine. She could put no flour on her wildfowl and it would be good. Seem like mine would be better with flour on it.

Part of what made this woman's mother a good cook was her ability to make good food with fewer expensive (that is, store-bought) ingredients.

Each family cook is a node in a food-sharing network that is of primary importance in maintaining social bonds in the community. Men provide raw food in different ways: sport fishing and hunting, commercial fishing, gardening, farming, and so forth. Whether they produce food for their living or not, men always have surpluses of something or other. Each man is a regular provider for the family cook in the household where he eats, but he also takes food to other family cooks as he wishes. Generally these cooks are affinal or consanguineal kin to him or friends of his family cook.

These men sometimes give a cook more than she can use of some item, but she is not at liberty to redistribute portions in a raw or wild state. She must invest some of her own labor before the food is truly hers to give away. She may, for example, receive enough fish for two family meals, dress all of them and send half to a friend. If for some reason she knows she cannot dress all of the fish, she is bound to tell the giver to leave half with her and take half to her friend. She cannot accept the entire load and give away half of it undressed. Similarly, she might accept more greens than she can use, cook the whole pile, and send parcels out at dinner time.

Tidewater is a food-producing town, and the men enjoy sport hunting and fishing in addition to their work as farmers and fishermen. As a result, local diets potentially have great variety. Table 3 gives a reasonably complete list of meats that are available and considered generally pleasing. Not all people in Tidewater eat or enjoy all of these

Table 3. "Edible" foods

Meat	Poultry	Fish	Shellfish
Beef/veal	Chicken	Spot	Crab
Pork/ham	Wild duck	Croaker	Oyster
Lamb/mutton	Canada goose	Speckled perch	Scallop
Deer	Snow goose	Bluefish	Shrimp
Squirrel	Coot	Drum	
Rabbit	Turkey	Flounder	
Frog	Dove	Mullet	
Turtle	Pigeon	Bream	
	Quail	Speckled trout	
	Blackbird	Rockfish	
	Woodcock	Panfish varieties	
	Snipe		

foods, but most people eat most of them at some time during the year. Furthermore, these foods are generally considered "edible" even if personal tastes vary. Some older people do not like lamb, for example, but they do not consider others perverse for eating it. The length and diversity of the list is such that one would almost believe that Tidewater people eat everything that walks, crawls, or swims. But they are particular in their selections and will not eat a variety of foods available to them, even though they know they are relished by some people from outside the community. Table 4 gives a partial list of these foods. The reason given for not eating these foods is almost universally an aesthetic one. People say the meat is too "wild" or too "strong" for their tastes. Derision is heaped on people believed to eat these foods, who are cast as lacking taste or sense. For example, out-of-town fishermen, the constant butt of local humor, are scorned for eating the bass they catch. Tidewater men enjoy the sport of catching bass, but they

Table 4. "Inedible" foods

Meat	Poultry	Fish	Shellfish
Raccoon	Crow	Eel	Clams
Possum	Pheasant	Bass	Mussels
Muskrat		Skate	Crayfish
Goat		Pike	
		Shad	
		Raccoon perch	
		Catfish	
		Carp	

throw all of their catch back. It is my impression that the people of Tidewater think that nonlocals who eat bass, skate, pheasant, and so on, have no ability to discriminate between the edible and the inedible. That is, they believe certain foods are *intrinsically* distasteful; anyone who eats and enjoys them must, therefore, lack powers of discrimination or necessary experience.

> I used to have friends come down here from Durham, and they didn't know what really good fish was. They'd get these old bass, which we wouldn't even eat 'em, and we'd go down there and that's what they'd have. So I sent 'em some fish one day, I think they were spots or bluefish, and she said "now they're the best fish I ever had in my life." See she'd never really been accustomed to cooking good fish.

Naturally, agreement concerning what is and is not edible is not total. Some prefer saltwater, some freshwater fish, for example. And all have tried "inedible" foods at some point in their lives. One waterman told me he had eaten possum and enjoyed it—but, he added, he was "three sheets in the wind" at the time. I presume he meant the alcohol in his system had dulled his ability to act according to his customary aesthetic values.

The man who keeps an elaborate flower garden also runs athwart local opinion with his belief that no flesh is intrinsically undesirable, and he runs counter to local norms in taking a hand at cooking indoors when he wishes. He once conducted an experiment on his wife and daughter to demonstrate that "inedible" foods taste good. The two women were due to go on a long shopping expedition to Virginia, and he knew they would be very hungry when they returned. On the day before the expedition he bought a bushel of oysters and made a great show of shucking them that evening. After the women had left for Virginia, he went to a local pig farmer who was castrating young pigs and procured a batch of "mountain oysters" (that is, pigs' testicles). When his wife and daughter returned from Virginia he was at the stove frying "oysters." He offered them each a heaping plate, which they accepted and ate greedily. Only when they had finished did he tell them what they had eaten. He claims to have proved his point, but his wife and daughter will not eat mountain oysters again, even though they admit they enjoyed them.

On the other side of the coin, some foods are held in esteem in part because outsiders are believed to dislike them. Hog jowls, souse, chitterlings, head cheese, greasy greens, cornbread, and fat pork are all ammunition in the modern war between the North and the South.

Yankees are chided for not liking these foods. Many of these items are difficult and expensive to obtain now, so they are no longer "po' food," but they are still sought out. Their contemporary value lies not in their cheapness but in their taste and in their value as markers that differentiate locals from outsiders. I have even known people in Tidewater to send packages of salted hogs' tails and feet to Northern acquaintances as a joke. The package is expected to bewilder and bemuse.

To an outsider the meat diet of Tidewater (quail one day, chicken gizzards the next) may appear an unusual blend of the exotic and the humble. But such adjectives are applied to these foods by people far removed from the land. For most Americans hunting is a rare sport, and therefore the products of hunting are rarities on the table. For the people of Tidewater hunting is commonplace, and its products are not treated as great delicacies. Goose, for example, is not served with the same exultance as it would be by, say, an Englishman. For the Englishman goose is a festive bird to be served only on special occasions. In Tidewater it is a commonly hunted bird served without pomp or ceremony. Indeed, in general game meats are accorded no unusual or extravagant care. Deer meat is cooked like cuts of beef, coot is jointed and fried like chicken, and duck and goose are plain baked. In fact, almost every time I asked a cook how she served a particular game animal, the description would include such phrases as "like fried chicken" or "like roast beef."

My husband's mamma made blackbird pie, you know the little old teeny birds. They were real fond of stewing birds and all. You made it just like you would a chicken pie. You made your pastry, or sometimes you'd make your pie crust, and stew those and put 'em in there. Then put another pie crust over it and bake it like that. And sometimes they'd stew it on top of the stove like a stewed chicken. You'd put your drop pastry in there like you roll out, like a flour dumpling, in there like that. So it was two ways you could do that.

One cook told me that in contrast to Northerners the women of Tidewater "overcook the meat and undercook the bread." They do not like meat to show any pinkness, and rare steak or beef is unthinkable. Northerners are said to eat "hard," that is, crusty, breads, whereas people in Tidewater prefer lightly cooked breads such as cornbread and spoon bread. Tidewater women also believe they eat breads more often and in greater variety than Northerners do.

These cooks also compare their tastes in cooking vegetables to those of Northerners. Green vegetables, both leafy and leguminous, are boiled for an hour or more with "seasoning," that is, fatback, salt pork, or hambone. Only the long cooking can impart the flavor of the seasoning meat to the vegetables. Also, many leafy vegetables, such as collards and mustard greens, require a solid boiling to tenderize them. Starchy foods, including potatoes and corn dumplings, may be cooked on top of the green vegetables. The seasoning meat is served along with the vegetable it has been cooked with.

Northerners are not the only "foreigners." Other Southerners may have different tastes and ideas as well:

> My husband's brother's wife lives down in South Carolina. I had a recipe of hers, the way she cooked quail, and it's sorta a little bit different from us. They use wine and all like that. Most people around here don't do that, it's sorta new for them. And I really have never done it. And, oh my Lord, there are some recipes for ducks with marinades of soya bean sauce and all of that stuff. But I never have done that.

A regular evening meal does not end with a dessert. Desserts mark a meal as special. At the simplest level a meal can be special because it is someone's birthday. Then, to mark the occasion, the family cook bakes a birthday cake to be eaten for dessert. The main meal of the day on Sundays is traditionally more elaborate than those of weekdays and in addition to extra meats and vegetables may include one or more desserts. Most favored are pies (lemon meringue, chocolate chess, pecan) and cakes (sponge and pound in various flavors). There are also a few perennial but short-lived seasonal favorites, such as strawberry shortcake. A very elaborate meal, particularly at Christmas and Thanksgiving, involves several different desserts, mostly pies.

Of the several "special" meals throughout the year, by far the most elaborate is Thanksgiving. Some households have enormous family gatherings at Thanksgiving (greater than at regular meals where an extended family eats together), at which prodigious amounts of food are prepared and eaten. It is, of course, mandatory to have a turkey or two, frequently with an oyster dressing, and common to have other poultry besides. Duck-hunting season is split in two unequal segments, the first of which stretches from the Monday before to the Friday after Thanksgiving, and so it is common to have fresh wildfowl alongside the turkey. Accompaniments may include some or all of the following: corn pudding, sweet potatoes, "Irish" potatoes, cranberry sauce, candied yams, and cornbread. Desserts always include pumpkin pie and mincemeat pie but may also include chiffon, chess, pecan, and other regular favorites. In most houses the Christmas meal is like Thanksgiving's but often on a smaller scale.

At the other extreme the main meal of New Year's Day is deliberately sparse. It is a local superstition that "if you eat poor on New Year's you'll eat rich the rest of the year." In consequence everyone eats black-eyed peas seasoned with salt pork of some kind. Many people prefer salted hog jowls, but feet or ears serve the same purpose. Even though such a meal is symbolic of the direst poverty, it is eaten with gusto and delight.

I cannot end a description of local dietary habits without stressing the central role of the hog in cooking. One indication of the importance of the animal is linguistic. The word "meat" is used locally, as elsewhere, to refer to the edible tissue of land animals but more often to refer specifically to cured pork. If someone says "pass the meat" when a piece of beef and a lump of salt pork sit side by side on the table, the request is unambiguous.

Scarcely a single meal passes in which some part of the hog is not employed. Lard is the principal cooking fat, cured pork is the chief vegetable seasoning, rendered bacon fat is used as a sauce for salt fish, salt pork is an essential ingredient of the local version of Brunswick stew, and the many cuts of pork are treated to every kind of cooking process: frying, boiling, baking, roasting, stewing, smoking, salting, grilling, broiling, and drying. This variety reflects both the versatility of the hog as food and the fact that at one time hogs were raised everywhere.

Although few people now keep hogs, the local diet retains the usages of former times. What was once a largely pragmatic consideration has become an aesthetic choice. Even with the dramatic escalation in recent years of the price of traditional "po' foods," which has eradicated economic reasons for buying them, such foods are still purchased because they are perceived as essential elements in most meals. Some cooks periodically prepare po' food to evoke memories of the past. One, for example, made haslet stew at the end of every fall. This watery stew of pig's heart and liver, with flour dumplings, was formerly made at hog-killing time to use up perishable items quickly. The practical need to make the dish is gone, but the taste for it remains.

It is eating "poor" that provides the hallmarks of good cooking:

> My husband's mamma was a lady that could take nothing and make something out of it. That's what I call a good cook. You would go to her

[75]

table and think, "Well, we're not going to have much for supper." And, I pray, she would have a variety of things. And, you know, you thought, "Well, we're not going to have much tonight." She'd have a little of this and a little of that, and it'd all be good. And she'd just mix it up good. Some can do that.

The great majority of Tidewater women do not have paying jobs outside the home. A great deal of their time is spent in cooking and caring for household functions, and what they describe as "leisure" activity is also geared toward the domestic realm. Needlecrafts were once a popular pastime, and the products could be put to use around the house. Recently, however, younger women have not been learning these crafts from their mothers as they did in the past, and the skills are rapidly dying out. Whether a woman sews or not is now a marker of age.

Quilting was very common at one time, and many old quilts are carefully preserved as mementos of older generations of women. The women in town who still quilt are of the oldest generation, and none of their children has adopted the craft. Cutwork, embroidery, and other needlecrafts are now scarcely practiced, but products of previous eras are cherished. I begin with an analysis of quilts which is slightly more detailed and formal than what has gone before because the construction and use of quilts provide insights into the aesthetic realm of women and the home. Even though only the oldest generation quilts, the work embodies values that permeate all homes. Formal analysis is also necessary because many of the quilts I surveyed look to the casual observer as if they were simply thrown together anyhow. What may appear scrappy and uninteresting is in reality highly structured and informative of general aesthetic values.

A quilt may be a single object of appreciation, but many elements combine to produce the overall effect. Some quilt scholars have devised long lists of these variables for detailed comparison of quilting styles, but for present purposes three variables will suffice: juxtaposition of geometric shapes, juxtaposition of colors, and quilting stitch patterns. Figures 17 and 18 show two "best quilts" made by the same woman. (A best quilt is made from bought material rather than scraps and is used for guest beds.) Both quilts use geometric shapes, color contrast, and quilting stitch to create striking overall effects. Red, white, and blue in the quilt in Figure 17 accentuate the concentric diamond pattern, while a trailing vine quilting stitch highlights the white areas (see Figure 39). The quilt in Figure 18 is a repeated block

[76]

Figure 17. Quilt LG 1

Figure 18. Quilt LG 2 detail

design made up of geometric shapes smaller than in the first one. The colors are more muted, and the quilting stitch follows the basket pattern rather than add a new pictorial motif. These quilts are considered very fine both because they are aesthetically pleasing and because they required many hours of painstaking work. I have more to say about these quilts later, but for the moment I turn to the quilts of the most prolific quilter in the community.

This quilter, whom I call Florence, has a collection of eight quilts and seven unquilted tops she has made. All but one are "scrap quilts" for daily use. (A scrap quilt is made from odds and ends of material, left over from other sewing jobs or from worn-out clothes, for the use

[77]

of family members.) An examination of this collection reveals certain aesthetic preferences that are not peculiar to Florence but common to local quilters and somewhat different from those of quilters from other parts of the South.

The quilts and quilt tops in Florence's collection could be classified in many ways. Quilt books frequently use pattern names from a standard compendium such as *The Romance of the Patchwork Quilt in America* (Hall and Kretsinger 1935), but (I will repeat the warning several times) Florence does *not* use names for her quilt patterns. As I consider the name to be an important aesthetic component of a quilt, for reasons explored below, I use a simple cataloguing scheme to refer to particular quilts. The first two letters identify the quilter by initials, the integer number identifies the pattern, and the decimal extension distinguishes quilts made according to the same pattern. Where possible the decimal extension indicates chronology. Thus FD 2.2 is a quilt made by Florence Doxey using pattern number 2, and it is her second example of this pattern. Although Florence used no names for quilts, she clearly identified quilts that used the same pattern, so that the cataloguing system records this recognition and does not identify each quilt by a separate number. Figures 19 through 29 show Florence's quilts in various degrees of detail.

To some quilters in the United States the name of the quilt is itself of no small importance. In some cases the pattern is a stylized representation of what the name suggests, such as Lone Star (Figure 30). Sometimes the relationship between pattern and name is more abstract, as in Jacob's Ladder and Flock of Geese (Figures 31 and 32). And sometimes there is no apparent relationship between name and pattern, as in Nelson's Victory (Figure 33). Quilters who use names may be consciously or unconsciously influenced by them in the production of quilts. They may, for example, be prompted to emphasize star patterns in a design with "star" in the name. Conversely, women who use no names may feel fewer constraints. They may think of all quilt designs in terms of generalized shapes rather than specific linguistic symbols and not feel the need to represent something as specific as a star, ladder, or lily. This is certainly the case in Florence's collection. Before looking at Florence's quilts in detail, however, we need to understand the components of a quilt design.

Juxtaposition of shapes and juxtaposition of color have a special relationship to the overall design of a quilt. The great majority of pieced quilt designs are made up from a few simple shapes: diamond, triangle, hexagon, and square. However, the pattern is not given

Figure 19. Quilt FD 1 detail

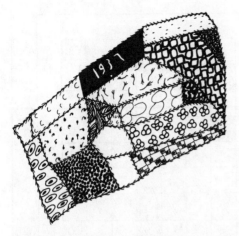

Figure 20. Quilt FD 2.1 detail

definition by the arrangement of geometric shapes alone. Choice of colors determines the overall pattern that emerges. Without color, for example, the Jacob's Ladder pattern appears as in Figure 34. Only when appropriate squares and triangles are shaded light and dark is the ladder defined (Figure 31). If the quilter chooses other shading patterns then different designs appear, such as Underground Railroad or Stepping Stones (Figures 35 and 36). One of the basic areas of creativity open to the quilter is the arrangement of colors within a basic geometric framework.

The quilting stitch, which holds the layers of the quilt together, completes the visual effect of the finished quilt. The quilter may follow the pieced design with her stitches or at least use the pieced design as a general guide (Figure 37), she may completely ignore the piecing (Figure 38), she may use large solid areas in the pieced design as frames for single motifs (Figure 39), she may create textured effects

[79]

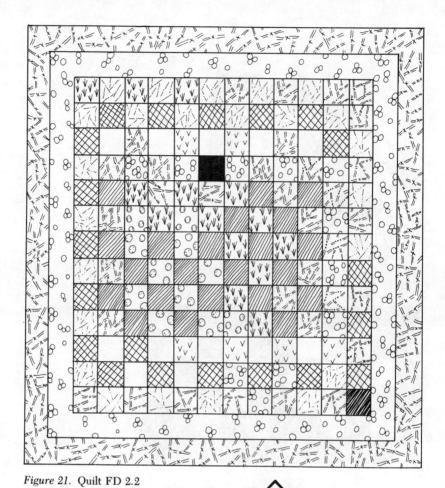

Figure 21. Quilt FD 2.2

Figure 22. Quilt FD 3 detail

[80]

Figure 23. Quilt FD 4 detail

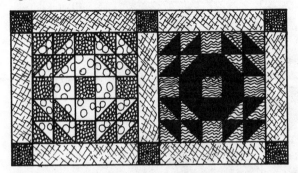

Figure 24. Quilt FD 5 detail

Figure 25. Quilt FD 6.1 detail

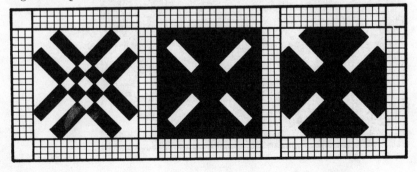

Figure 26. Quilt FD 7.1 detail

Figure 27. Quilt FD 8 detail

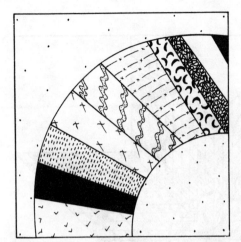

Figure 28. Quilt FD 9 detail

Figure 29. Quilt FD 10 detail

(Figure 40), or she may use any combination of these techniques. Thus the quilting may emphasize the pieced design or provide a counterpoint to it. Whatever the aesthetic relationship, however, a quilt top is *three-dimensional*. The texture and visual complexity added by the quilting stitch are fundamental ingredients in the final product and have too often been overlooked in design analysis. Moreover, the feel and texture of a quilt change over time as the quilt is used and washed. In other words, a quilt is not a two-dimensional, static, visual object but a three-dimensional, visual and tactile object that changes significantly through time. The history and destiny of quilts are important to any understanding of the aesthetics of quilts, and I treat them more fully later.

[83]

Figure 30. Lone Star quilt design

In Florence's collection most quilts are made up of repeated, incremental units. These units may be simple blocks of color, such as FD 2.2 (Figure 21), or more complex designs, such as FD 3 (Figure 22). Fourteen of her quilts are made up of repeated units, and only one, a crazy quilt, is not. In many of the quilts she has set the incremental blocks apart from one another with a set of internal borders called "sashing." These borders separate and emphasize each block. All but one of her quilts and tops have an outer border in addition to the regular binding that edges the quilt, and one has a strong double border.

The blocks within these internal and outer borders exhibit a high degree of geometric, but *not* color, symmetry. Of the patterns that are more than one-patch designs, nine are symmetrical around four axes and two around one. The former also exhibit 90°, 180°, and 270°

Figure 31. Jacob's Ladder quilt block

Figure 32. Flock of Geese quilt block

Figure 33. Nelson's Victory quilt block

[85]

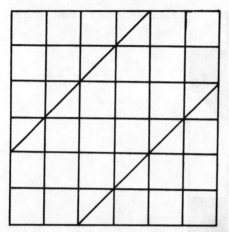

Figure 34. Jacob's Ladder uncolored quilt block

Figure 35. Underground Railroad quilt block

Figure 36. Stepping Stones quilt block

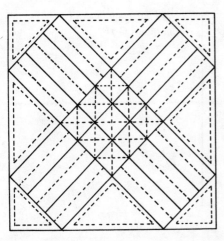

Figure 37. Quilting stitch following piecing design (from quilt FD 6.1)

KEY
—— Seam
---- Quilting stitch

Figure 38. Curvilinear quilting stitch with rectilinear piecing design

KEY
—— Seam
--- Quilting stitch

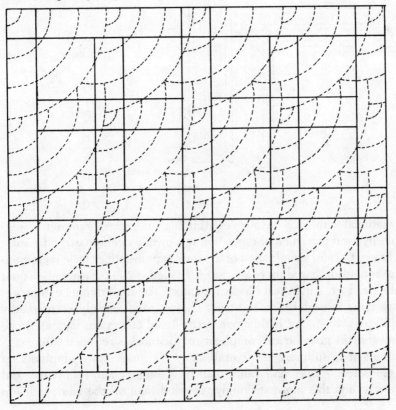

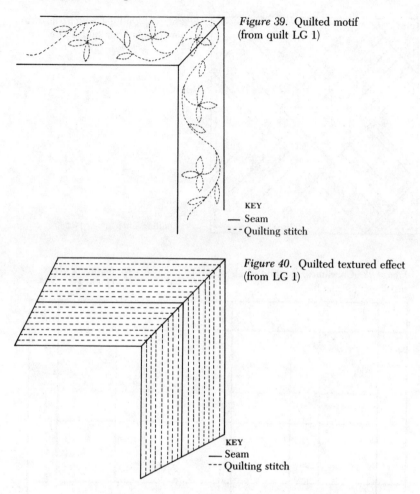

Figure 39. Quilted motif
(from quilt LG 1)

KEY
— Seam
--- Quilting stitch

Figure 40. Quilted textured effect
(from LG 1)

KEY
— Seam
--- Quilting stitch

rotational symmetry. However, this high degree of symmetry, regularity, and incremental repetition is radically deemphasized by color choice. Careful examination of the quilt tops identifies little incremental repetition based on color. FD 6.1 (Figure 25), for example, is not the product of identical blocks repeated. The underlying geometry is the same in each block, but color choice makes each block markedly different. Some are highly symmetrical and others are asymmetrical; in some the geometrical complexity of the block is revealed whereas in others it is submerged. Overall, there is much more emphasis on color, hue, shade, and value than on geometry and regularity, and nowhere is this more strikingly revealed than on the one patch top

Figure 41. Quilt AN 1

(Figure 21). Here Florence might have created a regular checkered pattern or one with a uniform color balance, but she has avoided such a mechanical approach to design. She has not arranged the colors uniformly, and the focus of attention is off center. One color is contrasted with a lighter one in one part of the quilt, with a darker one elsewhere. All of her quilts exhibit the same aesthetic qualities: geometric uniformity subordinated to complex color choice, with individual blocks contained within uniform borders.

Other quilts from Tidewater have the same basic features. The quilt in Figure 18, regular in its color choice because a best quilt, is not symmetrical overall. The baskets might have been set to form a concentric diamond pattern, but instead the pattern is broken and the diamond's center lies off center on the quilt top.

Another quilt fabricated locally uses color choice to break up the basic geometric configuration (Figure 41). The quilter evidently had sufficient material of each color to make the blocks uniform had she desired it. Instead she has created all of the possible combinations of the shapes which can be made with color choice while she preserved the underlying geometry. Figure 42 shows the basic uncolored block and along with Figure 43 reveals the method of piecing this kind of

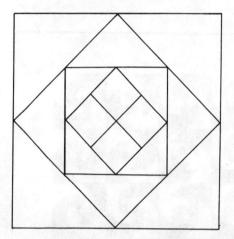

Figure 42. Quilt AN 1 uncolored block

block. First the quilter puts together four squares to make subunit I, alternating light and dark checkerboard fashion. Next she adds four right triangles to make a larger square, subunit II, again alternating light and dark. She continues adding triangles in the same fashion to make subunit III and then the finished block. One method of alternating lights and darks in the subunits produces a left-handed spiral pattern (Figure 44), another produces its mirror image, a right-handed spiral (Figure 45). But the quilter may take the left-handed spiral and rotate subunit I through 90°, producing a different pattern (Figure 46). She may do likewise with subunits II and III (Figures 47 and 48), or she may produce their right-handed mirror images (Figures 49–51). The simple alternation of light and dark in the subunits (which is, of course, only one method of varying the basic block) produces eight different patterns. Returning to the overall quilt, we can see that the quilter has employed all eight logical variations: she has played with design and construction technique in a series of variations on a theme. A schematic view of the placement of the different variations is shown in Figure 52.

It is also possible to arrange the blocks of this pattern to create a larger set of tessellating figures (Figure 53), but the Tidewater quilter has subordinated overall design to the individual blocks. The ultimate effect is one of considerable complexity. The effect of the tessellating pattern is to create a design unit larger than the blocks that make it up. Although the blocks in Figures 41 and 53 are drawn to the same size, the tessellating figures loom larger. Larger units may appear in the Tidewater quilt, but they are changing and ephemeral. This primacy

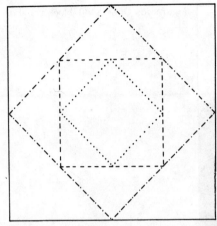

Figure 43. Quilt AN 1 showing block subunits

KEY
······ Subunit I
--- Subunit II
·-·- Subunit III
—— Block

Figure 44. Quilt AN 1 block variation 1L

Figure 45. Quilt AN 1 block variation 1R

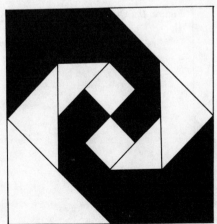

Figure 46. Quilt AN 1 block variation 2L

Figure 47. Quilt AN 1 block variation 3L

Figure 48. Quilt AN 1 block variation 4L

Figure 49. Quilt AN 1 block variation 2R

Figure 50. Quilt AN 1 block variation 3R

Figure 51. Quilt AN 1 block variation 4R

Figure 52. Quilt AN 1 block variation scheme

2L	1R	3R	2R	4R	1R
3L	4L	1R	3R	2L	1L
2L	3L	1R	4L	1R	1L
3L	2R	4R	2L	4R	3L

Figure 53. Quilt AN 1 block variation 1L, repeated in a tessellating design

in construction of the block unit over larger patterns is a general aesthetic principle in all local quilts. Internal borders, or sashing, around the blocks often help emphasize the block as the primal unit. Where sashing is absent, color choice preserves the integrity of individual blocks (see for example Figure 27).

As a general rule the scrap quilts of Tidewater exhibit a wide degree of freedom in color choice and variations on a theme, whereas the best quilts are regular in color and show few variations from block to block. The simplest and most usual reason given for these differences is that the scrap quilter is making do with whatever is on hand but the best quilter can buy enough material of each color to make all of the blocks uniform. But the quilt just analyzed gives the lie to this supposition. The quilter had enough light and dark material to make every block the same and to make a tessellating pattern. She did not make the quilt regular because she chose not to. The main reason is that best quilts are for public display and scrap quilts are for private use. The aesthetic values in the two realms are diametrically opposed.

Although the quilters of Tidewater use color choice to deemphasize underlying geometric patterns, their quilting stitches emphasize them. In all but one of Florence's quilts the stitches follow the edges of the geometric pattern (see Figure 37). The same is true of most other quilts made in Tidewater. Of the three variables, geometry, quilting stitch, and color, the first two show marked regularity and uniformity in all kinds of quilts, and the last involves a high degree of freedom and creativity in scrap quilts but is regular in best quilts.

The process of fabricating quilts in Tidewater is slightly unusual in comparison to many parts of the United States, where the production of a quilt is partly a joint effort. One or several women piece a number of tops, assemble sufficient batting and backing for all of the tops, and then invite friends to a quilting bee at which they quilt the three layers together following patterns marked by the owner. In Tidewater quilts are made from start to finish by one woman without the aid of others. This lack of joint effort mirrors the social realities of a Tidewater woman's life. Women do have small groups of friends who meet on regular occasions to play bridge, go grocery shopping, and perform chores that need several pairs of hands. But general social visiting is extremely rare. Many women told me they never visit their friends for a chat if they are well but will visit as often as possible in times of crisis. As one woman put it, "People here are not much on visiting you as long as you're getting along all right. But if you have a problem, get in trouble, they all rally round to help you." Her characterization was borne out by my personal observations. At one point Florence was

[95]

hospitalized for two weeks, and when she returned home she had a constant stream of visitors. In fact, she had so many visitors that on several days there was not a moment from sunrise to sunset when a friend was not in her sitting room, chatting. Before her hospital stay her only visitors had come for a specific task.

It is also true, as older needleworkers told me on several occasions, that every woman quilts in a slightly different fashion. Thus a quilt worked by many hands might be uneven in its overall stitchery. Singlehanded quilting obviates this problem.

The fact that quilts are made from start to finish by one woman affects them as aesthetic objects. Most quilters do not show their quilts to other women and display them in parts of the house closed to routine visitors, that is, the bedrooms. Quilts are not made for general public scrutiny or approval but are objects of private aesthetic value. Of course, best and scrap quilts are different: the former are used in guest bedrooms and are therefore on show to a limited public. The differences between the two types of quilt are highly suggestive. Best quilts use expensive materials, and are regular and uniform. Energy and artistry goes mainly into elaborate, painstaking quilting stitches, and best quilts are tributes to their makers' commitment to hard work. Scrap quilts are for family use only and allow the quilter to indulge her aesthetic fancies without adverse comment, since they will not be judged by outsiders. They may show an element of play that is missing in best quilts. These aesthetic decisions may be ultimately tied to the Protestant work ethic. That is, public craft should reflect well on a woman's industry and her ability to shrug off tedium, so best quilts are highly repetitive in design, with elaborate careful and uniform stitching. In private, however, a quilter may play as she works.

Scrap quilts, perhaps because they are made as fancies, are not cherished objects in the way that best quilts are. Best quilts are kept packed in camphor chests and brought out with reverence on special occasions. When they become too old to use, they are carefully washed and packed away as treasures. At this point they become like conceptual art works in that they may be stored in such a way that no one can ever see them. Some, for example, are cleaned, mothproofed, and stored in hermetically sealed bags. They are then permanently hidden from view, public and private, and discussed reverentially. Scrap quilts, on the other hand, are used and reused, roughly washed in the washing machine until they are shreds, and then demoted to some more mundane function. The pleasure of their creation does not make them lasting objects; quite the opposite. A quilt that was a

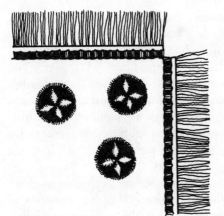

Figure 54. Cutwork placemat detail

pleasure to make is destined for ultimate destruction. I observed scrap quilts that had become shreds used as rags to clean motors, furniture pads, ironing-board covers; and one that had been especially tricky to piece because it involved a variety of inset diamond shapes ended its days as a shroud to bury a beloved family dog. Over the course of their lives these scrap quilts soften in color and texture, and several women commented on this process as desirable. They loved the feel and look of an old, well-worn, well-washed favorite. But this soft quality is the precursor to the material wearing so thin that it splits and tears, and then the quilt's days are numbered. From all of this we may derive a principle that applies to women's aesthetics in general, namely, that which is made with effort is of lasting value but that which is a joy to make has a limited duration. Best quilting is work, scrap quilting is leisure.

Elaborate embroidery, needlepoint, and cutwork are much more a thing of the past than quilts are. Some of the older women still quilt, but no one does fancy needlework. Those items which decorate homes are all treasured heirlooms, their owners confessing they are unable to do such work (Figure 54). Virtually all of these pieces were made at the turn of the century by younger women who had been trained in these crafts at boarding schools. These were the daughters of the few men in the town who could afford to pay for such an education: one kept a store and hotel, another was a doctor. When these girls came home from school, and before they were married, they visited one another regularly and stitched while they talked. This behavior contrasts to the more common practice in modern Tidewater of a woman doing her needlework alone, as in the case of quilting. The difference is undoubtedly a measure of economic standing. Most women in Tidewater pick up and put down their stitchery, snatching time for it between household tasks. The girls who embroidered had no chores, however, because the menial jobs around the house were performed by hired workers. Consequently they could visit when they pleased. But once they had children, these visits stopped. Their children, now in their seventies, display their needlework as mementos of a lost, genteel era. Such mementos also serve as subtle class markers for their present owners, indicating that their parents and grandparents belonged to a leisured class.

In modern times home-oriented, group leisure activities are few. Before the advent of television the home was one of many centers of leisure activity. Peer groups, especially youths and young adults, gathered to dance, sing, and play games. The older men and women in town remember these activities fondly and point to television as the cause of their demise. One man described television as "the greatest curse that's ever hit the United States. It adds nothing to you and it takes your time away from you." Before television, he said, "we had little dances, square dances mostly, when I was a kid. Once in a while we'd have a candy pulling. Five or six or a dozen young girls and boys would get together and they'd have a candy pulling. Most all the girls could play a piano. When it got into the eighteens and nineteen and twenty everybody had pianos that wanted them." One member of this generation who regularly played the piano for dances or singing parties has preserved a stack of sheet music—art songs, popular songs of the twenties, vaudeville songs, and college songs. On very rare occasions now two or three women gather at a piano or home organ to sing, but these are extraordinary events. The community at one time also had two fiddle players who played for dances at home. But the fiddle always had a suspect reputation, as the following story attests:

My grandfather was a fiddler and played for dances. I reckon that in my family there was a religious streak going right on down the family. It's in me. He used to play for dances back in the old days. He had a dream one night. And I don't remember the details, but I remember the outstanding things. Evidently there must've been some kind of subconscious conviction laying on his mind that he ought not to do it. He had a dream one night. Seems that he dreamed that he was playing for a dance, and that his fiddle—they called them fiddles in those days. I was a good-sized boy before I ever knew it was a violin—but his fiddle just broke open and a lamb's head rolled out down at his feet. And that was the last dance he ever played for.

[98]

The home now is rarely a place for any structured leisure activities. There are occasional parties on special days, such as birthdays, but regular gatherings are uncommon. If one thread runs through home leisure, it is that it is a predominantly female activity. Males of all ages spend their leisure hours outside the house, whereas the inside of the home is the woman's world. Those parties which are given are organized by women, and men participate with a thinly disguised reluctance. The local bridge club is a women's affair. The club meets at each member's home in turn, and the hostess of the night prepares for all of the women a dessert to be eaten with tea, coffee, or cola between the second and last rubbers of the evening.

Today television viewing is the most common home leisure activity. A few women gather to watch special shows, such as favored soap operas, but generally television keeps people isolated in separate houses. Should one follow local sentiment and see television as the modern cause of this isolation? The ethnographic evidence is ambiguous. Home parties are perhaps rarer but they do still exist, and, on the other side, many factors kept women isolated before the advent of television. As far back as living memory allows, women have worked alone in their own homes: to visit another woman during the day without a specific purpose is tantamount to idleness, quilting alone is the norm and always has been, and often when women do work together at home, as in preparing the evening meal, they are close kin. If women wish to congregate for work or other purposes, they do so outside their homes, most notably at the church. There, as we shall see, communal effort is normal.

[5]

Aesthetics at Work

It is convenient, and in line with local sentiments, to divide local full-time occupations into three classes: water activities, farming, and services. Each of these classes of work has its own aesthetic dimension, although it is quite limited in comparison with other factors. I consider each of these classes in turn, giving attention primarily to the aesthetic sphere whenever possible. However, as the practicalities of some occupations, especially fishing, are somewhat arcane, it will be necessary to venture into other, more general matters from time to time in order to provide a basis for understanding the aesthetic.

Gathering the wildlife of Tidewater Sound for sale has been a local activity for at least a century, yet it has rarely provided a complete family income. Today only one or two watermen do not have a supplementary income of some kind to see them through the inevitable lean times. In the past even the market gunners, who often made substantial sums during the season, had small farms or other businesses for additional income or support. All the watermen agree that to survive in the business one must have a keen eye for a dollar. Turning scraps of this and that into money is called "hustling" and might be called the major feature of all successful watermen. The term does not have the negative connotations it holds in other parts of the United States but is instead a mark of approval. The following story is a good example of a successful hustle:

One year V. B. caught around a thousand pounds of rock on one day. [Rock is customarily the highest-priced fish.] Now the buyers if they see a big catch of a high-price fish will slash the price. Instead of carrying his haul directly to the buyer he phoned ahead and asked what he was paying for rock that day. When the buyer told him the regular price, he carried in all thousand pounds. You see, the buyer had to stick to his price because he had given it out over the phone.

The story was often repeated as a model of how to make money out of fishing. The buyers are said to be rapacious middlemen who make money out of other people's hard labor. They have to be humored and placated because they can refuse to buy at any time on any pretense, but the watermen do not like them. Watermen tell stories of buyers who force them to sell to one company only and then refuse to buy a particular catch or who threaten to stop buying altogether if the catch is offered to anyone else: "Your buyers is what controls you. Just like up here. This fellah wants you to sell to him, but yet he wants to cut you off at a certain time. And if you go to sell to anyone else, then he gets hot and won't buy your fish, or crabs." They also tell of buyers who lie about the retail price of fish if they sell out of town, in order to get expensive fish cheaply. Watermen conceive of themselves as largely helpless in this situation, because they cannot both catch and market fish. Hustling remains their chief weapon against the buyers.

To the man trying to make a living out of the sound, every little helps. A road-killed raccoon will not remain on the roadside for long. A trapper will pick it up and freeze it until trapping season comes in, when he will thaw it and sell it with his other furs. At thirty-five dollars per pelt it is worth the effort. The waterman also learns to be a Jack-of-all-trades. He must know how to repair motors, nets, pots, boats, and all of his equipment. Having professionals take care of these repairs would be prohibitively costly and take his gear out of service at the wrong time. Furthermore, it is hard to take a faulty motor to the shop if you are three miles from shore.

Not only must the Tidewater fisherman be a general handyman, he must also master several different jobs and skills. He must be a skilled boatman, able to control a skiff with ease under power or with a poling oar; he must be acquainted with the bottom characteristics of the sound to find the best fishing areas and to navigate in fog; and he must be able to read weather signs both to profit from wildlife movements and to avoid personal danger. Watermen vary in their abilities in these areas and suffer or benefit in proportion. One extremely knowledge- able waterman can tell his exact location in thick fog, which can de- scend with alarming speed, by feeling the bottom with his poling oar. Others sometimes spend foggy nights in their boats. The year-round waterman must also handle two or three separate jobs, since no single one will keep him employed for more than six months. Options include commercial fishing, crabbing, eeling, guiding for sport fishermen, trapping, and guiding for duck hunters. There are also choices to be made within some of these categories. For example, a commercial fisherman may use haul seine, gill, pound, fyke, or submarine nets, although the last three are rare these days.

How each waterman employs himself throughout the year depends on a number of factors, some financial, some aesthetic. The basic choices are (in the winter) between commercial fishing, trapping, and guiding for hunters and (in the spring, summer, and early fall) between crabbing, eeling, and guiding for sport fishermen. Most watermen choose one activity from each group, but some combinations, though unusual, are possible. One may guide for hunters in the early winter and fish commercially for the rest of the season, or one may guide and trap. In the summer season some watermen both crab and eel, varying the number of each pot they set according to market prices and the size of each catch. In early spring before the crabbing grounds in Maryland have opened up the price of crabs is high, and it is profitable to set as many crab pots as possible. As the Maryland waters become more productive Tidewater fishermen who have the gear turn to eels.

The several dimensions to each water activity are tabulated in Table 5. This table shows equipment needed, number of people needed, regular expenses, whether the task must be done daily, and the advantages and disadvantages of each as articulated by the watermen. Items in parentheses are not absolutely necessary, but they make work lighter or increase profits. The crabber, for example, can reduce overhead by using gill nets to catch his own bait instead of buying it from a commercial bait dealer. All of these activities require a skiff and gasoline for the motor, which are not listed in the equipment and expenses columns.

No single activity is free of disadvantages, so the waterman cannot avoid compromises. The basic variables are high versus low income, stable versus irregular income, working alone (or with one or two friends) versus working with the public, and low versus high initial capital outlay. The first mentioned of each of these variables, which the watermen themselves offer as binary variables, is considered a good feature, whereas the second is considered undesirable. Because of fundamental relationships between the variables, each activity is associated with two desirable and two undesirable characteristics (see Table 6).

Table 5. Watermen's tasks

	Equipment	People	Daily	Regular expenses	Advantages	Disadvantages
Winter Trapping	100 traps, gun	1	yes	bait	potential high profit	irregular earnings, animal attack
Hunting	blind, gun, calls, 50+ decoys (waterdog)	1	no	none	stable income	shooting accidents, dealing with public
Commercial fishing (a)	haul seine, fishing skiff	3	no	none	high profit	high capital outlay, irregular earnings
Commercial fishing (b)	20–50 gill nets	2	yes	none	stable income	cold work
Summer Crabbing	100 pots (gill nets)	1	yes	bait	potential good profit	irregular earnings
Eeling	100 pots (crab pots)	1	yes	bait	potential high profit	irregular earnings
Sport fishing	Rod, baits	1	no	none	stable income	dealing with public

Table 6. Dimensions of watermen's activities

	Desirable	Undesirable
Trapping	high profit alone	irregular income high outlay
Hunting	stable income low outlay	low profit public
Commercial fishing (a)	high profit not public	irregular income high outlay
Commercial fishing (b)	stable income alone	low profit high outlay
Crabbing	high profit alone	irregular income high outlay
Eeling	high profit alone	irregular income high outlay
Sport fishing	stable income low outlay	low profit public

A man's choice depends primarily on whether he has the capital to buy, or can inherit, the equipment for the high profit/high risk occupations, which are generally preferred over the stable profit/low risk occupations. How much capital is needed is also a significant factor. A combination of commercial fishing in the winter and crabbing or eeling in the summer is highly desirable but the most expensive to get started. A combination of guiding for hunters in the winter and fishermen in the summer requires almost no capital but is extremely undesirable. (For combinations of occupations in terms of cost, see Table 7.) This progression is somewhat ladderlike, although the maturing waterman need not step on every rung. It would, for example, be undesirable to move from step 3 to step 2, which would involve a complete change of summer and winter equipment, trading the cost of the summer equipment down. A waterman would almost certainly move from step 3 to step 1. Very few actually reach the top because of the extreme cost of haul seine fishing. A waterman calculated for me that to get started in haul seine fishing with all new gear could cost over $10,000. Few watermen start at step 8 because of the general distaste for dealing with the public throughout the year. Most balance the year with one high- and one low-cost occupation.

There is not only a financial but a personal risk attached to these occupations. All watermen run the risk of drowning, and all have had

Table 7. Cost scale of water activities

	Summer	Winter
Greatest Outlay	1. Commercial fishing (a)	Crabbing &/or Eeling
	2. Commercial fishing (b)	Crabbing &/or Eeling
	3. Commercial fishing (a)	Sport fishing
	4. Trapping	Crabbing &/or Eeling
	5. Hunting	Crabbing &/or Eeling
	6. Commercial fishing (b)	Sport fishing
	7. Trapping	Sport fishing
Least Outlay	8. Hunting	Sport Fishing

friends and relatives who drowned. A man in heavy-weather gear sinks quickly if thrown overboard, whether a good swimmer or not. Hip boots ship water instantly and act like lead weights. In addition, two occupations have special dangers that make them undesirable. Guiding for duck hunters is especially hazardous because the hunters are usually inexperienced in the use of firearms, heedless of safety codes, and intoxicated or under the influence of alcohol while in the duck blind; daily the guides return with harrowing tales. The trapper runs the risk of being bitten and clawed by trapped animals. Because of these dangers commercial fishing is much preferred over the other two occupations. Hunting is preferred over trapping because of the characteristics outlined above, even though it is potentially more dangerous than trapping and involves dealing with the public. The act of killing to eat is greatly preferred over killing for pelts.

Local men like to stick to the rule "Only kill what you will eat" in all of their dealings with the wild. This maxim reduces the aesthetic pleasure derived from a number of activities including eeling, trapping, and bass fishing. Men dislike fishing for eels because they do not consider them edible (and believe they are exported to Europe or Japan) and cannot understand the desire to eat them. Local women do not wear furs, so the act of trapping is doubly pointless on the local level. Just like the local farmer who grows millet because he feels impelled by external market forces (eels regularly bring a dollar per pound), the watermen does what is necessary to make a living, but the desires of the outside world alienate him in aesthetic terms from his labor.

The decision to be a waterman is itself founded on aesthetic desires.

All watermen say they enjoy their work because of the beauty of the environment, and their behavior supports this claim. When they are not working for profit, they still spend much of their time on the sound. Some sport-fishing guides will bring their charges in when they have caught their limits and go back out immediately to fish by themselves. Jobs that involve guiding are disliked in part because they reduce the waterman's aesthetic appreciation of his surroundings. They say they have to spend so much time avoiding a fish hook in the face or a leg full of shot that they have no time to relax and look about them. Two watermen independently told me they loved the sights of the sound so much that on several occasions they have ridden to their duck blinds without guns, simply to observe the waterfowl.

The aesthetic pleasure derived from working on the sound is considered fair compensation for the lack of great financial reward, the hard labor, and the often repetitive chores involved. Crabbing, for example, is no less repetitive than most factory jobs on a production line. It mostly entails raising, emptying, baiting, and resetting one hundred or more crab pots, six days per week. All of the watermen in Tidewater have had jobs that were more regular and paid more than fishing, but the lure of the sound is mighty. One crabber, a qualified mason, turned down the opportunity to lay the foundations and brick veneer of a new, four-bedroom, two-story house, which would have paid well with no capital expenditure on his part, in favor of crabbing, which at the time was netting him fifteen dollars per day on those days when he could sell his crabs. Besides, watermen consider their work to be "real" in a double sense. They are in command of the process from start to finish, whereas the factory worker on a production line is responsible for a minute part of the finished product. Also, the products of fishing (with the exceptions noted) have a direct, obvious, and fundamental use. A fish caught in the morning can be in the pan by night. The products of the waterman's labor have direct aesthetic appeal.

Married men with children are usually forced to take out-of-town employment because the income from fishing is too irregular to meet daily needs. But a man who has started his working life as a waterman inevitably returns to that life upon retirement from paid employment. These older watermen may take on a year-round work cycle or may fish in the summer only. Younger watermen point with pride to men in their eighties who still fish regularly. Only severe physical infirmity can cause a waterman to quit his skiff.

Despite these strong aesthetic attractions, the life of the waterman has negative aesthetic components as well. Fish caught in a haul seine by the gills must be removed by hand, generally without gloves. In January the feel of slippery, icy fish for several hours on bare skin has no appeal. By contrast, the blazing noon sun of August on old fish boxes and crab bait can raise a mighty stench. Yet the waterman treats these aspects of his employment stoically. Not all aesthetic experiences are enjoyable; they must be weighed in the balance.

Perhaps surprisingly, watermen have little overt aesthetic interest in their boats. I could elicit aesthetic judgments about boats from only one man, and then about shad boats, a kind of sailing vessel used on the sound for fishing and hunting in the early part of the century:

> There's a lot in shaping a boat to make her look good. You could build a shad boat and it would look awful. Then another man could build one'd be just as shapey and nice-looking as a yacht. Wallace O'Brien could build the prettiest shad boat. They sailed those shad boats when I was a kid and they were good sailors.

This statement is unusual, but several hidden meanings make sense of it. The comparison to yachts is the significant point. Yachts sail across the sound regularly—north in summer, south in winter. Watermen use a vulgar phrase for them that likens them to inedible waterfowl. "They fly up and down here like a bunch of [expletive] geese, that are no use to no one." These yachts are pleasure craft; the watermen see them as idle toys that have no function. The above anecdote is pointing out that a working boat could be thought of as pretty as a yacht, yet it was functional. What is more, the men in them were better sailors than yachtsmen and worked harder:

> We used to carry ballast for sailing made out of canvas bags. They'd have a hundred pounds of sand and sewed up tight. To go on up against the wind to get where you wanted to go, it usually took three men to sail 'em. Two men would stand right a-straddle of the center board, and when the man would tack they'd shift that ballast from one side to the other, mighty quick. Two men can shift five hundred to a thousand pound of ballast right now. It was hard work but we didn't mind it. God damn it, I've shifted 'em. Shifted 'em for twenty miles.

Stories about boats and boatbuilding are rare, and no folklore is connected with the craft: no boatbuilding rituals or superstitions, no proverbs, no paintings or models of boats. Of course, boatbuilding itself is a traditional folk craft. All watermen know something about boatbuilding and have built or helped build at least one boat in their lives. They never use written sources but rely on their own skills learned by watching and helping expert craftsmen. There is, however, a general feeling that real expertise in building boats runs in families:

Pat O'Brien was the best boatbuilder in Tidewater. And every O'Brien that I ever saw around this section was a boatbuilder. James O'Brien, brother to Pat, is a good boatbuilder, and he's about seventy. His grandfather and his father before him, all the O'Briens just had the knack to build a boat. Pat could take a piece of wood to build a stem lining, and he'd take it and lay it out with a pencil and his finger against it as a guide, and lay it out, and take a hatchet and chop it out, and dress it off. When he put the side planks on, damn if they wouldn't fit. He just knew what the hell he was doing.

But expert or not, there is always plenty of free advice:

I know one time there used to be this feller, I've forgot his name. But he said that every time he got ready to build a boat somebody'd come round with their opinion, telling him how to build it. So one time they said that he set up two boats to build. And when there wasn't anybody around he'd work on one boat, when somebody'd come around he'd work on the other. So long as they were giving him an opinion he said, "I'm going to build this one to suit you, but that one over there I'm going to suit myself."

The opinions so readily expressed by watermen concern crafting the boat for practical purposes and have little to do with its aesthetic qualities. Yet no two boats, even two built by the same man, are alike, and a waterman can easily distinguish and identify them at some distance: "Each boatbuilder has his own way of building boats. I don't care who he is, he won't ever build two alike. There'll be a little bit of a difference in any of 'em. I've never seen anyone build two that were exactly alike." However, these distinguishing features—length, bow rake, draught, attitude—do not appear to contribute or detract from the aesthetic qualities a boat might have. No waterman is interested in the look of a boat except inasmuch as it reflects its capacity to be employed in certain ways.

Most watermen use flat-bottomed skiffs because of their clear practical advantages over other designs. Many of the bays and marshlands of Marsh County are extremely shallow (three feet or less), and only a flat-bottomed boat can navigate in them. Also, a flat-bottomed boat can rise on its bow wake and travel at full speed in much shallower water than one with a keel or V-bottom can.

The carrying capacity of a skiff is determined by its relative width, length, and depth, but which dimension is lengthened or shortened to suit the carrying needs of the waterman is determined by the speed and handling characteristics the waterman needs in the boat. A large fishing skiff used in conjunction with a smaller skiff for haul seine fishing must be large enough to hold several thousand pounds of fish and need not be fast or maneuverable. This kind of boat is, therefore, built broad in the beam and deep. A crabbing skiff is deep and long but narrow in the beam so that it handles easily but can carry a moderately large catch. A sport-fishing skiff is narrow and shallow, for carrying capacity is unimportant yet it must handle easily in the shallows.

Watermen paint their boats drab grey or green. They are fastidious about keeping their boats clean, and these colors make their job easier. Drab colors are also important for camouflage in hunting season. These boats have no painted ornaments and no painted names, only the mandated state registration number.

On the job, watermen dress for comfort and convenience, but they remain in working gear during leisure hours. They may not wear oilskins around town, but hip boots are a badge of their calling. In the winter they wear "Dr Roberts"–style hunting caps and in the summer baseball-style caps bearing motifs of personal significance.

The local farms are owned by a very small number of families, all of which have deep genealogical roots in the community. One old plantation family was buying and selling parcels of land in the area at least as early as the turn of the nineteenth century. These families now are survivors of the mid-twentieth-century technological revolution that led to the heavy mechanization of farms and their subsequent consolidation. Several farms in what has become the center of the town did not survive, and between 1935 and 1950 they were carved into building plots and sold or given away to family members. This platting has created a slight feeling of nucleation in the town. Those farms which have survived seem reasonably secure at present, but all of the farmers are deeply pessimistic about the future. All have such large amounts of capital tied up in farm machinery and loans that a bad harvest or a succession of poor years can spell ruin. These farmers have unwittingly and unwillingly become involved in the global commodities market and see themselves less and less as free agents. They are tied into a web of government grants and regulations, international politics, high-finance mercantile trade, and global supply and demand they scarcely understand. These forces are major influences on what they produce, which in turn affects the aesthetic dimensions of their labor.

The aesthetic judgments of the farmer at work are few, though not necessarily insignificant. What aesthetic judgments he does make are closely tied to practical decisions. The clothes he wears at work, for example, are chosen for comfort and convenience; they also mark him as a farmer to the rest of the world. When the farmer leaves his farm he does not change his clothes (jeans, workshirt, work boots, and feed cap)—he prefers to appear in public as a farmer. The only item of dress that is cause for remark is his cap. Each farmer wears a different cap advertising agricultural products of some kind, whether seed, fertilizer, or machinery. These are objects of some pride and a tinge of vanity. Farmers are so rarely out of their work clothes that when they dress differently, it is a cause for comment by friends.

Many crucial decisions on a farm are based on the perceptible qualities, especially the sight, of land, crops, and animals, and when these are combined with matters of taste and affect, as they sometimes are, they may be said to have an aesthetic dimension. The decisions when to plough, sow, and harvest are in economic terms critical. At each of these stages a bad choice can drastically reduce income by reducing yield. How the soil or the crop *looks* is the principal determinant in each of these cases. The act of inspecting a field is practical and technical rather than a question of taste, but it does have an aesthetic aspect. A sodden field in spring or a crop riddled with parasites is both economically and aesthetically displeasing, but a healthy stand of corn or wheat is pleasing. However, modern agricultural products have confused this aesthetic area.

In the past, crops were diversified and satisfied local needs for farm produce while also producing a surplus for sale elsewhere. Farmers grew crops they understood the need for and in growing which they had a great deal of family experience. Now to survive they grow what is suggested by county agricultural agents or in demand on the commodities market. Thus they grow soybeans, millet, and linseed, but they do not know what these crops are used for and hence do not know their value in human terms. These crops, in consequence, do not *look* as good to them as fields of corn or truck crops. Farmers idealize themselves as primary food producers, filling the tables of the community with things to eat. Modern crops weaken this vision and in turn affect the aesthetic appeal of their cultivated environment.

Finally, the decision to become a farmer has a major aesthetic aspect. Because the occupation is not financially secure, those who take it up must have other reasons for doing so. One of these reasons is aesthetic. All farmers agree they enjoy working in the open and appreciate the aesthetics of their rural working surroundings. Some contrast this open-air work to the close, unappealing environment of the factories that for them are the alternative to farmwork. Although farming is technical and practical, it rests on an aesthetic foundation.

The service jobs in town are not as male-oriented as farming and fishing. Most are run by husband-and-wife teams, a few by men or women alone. The two most important services for locals in town are the general stores and the eating establishments. Local residents use these services regularly, whereas other services—for example, legal, realty, home repair, and building supplies—are specialized and only occasionally used.

The stores have two distinct sources of business: locals and transients. Locals buy gasoline and oil, perishable items such as bread and milk, things they unexpectedly run out of, and small items such as candy and soda. They do their main grocery shopping at supermarkets in several large towns nearby, where the prices are lower and there is greater variety. Tourists, campers, and fishermen use the stores to buy the same kinds of things the locals buy plus a wide variety of groceries, such as tinned meat and vegetables, cleaning materials, paper goods, fresh meat, snacks, and so forth. The storekeepers estimate that about 80 percent of their trade is from transients, although this figure is nothing but a good guess because neither keeps records of who buys what. Nonetheless the figure is an important expression of who they think buys most, particularly as the stores are set up more for the comfort of locals than for transients.

The reliance on transient trade and the decline of local business were caused by the arrival of trunk roads. These roads gave local people a way to get to cheaper markets and outsiders a chance to gain quick access to scenic and sporting water facilities. The stores have had to change to accommodate these new circumstances. Before the new roads the stores survived exclusively on local business, and the people of Tidewater depended on the stores. The modern stores do stock some items not commonly found in groceries, such as car fuses, oilskins, and fishing lures, but in the past general merchandise was as important as groceries. The major store in town, now defunct, carried men's and women's apparel, piece goods, shot and powder, cosmetics, nails, horse collars, dishes, in fact virtually everything one might need.

The stores were also vital as creditors. Market hunters, fishermen, and farmers could buy items on credit and pay up when they sold their produce:

> I've heard some of the old heads say that this fellah, Field, furnished the powder and shot and the fellahs would go shoot the ducks and bring them here for him to ship and they'd pay off their bill. He let 'em have it 'till they killed enough ducks and he got it back, more or less of a barter thing. But there come a winter, it was very mild. There were no ducks. The ducks didn't come this far, it wasn't cold enough. And nobody could kill any ducks. They stood up around his store and pitched horseshoes, the gunners did, and finally he said to 'em, "Well boys, if we don't make it this year it'll be all right. I'll put it on the bill next year. You'll make it next year." That's the way Tidewater's always been.

Store credit was, and is, interest-free. Such credit is perceived as fundamentally different from interest-bearing loans, and the two go by different names. Interest-free loans are called "credit" or "bills," and interest-bearing loans are called "borrowing." Credit is acceptable, borrowing is not. The credit system built up a series of trading relationships between households and particular merchants which survive to this day, even though the stores have changed owners several times and it is the adult children and grandchildren of those households who now do the buying. Everyone in Tidewater shops at one general store only for day-to-day items. Each household has a deep sense of loyalty that outweighs practical considerations such as comparative cheapness. One woman told me emphatically, "My father and grandfather traded at that store, and I'm not about to go elsewhere just to save a few pennies." As Tidewater people are thrifty with earned money, this remarkable statement indicates a hierarchy of values. Loyalty to a trader who through the credit system has helped the family survive outweighs the desire to buy goods as cheaply as possible.

Loyalty to store owners is reinforced by continuing debt relationships. Every household in Tidewater keeps a line of credit with one of the stores, even though most have enough money in the bank to stay clear of debt. It is also common for people to buy groceries on credit when they have enough money in their pockets to pay for them. The line of credit is a symbol of loyalty and cohesiveness, not a practical necessity. Once I observed a storekeeper accuse a young farmer of taking gasoline for his truck without recording it in his credit book. Outraged at the accusation, the farmer demanded to know what he owed the storekeeper in credit, took out a wad of bills, paid the whole debt, and left the store. By paying his debt he severed his loyalty to the store.

Because of the change in their business the stores now look different. In the old stores the owner waited on the customer, but with the periodic inundation of transients there is no longer time for "old-fashioned service." The stores now are laid out like small supermarkets, and customers pick items from the shelves and pay at the cash register. But storekeepers still wait on locals who are old and infirm. The changes in the layouts of the stores have left little room for people to sit and chat, and many locals feel that the homelike coziness of the stores has been lost. At one store the changes have drastically reduced the practice of sitting and general visiting, but at the other the old ways are still going strong even though customers have to share social space with a stack of motor-oil cans on one side and cat food on the other.

The stores of the past had a homelike appearance that survives today. One store was a converted house; the other was built along the same lines as an old-style house but built end to the road, and the ground floor, the store, is one large room. Storekeepers of past and present feel that the homelike quality is essential for good business. Local customers, they believe, should feel comfortable enough to want to stay awhile. If for some reason a local must make a quick purchase, the owner will chide him, "Don't hurry."

There are two kinds of eating establishments in town. Three are takeout sandwich stands, and one is a sitdown restaurant. The former are very recent and cater exclusively to the transient trade. Their mainstay is American fast food: hamburgers, hot dogs, French fries, and fountain soda. The restaurant is also new, but there have been others of its type for a century. Its stock in trade is home-style specials, and it caters to both locals and transients. Tidewater men who work in town eat here at lunchtime, and they make up a substantial, convivial lunch crowd. They always eat the daily special if it conforms to local culinary norms. Any dish out of the ordinary by local tastes, such as stuffed peppers or spaghetti, finds no local takers. The owner, a widow, makes a point of creating a home atmosphere in her cooking and attention to customers. Even the name, "My Family Restaurant," evokes a homey feeling.

Creation of a feeling of being at home extends to all services in town. Most services are delivered in a special part of a family home or in an adjacent building. They run the gamut of legal services, television repair, haircuts, commercial bait and fishing gear, and general house repair. Only three services do not strictly adhere to this type: two are real estate offices, one a legal practice. All three are new, and the great majority of their customers are not local. Appropriately enough, though, one realtor works out of a converted house trailer, the other out of an office that is part of someone else's home. Only the law practice stands in splendid isolation, both physically and culturally. However, the lawyer is an out-of-town practitioner with offices in several counties and townships. He is the exception that proves the rule.

A few general points can be made about the aesthetics of work. Tidewater people at work are generally isolated from one another. Farmers, fishermen, barbers, and lawyers work by themselves or with one other person. In consequence, the aesthetics of the work situation is highly personalized. The farmer and waterman gain personal, not shared, aesthetic satisfaction from their environments. The service people run their businesses from buildings or offices laid out to suit their own tastes. In many ways the man (or woman) at work is as isolated as the woman at home.

The association between work and home is strong and important. Watermen usually have docks in their yards and use their barns for storing equipment. Farmers live adjacent to the fields they tend, and service people work out of their homes. The physical association with home varies from job to job, of course. The waterman works at a great distance from his home, the farmer works nearby, and the service person works in his home. The distance of employment from home is strongly correlated with the stability of each job and the amount of aesthetic *control* that is exerted in each sphere. In essence, the farther from home the job takes place, the less aesthetic control the worker seeks to wield.

The waterman does nothing to change the aesthetics of his environment and claims to have no aesthetic interest in the things that of necessity he brings into it, such as boats and nets. His aesthetic pleasure is derived entirely from nature in the raw. Many who seek aesthetic satisfaction while at work ride out to a favorite deserted spot, away from floats and crab pots and out of sight of houses on the peninsula. There they sit or stand and gaze beyond the confines of the skiff at a soundscape devoid of artifacts. The waterman is also acutely aware at all times that his survival, while assisted by appropriate behavior, is not assured by attempts on his part to control this environment.

The farmer gains aesthetic pleasure from domesticating nature. He transforms segments of the natural environment through careful cultivation. But he works in nature and must continually deal with such realities of the natural world as pests and weather. The products he works with are partly natural, in that they are plants and animals, and partly controlled, in that they are domestic varieties grown under regulated conditions using commercial feeds, fertilizers, and pesticides. His measure of control is midway between the waterman's and the service person's and analogous to the aesthetics of gardens, which lie midway between houses and wilderness.

The service person totally controls and transforms his environment: it is entirely an artifact of his making. In the general stores, for example, all products are laid out with bureaucratic efficiency, cleaning products in one aisle, automotive supplies in another. Even goods of natural provenance, such as fruits and vegetables, are carefully controlled. Identical cans of pineapple segments sit in neat ranks and files, just like the motor oil two rows over. Everything is itemized, indexed, and inventoried.

This diversity in aesthetic control is matched by the economic stability of each occupation. The waterman's is the most unstable. He has little way of knowing what he will earn from day to day, there are no government programs to ease his losses in bad years, no insurance companies will insure his gear, no bank will accept his equipment as collateral for a loan, and no county or state programs educate him in better ways to do his job. Farming has its risks, but the farmer has a certain amount of state and federal protection. He can insure his equipment and borrow against his holdings. He can predict with some accuracy what his profits will be, and the county agricultural extension agent is always available to give free advice. Services are almost all stable, with regular, predictable incomes.

The degree of control the worker exerts over the environment is, perhaps logically, proportional to the amount of control he is perceived to exert over himself. Watermen are characterized as "wild" and "roosters" and are generally thought of as rough and unruly. People in services, on the other hand, are seen as orderly and respectable. Farmers, too, tend to be seen as in control of themselves. One principal index of such control and respectability is church membership and activity. Men in services and farmers are active and engaged members, fishermen either do not attend or are reserved in their involvement. However, speculation about the relationship between aesthetic domains requires exploration of the church in some detail.

[6]

Aesthetics of the Church

The church in Tidewater is the locus of an extremely wide range of aesthetic forms, including architecture, music, poetry, storytelling, oratory, drama, and food. At all church functions different combinations of aesthetic forms work together to create complex aesthetic environments. I consider the main events of the church in turn, because it is easier to see this complex realm at work than to try to understand aesthetic forms in isolation first and then put them together. I also consider several situations of conflict, because they make the role of church aesthetics very clear. To start, though, I set the stage by detailing the historical development of the church's architecture and attendant aesthetic decisions. A detailed understanding of the development of the architectural space and its internal and external decoration is important not only because this space frames other aesthetic forms but also because conflict over the aesthetics of the building began a major schism in the church.

Tidewater Missionary Baptist Church was granted a charter in 1893 and began with a membership of eighteen. There is no record of the exact date of construction of the building, but church records indicate that the first wedding took place there in 1898. Between the founding of the church and the construction of the building, the congregation met in an old schoolhouse.

From its founding until the late 1950s the church was on a circuit—known locally as a "field"—because it had insufficient income to support a full-time preacher. For most of this time there were four churches on the field, so Tidewater had one morning and one evening service per month. During the 1950s the church underwent considerable reorganization, including significant architectural changes. Over the decade the congregation added a Sunday school building to the rear of the church, installed a choir loft, veneered the church exterior in brick, put up a bell tower, bought a parsonage, and hired a full-time preacher. All of these changes required extraordinary, concerted fund raising, which has not been equaled since.

Because the church is not well-endowed or located in a high-population area, it does not attract established preachers. Most of the preachers are young men straight from the seminary, who stay for three or four years only and then move to another charge, either of their own accord or, more commonly, under pressure from the congregation. Younger preachers are often fired up to make sweeping changes, particularly in the church's aesthetics, but the influential members, all of whom are direct descendants of the founders, treat change with circumspection. Many of the aesthetic values of the congregation have been clearly articulated because of ongoing battles with preachers.

When it was built, Tidewater Missionary Baptist was a simple edifice. The town doctor donated the land, and local people contributed materials. Wood for the frame came from logs cut from the swamp and taken to the town sawmill, where they were rip cut and dressed. The sanctuary was built as a forty feet by sixty feet rectangle with a flat ceiling fifteen feet high (Figure 55). The pulpit was set in a trapezoidal recess at the rear of the sanctuary. The interior walls and ceiling were dressed with a thin lath paneling and finished with a hand-rubbed palm oil. This operation was supervised by an English boatbuilder, and the members have been proud of the job ever since. The wood has a bright, burnished luster that has never needed cleaning or retouching in any way. (One young preacher in the 1960s suggested the interior was too dark and should be painted white. He was soon gone.) The subfloor was made from rough hewn boards sawn from drift lumber that had been salvaged from county waterways, and later a pineboard floor was added. Twin double doors at the front of the church led into a vestibule as wide as the church and six feet deep. Matching doors led from the vestibule into the sanctuary.

The exterior of the building was originally plain and conformed to standard building practices of the 1890s. It had a gable roof with two symmetrically placed doors in the gable end facing the road. Wooden steps led up to each door, and a peaked window was centrally placed between the two doors. Each side had six partially colored windows, with two at the rear illuminating the pulpit. The whole building was sheathed in white clapboard.

[117]

The original furniture was handmade by local craftsmen. At the outset pulpit and pews made up the total inventory. There was no baptistery incorporated into the church, because at the time it was customary to baptize new members in Tidewater Sound. The practice continues to this day. The pulpit, which is a simple Bible stand, was made by the local blacksmith, and the pews were made by various members. At first the church was lit by kerosene reflector lamps hung by chains from the ceiling. A pump organ provided the music and was located to the right of the pulpit. A photograph taken in 1900 of the interior of the church shows no ornamentation at all. The pews were severely functional, without bead or molding. Only the pulpit was carved.

Until the 1950s exterior and interior changes were minor. The organ was exchanged for a piano in 1913. In the early 1930s the kerosene lamps were replaced by electric lights powered by a generator in the vestibule. Later in the decade the aisles and pulpit area were carpeted.

In the 1950s alterations completely changed the exterior and somewhat modified the interior. A two-and-one-half story extension was added to the rear of the building by extending the building straight back and adding short gabled tees to the side. Uncharacteristically for the town, both the sides and the rear of this addition were fenestrated asymmetrically. This addition, called the "educational building," was built to accommodate the various Sunday school classes that previously had met in groups in different parts of the sanctuary. Two doors opposite the vestibule doors now lead from the sanctuary into this extension.

A choir loft was added by moving the pulpit out from its alcove. The floor was banked in three tiers with seats for sopranos on either side of the pulpit, altos on the next level directly behind the pulpit, and tenors and basses on the highest level behind them. Prior to this structural alteration the choir had sat on the preacher's left, beside the piano. Members agree that these alterations did not significantly alter the aesthetics of the interior, which they have always cherished and wish to preserve (see Figure 56).

By contrast, the external appearance of the building was radically altered. The addition of the educational building enlarged the profile of the church, but the brick veneer and its concomitant changes were the most dramatic in the architectural history of the church. It was at this time that influential members of the community were starting to build brick houses for themselves. They came to consider brick facing

Figure 55. Original church plan

4 ft

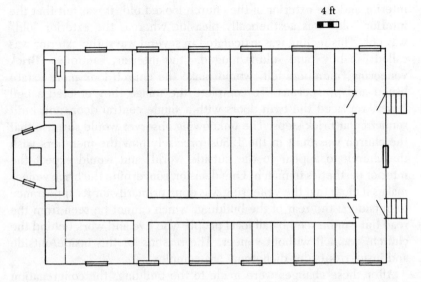

Figure 56. Present church plan

4 ft

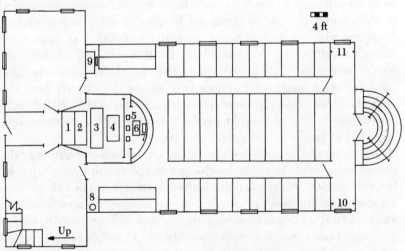

Up

1. Pew (tenors and basses)
2. Pew (altos)
3. Pew (sopranos)
4. Organ
5. Ceremonial chairs
6. Bible stand

7. Communion table
8. American flag
9. Piano and bench
10. Coat rail (men)
11. Coat rail (women)

as an index of prosperity, stability, and security. Although both the interior and the exterior of the church looked old, it was felt that the interior "old" was aesthetically pleasing whereas the exterior "old" was not. This feeling was articulated in several ways: the exterior was called "shabby" and "old-fashioned," the interior, "antique." Brick veneering, members felt, would make the church look more established and prosperous. To complete the image they erected a bell tower, replaced the twin doors with a single central door, and built semicircular brick steps. The unknowing observer would surmise that the church was built in the 1950s (precisely how the members wish the church to appear to the outside world) and would expect the interior aesthetics to match. One decision concerning the brick veneer makes it clear that the veneering was done primarily for its appearance to outsiders: the rear of the building, which cannot be seen from the road but can be seen by all local people who live and work behind the church, was left without veneer. The reasons for this inside/outside and insider/outsider dichotomy are complex.

After these changes were made to the building, the congregation decided to leave the field and hire a fulltime preacher. To some extent the concerted efforts to modernize and expand the church building were experiments to see if the members were sufficiently committed to the church to risk the financial burden of a fulltime preacher. Members also wanted to make sure the building was impressive enough to attract several candidates for the position, so that they would have some choice over whom they hired. To house the new preacher they bought a dwelling adjacent to the church from the granddaughter of the doctor who had donated the land for the church. This house is one of the old period 1 houses with a two-story ell, screened-in porches, and open living room.

It is important to note that the expansion and modernization of the church were made possible by changes in the community caused by the new roads. Children of older families settled down in Tidewater in greater numbers than previously because housing became available, and new families began to move in to the area and commute to jobs in Virginia. They expanded church membership enough to go to a fulltime preacher, but the presence of the two factions was to lead to trouble.

In the 1960s two relatively minor changes were effected to the interior of the church. In 1962 the members voted to change the old pews, but there was disagreement as to what would go in their place. The preacher wanted to paint the sanctuary white and to buy pews with white ends to brighten up the space. The idea of painting the walls was met with coldness, but a few favored the white pews and debate dragged on for months. The white pews were eliminated from consideration at the first business meeting at which the pews were discussed, by a narrow margin. At the next meeting this vote was rescinded, again by a narrow margin. At a third meeting a committee was selected to choose the pews, and there were no more votes in open meeting. The committee was a coup for opponents of the white pews, as committees are always chosen from the same pool of established members of the church. Normally these members can be relied on to give every point of view a fair hearing and come to a just and equitable decision. In this case, however, all of the members of the pool had opposed white pews from the very beginning. As soon as the committee met, it dropped the white pews from consideration without debate and ultimately selected oak pews that resembled the old, handmade ones. The tensions that inevitably arose subsided because the issue was handled diplomatically. They lay dormant until an issue of greater aesthetic import arose.

In 1969 several large donations made the purchase of an organ possible. It was installed between the pulpit and choir loft in a specially designed well. This action completed the movement of the music from the side of the sanctuary to the center. It also indicated support for a certain style of church music and marked the end of a long debate over what was appropriate. This "row" is discussed below; for now it should be noted that members see piano music and organ music as diametrically opposed in aesthetic terms. The piano is visceral and basic, good for belting out old favorites at the top of your voice and therefore especially suited for encouraging children to sing out. Piano players in the community play by ear, picking out melodies and harmonies as they can. This style of playing is generally considered suitable for the instrument and, according to several informants, was the basic accompaniment for singing in the church until the 1950s. The organ is mellow and sophisticated, more suited for singing "softly and tenderly." It is more of an adult, intellectual taste, and organ playing, it is felt, requires professional music training. For these reasons the piano, which remained in the sanctuary after the organ was installed, is used for Sunday school singing, and the organ is used for worship services.

Members are well aware that the outside of the church is aesthetically at odds with the inside, and (like the owners of brick houses furnished with antiques) they are pleased with the dissonance. The modern outside projects one image to outsiders, the old interior a different one to insiders. Members love to watch the faces of newcomers as they enter the sanctuary for the first time. They know they are expecting a modern interior and anticipate they will be surprised and delighted when they see the old woodwork. All intimations of modernity are carefully hidden: heating and air conditioning ducts are under the floor, and the organ sits in a camouflaged well. Even the electric lights are in the style of oil lamps. Entering the church is like stepping back a century.

At present there are no plans to change the church structure or furnishings. All building efforts are being directed toward the building of a new parsonage. This project is likely to cause problems because the old methods of fund raising and volunteer labor are failing to produce results. Inflation is depleting the building fund as fast as it can be augmented, and modern building codes require the services of hired contractors. These factors will eventually require the members to take out a mortgage, but the move will cause turmoil because many of the older members oppose usury. Sentiment vehemently favors paying as you go:

A.T. This fellah that we had preacher then said one thing to me that I didn't like, and I don't like yet, and wouldn't have him as preacher on account of it. I said, "Church is nearly 'bout out of debt." He said, "Yes, and let's get it back in as quick as we can. Get it just as far in debt as you can."

E.M. Well I know that went against your grain, Amos, 'cause I know you.

A.T. I like to keep everything out of debt. I like to be out of debt.

E.M. Yeah, yeah, I know. But that's the psychology of the present-day ministry.

A.T. My God, they can take their psychology and go to the devil with it.

E.M. Well that's the way you feel about it. But that's the psychology of the present-day ministry.

A.T. That's not the proper psychology. Get out of debt and stay out of debt.

E.M. That ain't the way the preachers look at it. If they can get their congregation in debt, build a new church, build this, that, and the other, get 'em in debt. Then everybody'll put their shoulder to the wheel and push.

A.T. Yeah, they get everybody in debt.

The conflicts between the "present-day ministry" and local sentiments are complex and central to an understanding of the dynamics of the community.

Several kinds of events are primary in the workings of the church. I begin with the most common and regular, Sunday school and regular worship services, and move to services and events that occur only annually or infrequently, such as Christmas services, baptisms, revivals, fund raisers, and so forth. No church-sponsored event does not have a major aesthetic component, and some events consist of nothing but aesthetic forms. Thus the shape of these events as a whole and their use and manipulation of aesthetic forms must be covered in some detail to make clear the interplay of forms.

Sunday school has two separable aesthetic arenas: the aesthetics of the services themselves, basically involving music and narrative, and the capacity of each class to contribute ideas, time, labor, and money to the upkeep and improvement of the appearance of the church.

Sunday school meets every Sunday morning at the church at ten o'clock, the hour before worship service. The Sunday school has a recorded membership of one hundred fifty-one, but attendance is usually between sixty and ninety. Even at this rate Sunday school is better attended than worship service, to the general concern of members and preacher alike. People give many reasons for preferring Sunday school: dislike of long sermons, need to get home to fix dinner, inconvenience of keeping small children in church, and so on. But the most commonly cited reason is that Sunday school is more intimate than worship service, and this perception is reflected in the aesthetic forms of the two types of service. Also, Sunday school classes are made up of peer groups. An extended family of grandparents, parents, and children can come to church together, and each individual will be able to go to a different class to receive instruction at his or her level of maturity. Teaching, particularly in the older groups, is also by peers. The different classes are as follows:

Preschool	
1st and 2d	grades
3d and 4th	grades
5th and 6th	grades
7th and 8th	grades
9th through 12th	grades
College age	Men and women from college age to thirty
Young adult	Married couples between thirty and fifty
Women's	Women of retirement age
Men's	Men of retirement age

Sunday school opens with all of the classes together in the sanctuary. Generally the peer groups that form the classes sit together, with

[123]

younger children in the front rows of pews, older couples and women in the middle, and men at the back.

The sanctuary is decorated each Sunday by women on a rotational basis, the assignment being given by a standing committee. Decoration usually consists of a flower arrangement on the communion table and conforms with the seasons: bulbs in spring, dried and everlasting flowers in the fall. On special occasions the decoration may be handled by the flower committee plus additional helpers and is, in consequence, more elaborate. At Easter, for example, the windows and choir loft are filled with Easter lilies and spring bulbs. Also, some women commemorate the anniversary of the death of a relative with elaborate floral displays.

Activities begin with the Sunday school director taking up his customary place, standing just in front of the first row of pews and announcing the first hymn of the day. This is always a stirring favorite, accompanied on the piano by one of a number of people who are willing to play for Sunday school. Most of these people play by ear, and youths are encouraged to try. The music director for worship services has little or nothing to do with Sunday school music. If possible, the hymn has topical or seasonal associations. Examples include "America the Beautiful" (Sims 1956: # 489), "Battle Hymn of the Republic" (# 488), and "Come, Ye Thankful People, Come" (# 490). Few of the hymns used in the Sunday school service are also used at worship service. The Sunday school hymns are all considered "easy to sing," meaning that they are in straightforward meters (commonly 4/4) with the words fitting the notes syllabically, that is, one syllable per note. "America the Beautiful," for example, fits this model precisely.

After the hymn the Sunday school director reads the announcements he has prepared. These typically include information on the sick and news about future special events. Anyone in the congregation with more information on these matters contributes it. The floor is then opened for other announcements, which generally include more of the same.

Following the announcements the director gives a devotional thought. These thoughts fall into three broad classes: homey tales, sometimes illustrating the spirit of a special Sunday such as Mother's Day; inspirational tales, to encourage the congregation to participate in a fund-raising drive; and petitions, to support state or local legislative actions of church interest. The director almost always reads from a prepared text when giving the devotional thought, and his delivery is plain and unmodulated. The thoughts are accompanied by readings from the Bible.

Devotional thoughts for special Sundays are homey tales frequently involving children. For example, on Mother's Day the director read the story of a little boy who was saving his pennies to buy a ball. When Mother's Day came around he took his savings and bought his mother a bottle of perfume. His mother cherished the perfume and on discussing the deed with her husband decided she would not return the boy's kindness by buying him the ball that he could not now afford, because to do so would detract from the sacrifice he had made. The reading was John 12:1–8, the story of Mary and the pound of ointment.

On regular Sundays, when no burning political issues are being discussed in the community, the director reads tales with an overt moral content. One was the story of a mother and children who were having breakfast at the counter of a diner. Because the diner was crowded, they could not sit together at the counter. One of the young daughters called to her mother, "Don't they say the blessing in this place?" The man at the counter said "Yes, will you say it?" As she prayed every head in the diner was bowed. The reading was Isaiah 11:6, "The wolf shall dwell with the lamb, and the leopard shall lie down with the kid. The calf and the lion shall abide together, and a little child shall lead them."

When the director wishes to mobilize the congregation on political issues, he abandons the story format and simply recites pertinent facts or exhorts them to action. When liquor by the drink was coming up for discussion before the North Carolina legislature, he recited statistics on drunk driving and compared them to those on murder, rape, and arson. He stated that more people were arrested for drunk driving than for these other crimes combined and then urged members to lobby against liquor by the drink. The reading was Genesis 3:1–13, the story of Eve and the serpent. When liquor by the drink passed, he read the story of Aaron and the golden calf, Exodus 32:1–6, and simply remarked that North Carolina had taken the wrong lead and was following its own golden calf.

Whether he is telling stories or calling for action, the director uses a narrative style that is very simple and largely unmodulated. He talks in a conversational manner, and because of his proximity to the congregation he need not raise his voice much. This style, and the style of teaching in the classes, which is similar, differs markedly from preaching style.

After the devotional thought the director asks a member of the congregation to lead the morning prayer. The prayer is usually tripartite. It begins with thanks for blessings, such as health, ability to attend church, and the general wellbeing of the members present. The middle, and longest, section is a plea for blessings on the sick, bereaved, and troubled, both in Tidewater and throughout the world. Individual church members are mentioned by name, as are people of national prominence. Blessings are also asked for the country and community in general. The final section is a formulaic closing that asks for guidance for Sunday school teachers and the preacher and ends with one of several stock perorations.

The general meeting concludes with the singing of the first and last verses of a hymn, usually a children's favorite such as "Jesus Loves Me" (# 512) or, at Christmas, "Away in a Manger" (# 77). At the end of the hymn all except the men's class file out and go to their respective classrooms. The men meet in the sanctuary.

Each class is run differently, but there is a clear division between adult and youth classes. Adult classes have their own polity with officers, a treasury, and a democratic decision-making process. Youth classes are run by adults and lack this polity. They are opened with a prayer and consist of a mixture of instruction and activities, the ratio depending on the age of the group. Since the youth groups play only a very minor role in the aesthetics of the church, the adult classes are the main focus of my attention.

The aesthetics of the individual rooms in which the classes meet contrast with the aesthetics of the sanctuary in a significant way. No graphic art or decoration of any sort appears on the sanctuary walls. The classroom walls, on the other hand, are liberally adorned with pictures of various provenance. The rooms of the children's classes are decorated with the pictures they make each week as part of their instruction. The women's classroom, which also serves as the choir's robing room and the meeting place for several women's groups and committees, such as the Missionary Union, is more formally decorated with pictures donated by members of the class. These include a framed tapestry copy of da Vinci's *Last Supper*, a lithograph of Christ at Gethsemane, and a head of Christ. In general, each class is responsible for the appointments of its room, although in the case of the children the adult teacher helps out a great deal with donations and suggestions. The men meet in the sanctuary and so do not have to concern themselves with these matters.

All of the teachers, except in the men's class, are women, and the men could have a room of their own if they desired it; a clear split between men's and women's aesthetics is evident and in line with other aesthetic decisions in the church (and in the home). That is, the

men prefer not to have to make aesthetic decisions about their environment, whereas women take an active hand in shaping theirs.
Both men and women of the church readily and often articulated these
sentiments to me. As one woman said, for example, "When you see
the men getting ready to do something around here, it's the women
that are pushing, and the women who end up doing it all."

The adult classes begin with a collection and a discussion period.
Sometimes the sick or bereaved who are of special interest to the class
are discussed in greater detail than in the general meeting. Action to
be taken in regard to the sick, such as sending flowers, is discussed
and voted on or decided by general consensus. Sometimes more complicated issues must be discussed, because each class may autono-
mously make decisions concerning church structure and decor. Supposedly the full congregation should vote on these decisions also, but
provided that the change a class wishes to make is not too drastic,
there is no need for general deliberation. The women's class, by far
the most active in this respect, bought the present carpeting for the
sanctuary without consulting the full congregation. When the men's
class proposed to build a choir loft, however, other members suggested that the matter was too important to be handled at the class
level. Older children's classes are sometimes encouraged by their
teachers to take on small fund-raising projects to provide modest items
of adornment for the sanctuary. A brass urn that usually holds flowers
on the communion table was supplied by one class, the collection
plates by another. These fund-raising activities generally involve aesthetic forms also. One class put on a religious play to raise money,
others have sold homemade ice cream or baked goods. They may also
take up special collections, which is the norm for the men's class.

After class business has been transacted the president of the class
reads the Bible passage for study and gives a short prayer. The reading
is quiet and intimate, with little inflection; the prayer usually requests
receptive hearts for the listeners and inspiration for the teacher. The
teaching program for the Bible classes comes from booklets printed by
the Southern Baptist Convention. Thus the reading material, and to
some degree its interpretation, is not peculiar to Tidewater. The convention supplies a teacher's manual with special instructions for
"young," "median," and "senior" adults. Inexperienced instructors
lean on these manuals heavily, but those with many years behind
them use the manuals as a foundation for their own interpretations.

During the year I attended Bible classes, there were four themes
for the lessons:

1. The Early Church (Readings from Acts)
2. Nature and Mission of the Church (Acts)
3. Discipline and Commandments (Exodus, Matthew, and various Epistles)
4. Basic Christian Beliefs (diverse readings)

Each lesson contains an overt or covert moral message. The biblical passages are of two kinds. Materials in sections 1 and 2 consisted mostly of historical anecdotes, whereas sections 3 and 4 used plain moral instruction. Teachers found it consistently easier to teach the former. Anecdotes such as the miraculous death of Ananias and Sapphira (Acts 4:32–5:11) and the stoning of Steven (Acts 6:1–8:3) were first probed for their historical and descriptive content in a personal, conjectural manner. In the case of Ananias and Sapphira, for example, the teacher tried to analyze their psychological motives for withholding part of their fortune by imagining what they said to each other the night before they presented themselves to the apostles. From this theme he moved to the general moral: it is wrong to withhold part of oneself from God, and the commitment to Christianity must be total.

Teaching on straight moral principles proved more difficult. Without anecdotal material to begin the lesson the teachers found very little to say other than reiterating and paraphrasing the biblical passages. Teaching on the Ten Commandments was less problematic, because these could be fitted into a historical context and expounded upon in that light. In the lesson on the "new" commandment to "honor thy father and thy mother" the loophole of "corban," whereby a man could legally refrain from supporting his parents without breaking the commandment, was discussed. This loophole provided the necessary historical/descriptive materials from which the teacher could tease appropriate moral principles. But verses such as "Thy word is a lamp unto my feet, and a light unto my path" (Psalms 119:105) proved more challenging to develop as instructional themes because they did not lend themselves to anecdotal speaking.

At 10:50 the general secretary/treasurer of the Sunday school rings a bell to warn the classes that it is time to conclude. The bell was formerly used by residents of a nearby island to warn boats of the nearness of the shoreline in times of fog. The end of the teaching section of the Bible classes marks the end of Sunday school.

Where Sunday school is intimate, with little emphasis on formality of aesthetic forms, the regular worship service places great emphasis on controlled aesthetic forms. Take, for example, the role of music in the two services. For Sunday school the piano accompaniment is un-polished, and there are no formal musical offerings or presentations. The service ends with the minimally musical ringing of a bell. By contrast, the worship service has a formally trained choir decked in special robes and assigned a focal place in the sanctuary. Their singing of special pieces frames the service (see outline below), and their presentations punctuate it. Music is supplied by a formally trained organist. Other aesthetic forms, such as narrative and oratory, are similarly distinct. Thus the regular worship service consists of aes-thetic forms that work in conjunction to create a unified whole that also has a distinct and recognizable pattern.

Regular services are held every Sunday morning at eleven o'clock. The order of regular services rarely changes and is printed in a formal order of service handed out to the congregation as they enter. In addition, the hymn numbers are announced on a board beside the choir loft. The order is as follows:

Prelude	Organist
Call to Worship*	Choir
Invocation	Pastor
Response*	Choir
First Hymn	All
Welcome and Announcements	Pastor
Responsive Reading	All
Silent Prayer	All
Morning Prayer	Church member
Second Hymn	All
Offering	All
Doxology	All
Special Music	Choir
Message	Pastor
Hymn of Invitation	All
Benediction	Pastor
Response*	Choir
Postlude	Organist

Sometimes the youth choir replaces the regular choir, in which case the items marked with an asterisk are omitted.

Before I deal with the individual components of the service, a few points about the overall structure are needed. The roles of the choir, preacher, and congregation are balanced in two ways. In terms of discrete events there is a general symmetry, the turning point being the morning prayer given by a church member. Action in the order of service shifts from the choir and preacher to the entire congregation, with the morning prayer in the middle of a cluster of events involving all, and then back to the preacher and choir. (This list and order of participants is printed in the church handout.) Members also describe the service as split into two equal halves. The first half includes all events up to the sermon and takes about thirty minutes, and the second includes the sermon and the closing events. During the first half the congregation can sing, read responsively, and generally be engaged in an active, physical way, standing and sitting as appropriate. In the second half, until the end, they sit still and listen.

The organist of the day enters the sanctuary about five minutes before the service is due to start and plays selections. She always plays them slowly and softly, even if they are tunes marked to be played faster. The members of the congregation seat themselves during the Prelude according to a well-known but unwritten seating plan (Figure 57). Older husbands and wives do not always sit together, and children rarely sit with their parents. Those families or couples who do sit together are marked as especially devoted to each other and to the church. The back row where the men sit is jocularly called "amen corner." These men are attentive and loyal but entirely passive. They do not sing the hymns or give outward signs of emotion.

Men greet newcomers with a handshake during the Prelude. This is the only time in Tidewater when men shake hands and is formally designated "the right hand of fellowship." Women do not shake hands at this time. While the members are talking quietly in the sanctuary, the men and women of the choir put on their robes in a room at the front of the sanctuary which is also the classroom for the women's Sunday school. The activity of the choir is jovial and boisterous but hidden from the sight and hearing of the much more subdued congregation. Choir members enter the room through the back of the church, not through the sanctuary, so that their characteristic ebullience will not spill over into church. The choir's robes are gold with white collars for the women. The youth choir wears red, and at one time there was an infant choir that wore white. Just before eleven the pastor enters the choir room and says a short prayer asking a blessing on the choir. The choir then files out into the sanctuary and stands in place in the choir loft. The preacher enters last and sits, out of sight of the congregation, behind the pulpit.

On the sounding of a chord on the organ the choir members raise and open their hymn books with military precision and sing the Call to

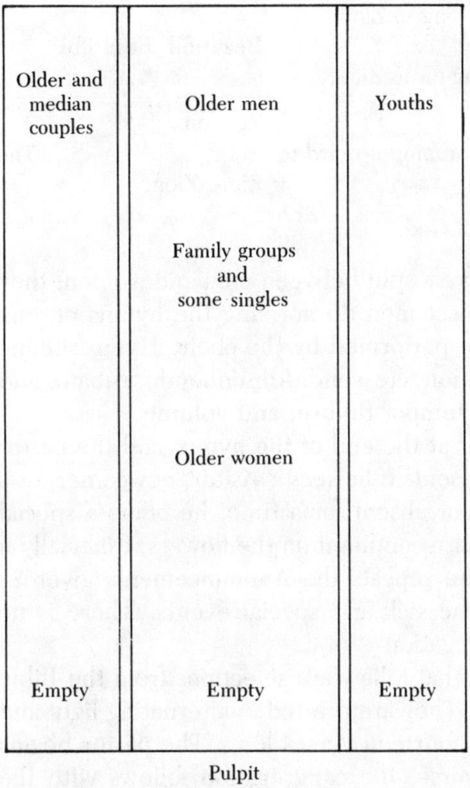

Figure 57. Church seating plan

Older and median couples	Older men	Youths
	Family groups and some singles	
	Older women	
Empty	Empty	Empty

Pulpit

Worship, either "The Lord Is in His Holy Temple" (# 515) or "Glory Be to the Father" (# 524). The choir remains standing.

The preacher stands and recites from memory a short formulaic Invocation. This is followed immediately by a Response from the choir, which is either "Almighty Father Hear Our Prayer" (# 529) or "Hear Our Prayer O Lord" (# 530).

The preacher announces the number of the First Hymn, and the congregation stands while the organ plays the tune of the first verse. The choir director or organist chooses the hymns and not the preacher, although the latter occasionally makes suggestions. Both the director and the choir prefer the first hymn to be an old favorite that everyone can sing with gusto, such as "He Keeps Me Singing" (# 307), "To God Be the Glory" (# 41), or "We're Marching to Zion" (# 308). These hymns frequently have refrains with some verbal counterpoint in them, as in the last-named:

[131]

Female voices:	We're march – ing to Zion,		
All voices:		Beautiful, beautiful,	
Male voices:	We're marching on to Zion,		
Female:		Zi – on,	
All:	Zion; We're marching upward to		The
Male:		Zion, Zion,	
All:	beautiful city of God.		

As these counterpoints involve a split between men and women, they are rarely heard, because most men do not sing the hymns or sing softly. Nonetheless, they are performed by the choir. Hymn singing involves virtually no modulation (crescendo/diminuendo, rubato, and so on); it maintains an even tempo, timbre, and volume.

Choir and congregation sit at the end of the hymn, and the pastor extends a Welcome to all present. If he sees a visitor, newcomer, or a member who has been sick or absent for a time, he offers a special personal welcome. He may also comment on the flowers, especially if the display is lavish. Next he repeats the Announcements given in Sunday school concerning the sick and special events. There is no participation from the congregation.

The Responsive Readings that follow are selections from the Bible pursuing a particular theme. They are printed in alternating light and boldface type and are about fourteen verses long. The pastor begins the reading with the first verse, the congregation follows with the second, and so on to the end. The preacher chooses the reading to complement the topic of his sermon, or, if that is not possible, he picks one that contains a verse germane to some part of his message. These are not read with much verve or particularly in unison. Each member reads at his or her own pace, and many, especially the men in amen corner, do not read at all.

The pastor begins a short period of meditation and Silent Prayer by calling upon a male church member to lead the morning prayer. At this point the organist plays a short selection in the same manner as the prelude pieces. The organist stops playing after a minute or two, and this is the signal for the start of the Morning Prayer. The prayer follows the same format as the morning prayer in Sunday school, leaving out blessings for the teachers.

For the Second Hymn the choir director may choose another old-time favorite or, more often, a subdued one. Examples include "When We Walk with the Lord" (# 260), "Amazing Grace" (# 188), and "Breathe on Me" (# 174). Midway through the year I observed the services, the music director had a change of heart about the second hymn. At the outset she chose slower hymns without refrains or hymns that were slightly unusual or rarely sung in the church. She told me it would never do to have the first hymn fall flat because the congregation found it tricky, but the choice of the second one could be slightly more adventurous. By midyear, however, this policy had to be discarded because the second hymn seemed to lack all spirit, and she introduced more oldtime favorites with refrains. During the last stanza of the hymn two deacons walk forward and stand in front of the pulpit. At the end of the hymn all remain standing.

At this point the pastor may do one of two things: he may ask a deacon to say a prayer of Offering, or he may say one himself. The incumbent prefers to delegate the task, but not all of the deacons want to do it. The preacher knows who is and who is not willing to partici-pate in prayers because he has consulted all of the men in the con-gregation on this point over the course of several years. If neither of the deacons up front is on the "willing" list, he says the prayer himself. After the prayer congregation and choir sit, the deacons take collec-tion plates from a table in front of the pulpit and pass them around the congregation. The plates are not passed through the choir loft. At this time the organist plays more selections.

At an unobtrusive signal from a member of the choir the organist stops the selection, often in midphrase, and strikes a resounding G major chord. On this chord all stand and sing the Doxology, "Old 100th" (# 514). At the end all sit, including the pastor.

Although the choir and choir director would prefer to be more ambitious in the Special Music, there are major constraints on what they can attempt. The sopranos and altos are moderately strong when all are present, but there is no one to sing a tenor line (the lone "tenor" follows the melody), and the basses find it difficult to learn and hold a line that deviates too drastically from a simple thirds and fifths harmony. The director also has difficulty getting members to turn out for practices regularly, so that it is hard to work on new pieces consis-tently. To overcome these problems the director chooses hymns or hymnlike sacred songs for the special music. These may be hymns that are rarely sung by the congregation or new and unusual settings of familiar hymns.

The choir has traditionally sung "softly and tenderly," as one old member put it, and therefore chooses pieces suitable for low, dulcet tones. Songs of this sort include "Love Is the Theme" (# 293), "He Touched Me," and "Near to the Heart of God" (# 301). To bring a degree of tonal variety to the music the director sometimes has different voices sing different sections of the songs. For example, men and women may alternate verses, or two members may sing the verses as a duet with the full choir singing the chorus. Solos are rare.

At one period in the history of the choir its customary style of music was replaced with music of the camp meeting style. This change caused a major schism in the church, but as it has ramifications beyond the scope of the current description, it is discussed later. After this fracas the choir determined to pay careful attention to control, timing, and enunciation. This preference is noteworthy because none of the choir members has had voice training, and most have only a rudimentary knowledge of music, gained through choir rehearsal. The basses, for example, have a good ear for singing thirds and fifths; they determine the "correct" note to sing by judging the relative positions of the notes on the stave and singing a third or fifth up or down. Therefore, the harmonies they sing may or may not be as written. Most of the sopranos follow the organ melody rather than sight-read.

Special songs that are neither hymns nor hymnlike are rare and reserved for special occasions. They include choral settings of "Bless This House" for Thanksgiving and "I Heard the Bells on Christmas Day" for Christmas. Although these settings are more complicated than is usual, the choir is comfortable with them because they perform them every year.

Regardless of what the choir thinks of its own performance, all church members praise its efforts, and there is never any adverse or constructive criticism. Being a choir member is considered commendable and not to be disparaged: it is an outward display of concern for the church. Almost all of the choir members are church officers, Sunday school teachers, or committee members. As a group they are a potent force in the church, and they can turn their power against the church if they are angered. An alto once told me it is common to say that "the devil sits in the choir."

At the end of the special music the choir sits, and there is a short pause while the members put away their music and the congregation gets comfortable. The service to this stage has taken about thirty minutes, leaving about the same amount of time for the pastor to deliver his Message. It is not feasible or appropriate to conduct a lengthy analysis of a year's worth of sermons here, but I include outlines of representative examples in an appendix to this book. What follows is a general summary of fifty sermons prefaced with a few remarks on the congregation's likes and dislikes.

Members prefer sermons that are stylistically the opposite of Sunday school lessons. Sunday school lessons should be anecdotal, drawing moral principles from historical narratives; they should be intimate, with little vocal modulation and gesticulation; and they should be less concerned with straightforward exhortations to lead a moral life. Conversely, a sermon should not be excessively anecdotal, although a degree of storytelling is permissible; it should be delivered with constant vocal modulation, the crescendos resounding throughout the sanctuary; and its main thrust should be a direct appeal to live a moral life. This, in essence, is the local distinction between teaching and preaching. Teaching is an intimate, personal act, whereas preaching is a theatrical, distant one. Descriptions of preachers emphasize vocal quality and dramatic delivery as the keys to good preaching:

> Boy! He's a natural. Yes sir, he's a natural. He's a bass tone, and he gets down low, you know. And he lets up at the right time, and all. He's just a natural-born preacher.

> He seems to be the evangelical type. He's got the right kind of a voice for it.

> He's a grand preacher. He's got the voice and the mannerisms. He's just a gifted preacher, that's all there is to it. He could move you right down inside of you.

A good Sunday school teacher, by contrast, provokes these reactions: "I like Tommy's teaching. He really knows the Bible, and I feel like I'm learning something." Although the semantic import of sermons is not insignificant, the general mode of performance is of prime aesthetic importance.

The difference between preaching and teaching is also emphasized by the positions from which preacher and teacher deliver their messages. The preacher stands on a platform behind the pulpit, whereas the Sunday school director stands on the main floor, on a level with the congregation and directly in front of them. Sunday school participants fill the front pews directly facing the director, but for regular worship service the first five rows are left vacant.

The most notable aspect of the pastor's sermons is their constant reference to the humble or what he calls the "ordinary." He frequently praises "ordinary" people and tells the congregation that even though they are not rich and famous, nor live in a fancy town, nonetheless they are precious to God. One whole sermon even had as its central theme "the glory of being ordinary" (see Appendix). For this sermon the preacher began with anecdotes that showed how apparently insignificant people can do great things. One involved the last football game of the regular season for the University of Alabama team of 1937. With only seconds on the clock the score was tied, but Alabama was within fieldgoal range. An unknown kicker kicked the fieldgoal, and Alabama went on to the Rose Bowl. The unknown kicker brought about a great victory.

The pastor often refers to the ordinariness of biblical figures. He frequently takes his text from the minor prophets (Amos, Hosea, Micah, etc.) and professes that his favorite verse is Micah 5:2, "And thou, Bethlehem Ephrata, art a little one among the thousands of Judah: out of thee shall he come forth unto me that is to be the ruler in Israel." He also prefaces remarks about, or quotations from, the minor prophets with a statement on their humble origins. Amos, for example, was a herdsman and a dresser of sycamore trees.

The pastor often includes in his sermons segments of Matthew 6:25–30 (God's eye is on the sparrow), usually in connection with the common exhortation to the members not to think of themselves as unknown or ordinary to God. In this light he sometimes compares members of the church to biblical figures. On occasion he has also compared Tidewater to Bethlehem. But never once has he compared the fishermen in the gospels to the local fishermen, even when the main text of the day was Luke 5:4–9, the calling of the disciples who were fishermen and the miraculous draught of fishes.

Finally, he sometimes tells tales of the famous and their miseries to make the point that it is better to be an unknown Christian than a famous non-Christian. Once he recited a list of famous people who had committed suicide, which act he considers to be the logical consequence of atheism. People who have no God have no reason to live, he argues, and people with a God, no matter what may befall them, always have a reason for living.

Many sermons concern what God or the devil does for humans. The central message is always that God is a force for good and the devil for evil. More specifically, the world is the province of the devil and is generally evil, but God does intervene when necessary to right wrongs. Those people who follow the devil are tricked into believing that the pleasures of the world are worth having. Those who follow God have the strength of will to resist the devil's trickery. These sermons express a clear dichotomy between good and evil, and what is good or evil is determined by biblical authority, not reason. The pastor rails against situational ethics and maintains that the Ten Commandments are moral absolutes whose interdictions may not be overruled regardless of circumstances.

He preaches many more sermons on God's work than on the devil's. Those on the devil are covert exhortations to specific action. He may, for example, preach on the devil's trickery and the punishments for succumbing to it, then imply that temptations not to give to the building fund are caused by the devil. Whereas sermons on the devil and his works are generally received well, demands for action or complaints about its absence are not. Pleas for money are particularly disliked, because members feel that contributions are a personal matter and not a subject for public discussion. They also do not like being taken to task for alleged wrongdoing. On the whole the preacher respects these sentiments, although he did once deliver a sermon on people who find a preacher's words too harsh.

Despite his adamancy that no issue is taboo, the pastor never preaches on doctrinal matters, difficult biblical exegesis, or live political points of debate. In any congregation, he explained to me in private, there is a wide range of opinion in these areas and it is not his job to stir up controversy. In relation to the Genesis account of creation, for example, he said he had made his mind up but he also respected the opinions of others and so would never preach on this text. Here again, Sunday school teaching is quite different from preaching. Sunday school teachers and the director frequently air their views on doctrine and politics.

Death and dying are frequent secondary themes in the pastor's sermons. On one occasion he linked death to his major theme of the "glory of being ordinary" by suggesting that the length of one's obituary indicates whether one is a "somebody" or a "nobody." But most often he uses the thought of death or dying as a warning to be constant in the Christian faith. As no one knows when he or she will die, it is important not to let one's faith flag. Death may strike at a moment of indecision or lack of faith, with eternal consequences.

The preacher also makes clear distinctions between aesthetic experiences that are sinful and those which are acceptable and even beneficial. Alcohol and sex figure prominently in the first category, music in the second. For the most part he does not identify what he means when he talks about "sin" or "the devil's work," preferring to keep his remarks and tirades on a general level. When he does get specific however, the sins he most commonly mentions are alcoholism and various sexual sins, such as adultery, pornography, and prostitution.

He once gave a lengthy discourse on the David and Bathsheba story to illustrate the problems inherent in sexual license and on another occasion glossed Amos' prophesies against Israel as a condemnation of sexual libido in the country. Otherwise the alcoholic is the proverbial sinner.

Music, on the other hand, is not merely acceptable but of fundamental evangelical importance. Twice he told the story of Ole Bull, the popular nineteenth-century virtuoso violinist, going to John Ericsson, a naval engineer, with a technical problem concerning the construction of his bow. To illustrate his problem he played a little for Ericsson, who was supposedly a practical man with no interest in music. On hearing Bull he said, "Don't stop, I didn't know what I was missing." The preacher likened this sentiment to the first experience of Christianity. He also told of an urban church minister who decided to open his church to sinners—alcoholics, drug addicts, and prostitutes—on a regular basis but could not decide how to persuade them to enter in the first place. He solved the problem by getting Louis Armstrong to play "When the Saints Go Marching In" on the church steps.

The structure of the sermons varies and is often loose, with the pastor pursuing tangential themes as he sees fit. He has only a rudimentary outline from which to speak, and many of his discussions are impromptu. He will, for example, incorporate material he has heard from the Sunday school teacher that morning (he is a member of the men's class) if it bears on the general theme of the day. The congregation does not favor this style and feels the thread of argument is often lost or submerged in the detail and maze of secondary themes. The sermons they like best are those in which he lays out a simple structure and then rigorously follows it. One such sermon started with the pastor describing a picture of a cat hanging upside down from a tree limb by its claws. The caption to the picture was "Hang in there baby." He then said he was going to give the members a hand to "hang in there" with. This was:

1st finger	new chance
2d finger	new status
3d finger	new power
4th finger	new security
Thumb	faith

He expounded on each of these topics in turn, returning from time to time to the hand metaphor. This kind of neat, firm structure is well received by the congregation. After a well-structured sermon with plenty of booming crescendos and admonitions, the congregation genially remark to each other on how good it was.

Toward the end of the sermon the preacher changes from the hortatory style to one of invitation. The change is not abrupt but smoothly executed. At the very end he invites anyone who wishes to come forward and be baptized. This invitation most often includes quotations or paraphrases from the day's hymn of invitation. As he makes the invitation he descends from the pulpit and stands just in front of the first pew. He then announces the hymn of invitation.

The Hymn of Invitation is always one of a small stock of hymns reserved for this special purpose. The most common is "Jesus Is Calling" (# 229), and others include "Out of My Bondage, Sorrow and Night" (# 233) and "Lord I'm Coming Home" (# 237). In these hymns the commonest metaphor for the desire to be baptized is coming home, as the following segments show:

> I've wandered far away from God,
> Now I'm coming home.
>
> (# 237)

> Come home, come home,
> Ye who are weary come home.
> Earnestly, tenderly, Jesus is calling,
> Calling, o sinner come home.
>
> (# 236)

> Jesus is tenderly calling thee home,
> Calling today, calling today.
>
> (# 229)

These hymns also make constant reference to transformations:

> Sin had left a crimson stain,
> He wash'd it white as snow.
>
> (# 225)

> Out of my bondage, sorrow, and night,
> Jesus, I come, Jesus, I come;
> Into Thy freedom, gladness, and light,
> Jesus I come to Thee;
> Out of my sickness, into Thy health,
> Out of my want and into Thy wealth,

[139]

Out of my sin and into Thyself,
Jesus I come to Thee.

(# 233)

Unlike the other hymns in the service, these hymns of invitation may involve some modulation, and in one of the most commonly used, "Softly and Tenderly" (# 236), the singers follow crescendos and sustains marked in the music. The marked meters of many of these tunes (%, %) are uncommon in comparison with other hymns in the general repertoire. Also, the syllabic meter of the commonest hymns of invitation, unlike all other popular ones, is irregular.

If the preacher does not already know someone is thinking of coming forward, he will stop the hymn after two verses and proceed with the benediction. If he thinks or suspects that someone might come forward, he will keep the hymn going or stop after two verses to renew the invitation and then continue with the hymn.

On rare occasions someone comes forward to be baptized. This act is rare simply because the vast majority of people who attend the church are already baptized. What is more, many members of the church told me, it is highly unusual for anyone to come forward except at revival time. During the year I was there only one person came forward during a regular service, and she did so the week before revival. She had made a firm decision to come forward *not* during revival to demonstrate clearly that her act was calculated and not part of a general emotional ferment. However, she came forward near revival so that she could be baptized with those who would come forward during the revival. When someone comes forward, the hymn is allowed to run its course, because the lead of one may be followed by others. At the end of the hymn the preacher turns the candidate toward the congregation and begins the following formulaic dialogue:

Pastor:	What does the congregation wish?
Any Member:	I move that he [or she, or they] be received.
Pastor:	Is there a second?
Any Member:	Seconded.
Pastor:	All those in favor say "aye."
All:	Aye.
Pastor:	Any opposition.
	Silence
Pastor:	There is no opposition. I invite you all to extend the right hand of fellowship to the new member[s] after the benediction.

Theoretically any member of the church could oppose a candidacy, and in such a case the candidacy would have to be refused because votes for acceptance must be unanimous. However, in the history of this church no one has ever been denied acceptance.

It is also possible for people to come forward for reasons other than the wish to be baptized. Some older people or couples come forward to rededicate their lives to Christ, which involves a simple statement to the preacher while the hymn continues. Also, a member may come forward to express a desire to be ordained. Both acts are rare. I observed the former once. Because the act of coming forward at a regular service, for whatever reason, is rare and not usually antici- pated, the hymn of invitation does not occupy the pivotal place it has at revival. In worship services the preacher often stops it after two verses and moves on to end the service. Revival is a different matter, and that I consider, in contrast to the regular service, below.

The Benediction is normally a short, formulaic prayer of dismissal given by the pastor or a member of the congregation. If the regular choir is singing, the pastor gives the benediction, because the choir's response gives him time to go to the exit to greet people as they leave. If there is no choir, or if the junior choir does the singing, a member gives the benediction and the pastor leaves the sanctuary at that time. The Response is always "Grace, Love and Peace Abide" (# 539), and it marks the end of the service. At the end of the response the congrega- tion begins to stand and move about.

As soon as the response has ended people begin to file out of the church, exchanging a greeting with the pastor on the way. Many members of the choir disrobe and leave quietly by a back door without greeting the preacher. Meanwhile the organist plays a few selections in the same manner as for the prelude. If someone has accepted the invitation to be baptized, the entire congregation comes forward to greet him or her. The men shake hands, and the women hug and kiss. Outside the church such physical contact is extremely uncommon and reserved for greeting kin who have been absent from the community for a long time. Outside, the men of the congregation gather for a few minutes to chat before dispersing to their homes for the traditional Sunday meal.

A few special services are held annually, such as those connected with revival, Thanksgiving, and Christmas, some that are held more often, notably communion, and some that are held as needed, such as baptisms, weddings, and funerals. Special services of the first kind may be less formal than the regular ones: the choir is not always present, and when it is it does not sing all of the formal responses. Also, the congregation may be less formally dressed. Members feel less obliged to attend, and so on occasion these extra services are sparsely attended.

The church holds a revival annually at the end of July or beginning of August. The services are held from 8–9 P.M. Monday through Friday of the chosen week. Despite the avowed intent of revival to "save souls" most people in Tidewater, both regular churchgoers and nonmembers, described revival to me as entertainment and spoke of it in the same breath as musical shows or the movies. One man, in the process of telling me about entertainment when he was a boy, said: "Revival was one of the highlights. When it came everybody went. We used to have evangelists come down here and put on good singing, and good music, and preached a good sermon. That was a highlight of our entertainment in this section before cars got too thick." He added, "We met the girls at prayer meetings and revivals and walked home with them."

The revival serves two functions besides entertainment: it is designed to buttress the faith of old members and to attract new ones. In Tidewater Missionary Baptist Church many of the nonmembers who attend the revival services are youths, and a certain portion of the evangelism is directed toward them. But the meetings are generally well-attended by people who do not attend regular services. Revival still has strong entertainment value, and boys are still attracted by the prospect of walking girls home.

The first night of the revival has no special theme, but the others are directed toward particular segments of the congregation. They are as follows:

Service #2:	Officers
Service #3:	Youths
Service #4:	Families
Service #5:	Members

On each of these nights the relevant groups are encouraged to attend en masse, and the sermon has an appropriate slant.

The order of service for revival meetings differs from that of regular services. There is less choir and more congregational singing. Also, the sermon is longer (forty minutes or more), and the invitation is more elaborate. The order is as follows:

Prelude	Organist
First Hymn	All
Greeting	Pastor
Second Hymn	All
Prayer	Church member
Third Hymn	All
Offering	All
Special Music	Choir
Message	Visiting evangelist
Hymn of Invitation	All
Benediction	Church member
Postlude	Organist

The differences from the regular service in basic structure and juxta-position of aesthetic elements are of interest. The formal role of the choir is much reduced: there are no introductory and concluding pieces or responses; only the special music remains. Instead, there is more congregational singing, all of the hymns being stirring, oldtime classics. In essence the services consist of songs and sermon both aimed toward the time of invitation. Where regular services have a symmetric circularity to them, the revival services are more linear, driven by the specific purpose of getting people out of their seats during the invitation.

All agree that "good singing" and "good music" are essential ingre-dients of a successful revival. Many people come specifically "to have a good sing," so that there is a good deal more volume than on regular Sundays. Standard hymns include "Lord Send a Revival" (# 333) and "Stand Up, Stand Up for Jesus" (# 415), with their explicit revival messages. Hymns with a syncopated or responsive chorus are espe-cially popular. Examples include "Standing on the Promises" (# 266) and "Are You Washed in the Blood?" (# 192). The singing is so vig-orous that on one night, at the conclusion of "Amazing Grace" (# 188), the preacher asked the congregation to sing one verse again, a capella, because he was so impressed.

The regular pastor conducts most of the service, turning matters over to the visiting evangelist after the special music and resuming his usual role after the invitation. Other aspects of the service—prayers, offering, special music—do not differ significantly from those of regu-lar services. The invitation is special.

The evangelist who is to preach the sermons is chosen at a business

[143]

meeting in June. Usually the members decide the issue, but the pastor may suggest names for consideration. In most church matters the members do *not* take their lead from the pastor and, more often than not, resent interference. In my year of field observation the evangelist was an old college friend of the pastor's from Tennessee. Bringing someone such a distance is not normal, and a few of the members quietly grumbled that his travel expenses were high.

In most respects the congregation expects revival sermons to be like regular sermons. Biblical exegesis, politics, and local problems should be eschewed, the delivery should be powerful and well-modulated, and the content primarily concerned with moral principles without excessive use of anecdotes. Yet revival sermons are expected to be more passionate than regular ones: they are expected to "save souls," and the congregation "comes for a show."

The texts for the revival sermons in my year in Tidewater were all famous historical or inspirational passages:

#1	Exodus 14:10ff.	The crossing of the Red Sea
	Philippians 4:10	Revival
#2	Matthew 16:13–20	Peter's confession
#3	John 3:1–16	The "born again" doctrine
#4	Ephesians 6:10–16	The armor of God
#5	Acts 9:26ff.	Paul's zeal after conversion

The sermons preached on these texts did not conform to the congregation's expectations, and some disappointment was voiced privately. All contained lengthy anecdotes that frequently displayed erudition on obscure topics. Each also contained long stories about the evangelist's own life and work in the church.

The first sermon opened with a testimonial on the evangelist's conversion and calling. He followed with the story of his first conversion of another man. He then drew a New Testament from his inside jacket pocket and showed the congregation a list of names he had written in the flyleaf. It was a list of people whom he knew and loved who were not baptized. The first sermon, then, was more about his own credentials as an evangelist than a straightforward evangelistic message.

His long tales may best be illustrated by one from the Thursday night (outlines of two of his sermons appear in the appendix). The text for the evening was Ephesians 6:10–16, concerning the need to put on God's armor. The last verse (16) was the point of departure for the story:

14. Stand, therefore, having girded your loins with truth and having put on the breastplate of justice,
15. and having your feet shod with the readiness of the gospel of peace,
16. in all things taking up the shield of faith, with which you may be able to quench all the fiery darts of the most wicked one.

He told a story concerning the ingenuity of the Roman army. They had broadswords that could cut a man's head off at a single blow, they were highly disciplined and virtually invincible. However, they met an enemy that blew poison darts at them. Before they could get close enough to use their swords they came in range of the darts and suffered many casualties. The Romans, therefore, made large, teardrop-shaped shields out of light wood. They were light to carry and afforded the soldiers complete protection from the darts. Soon the enemy discovered that the wood became very dry after months on campaign, so they dipped their darts in tar and set light to them. The wooden shields burnt easily. To overcome this new difficulty the Romans killed wild animals and stretched their skins over the shields. Now the flaming darts could not ignite the wood. The evangelist then exhorted the members to carry their own shields of faith, and he moved to the next anecdote.

Many members felt his anecdotes were too long and involved. Several said that his sermons were "storified." They were not really interested or excited by their content, nor did they feel they were spiritually uplifting. They wanted more zeal and fire, less instruction. Stories are for Sunday school, the pulpit is for action. There is also an important distinction to be drawn about stories: the stories the Sunday school teachers tell, which are universally enjoyed, are Bible stories, whereas the anecdotes the preachers tell are generally not biblical in origin. The art of spinning a tale is locally associated with lying (see Chapter 7), and so for the preacher to indulge in such behavior is suspect. But Sunday school teachers can tell stories because the Gospel is the truth: it cannot be confused with lying. Several favorite Sunday school hymns—"I Love to Tell the Story" (# 141) and "Tell Me the Old, Old Story" (# 222)—make it clear that telling the Gospel story is special. Also, the Sunday school director does not *tell* stories but, rather, *reads* them, so that even though these anecdotes are not biblical, he does not risk being styled a liar. The aesthetic form of storytelling—embellishment and dramatic presentation—are absent in his act of reading.

On the Wednesday night, youth night, much of the sermon was

directed toward the youths in the congregation. After the youth choir had performed its special music, the evangelist asked them to leave the choir loft and sit at the front of the church. His text for the night was John 3:1–16, Jesus' debate with Nicodemus which includes the famous passage: "Amen, amen, I say to thee, unless a man be born again of water and the Spirit, he cannot enter the Kingdom of God." The bulk of the sermon concerned the evangelist's desire to "save lost souls" and the constant need for Christians to seek the conversion of others. His one rebuke of the congregation came in this sermon. He upbraided the members for not actively seeking to convert people in the community.

The invitation at each meeting was long and sometimes entailed more than the request to come forward and be baptized. On the first night the evangelist asked people to come forward to say they would bring someone with them on the following night. On the last night he separately asked all deacons and all women to come forward to shake the pastor's hand. The central invitation to come forward and be baptized was much longer than at regular services.

On Wednesday night the invitation was the longest of all and was not interrupted with other calls to come forward. The hymn "Just as I Am" (# 240) has six stanzas. After one stanza the evangelist stopped the hymn and gave a special invitation to the youths at the front. After three stanzas the pastor stopped the hymn and repeated the invitation. The hymn went the full six stanzas, but no one came forward. As it later turned out, the youths had all been motivated to come forward but preferred to discuss the matter with their parents and the pastor before proceeding. Their decision influenced the final part of the sermon and the choice of hymn of invitation on the next night.

In place of the invitation on Thursday the evangelist told a variant of a popular story:

> At one time in the United States breaches between father and son were fairly common. Father and son would argue until eventually the son left home. One particular boy had such a fight and left home. One day, years later, he decided to try and return home. He went to the train station and bought a ticket. He found that he had three cents left over so he bought a one-cent stamp and a postcard. On the card he wrote a message to his mother. He wrote, "I'm coming home. You remember the apple tree by the railroad track. If you want me to come back tie a white handkerchief on the tree. If father is not reconciled don't do anything, and I will keep on going." On the journey he was very excited. He told the conductor his story and asked him to look out of the window for him.

He was too nervous to look for himself. He said "If there is a white handkerchief in the apple tree, I will be getting off at the depot." He waited and waited. Finally, when he knew that they must have passed the tree, he went to the conductor and asked if there was a handkerchief hanging in it. The conductor said, "No." The man's heart fell. Seeing this the conductor's face lit up. He said, "I saw sheets, towels, and pillowcases that covered the tree."

After this the evangelist said, "Now it is your turn. Come home tonight." The hymn of invitation was "Softly and Tenderly" (# 236), with the refrain:

> Come home, come home,
> Ye who are weary come home;
> Earnestly, tenderly, Jesus is calling,
> Calling, O sinner, come home.

Four of the members of the youth choir came forward. They caused a considerable stir among the congregation, and after the prayer of dismissal many of the members of the congregation jubilantly hugged and kissed the four youths. A fifth youth who was still undecided came forward the following night.

New members are baptized in Tidewater Sound on the first convenient Sunday after they have come forward. The five youths who came forward on the Thursday and Friday of revival were baptized two weeks later, along with a boy who had come forward at the beginning of the week and the woman who had come forward several weeks earlier but who preferred to postpone her baptism until after the revival so that only one service would be needed.

The congregation and candidates gathered at 2 P.M., at the edge of the sound, at a favorite picnic spot. Members were not dressed formally but wore T-shirts and shorts or slacks. Male and female candidates alike wore old jeans or shorts and open-neck shirts. The pastor wore his gardening clothes.

The general air was not one of solemnity or emotion. Many members paid only bare attention to the baptisms, and all behaved as if they were at a picnic. They later asserted that the baptism itself was simply the completion of the previous acts of decision: coming forward and acceptance. The most highly charged and significant act was coming forward, which was the principal point of transition. What followed were the inevitable consequences of that crucial change. From an anthropological perspective the baptism is not a rite of passage in itself but the end of a process that begins with spiritual conversion. By coming forward and being voted members of the church, the candidates have already begun new roles. The baptism marks the end of the period of transition.

Before beginning the service the pastor called the candidates together to instruct them on the mechanics of the baptism. Then he called the congregation together and began the service. In the past the service had begun with communal singing of "Shall We Gather at the River?" (# 481). This tradition had been discontinued at some point, although no one was quite sure why.

The pastor began by relating the story of Philip and the Ethiopian eunuch from Acts 8:27–40. He recalled verse 36: "And as they went along the road they came to some water; and the eunuch said, 'See, here is water; what is there to prevent my being baptized?'" The pastor then said, "There is water here. What hinders these people from being baptized? Nothing." He then offered a short prayer and waded into the water until he was waist-deep.

Each candidate waded into the water in turn to be baptized. The candidates crossed their arms across their breasts, hands on shoulders. With his left hand placed where their arms crossed and right hand held high the pastor said, "—[name]—, I baptize you my sister [brother] in the name of the Father, Son, and Holy Spirit." After this he placed his right hand on the candidate's back and immersed him or her, face up.

For the candidate baptism by total immersion has special aesthetic (perhaps better described as anaesthetic) qualities. Four of the five senses are shut off during the immersion. The candidates close their eyes and mouth, shutting out sight and taste. Without air there is no sense of smell, and their hearing is muted. The sense of touch becomes all-important, because the water completely surrounds each candidate's body, loading it with sensation. After baptism the candidates discussed their experiences with one another, and all agreed that it "felt strange"; but what exactly constituted the strangeness was hard to articulate. Certainly all were good swimmers who had been under the water in the sound many times, so that in a general sense the experience was not novel. My interpretation is that this was the first time each had concentrated on the affective experience without other distractions, such as the mechanics of swimming, pulling attention away from contemplation of the affective states engendered.

After all seven candidates had been baptized the preacher called the congregation together with the new members, streaming water from their clothes, and recounted his own baptism in a river in Tennessee. He followed this story with a prayer of dismissal.

Baptisms, weddings, and funerals are locally considered to be the three major rites of passage. However, weddings and funerals affect the church community quite differently from baptisms: they may not involve the whole church community and, in some cases, involve many more people from outside the church than from within its membership. In one wedding I witnessed, for example, neither bride nor groom attended the church, and most of their friends and relatives were not church members either. More important for present purposes, wedding and funeral services are entirely prescribed and formulaic. Aesthetic elaboration is restricted to small changes in the layout and decor of the sanctuary.

The wedding ceremony involves more changes in layout. The pulpit is removed and replaced by two seven-candle candelabra. The church is decorated with white flowers, and the pastor wears a black robe— the only occasion the pastor wears clothes that identify his calling. Funerals frequently take place outside the church precincts because the people of Tidewater have their own family burying grounds. The mechanics of the operation are handled by undertakers, with the pastor leading the service. At both weddings and funerals the service is taken directly from the Southern Baptist Convention manual of services.

At funerals and weddings the participants dress at their most formal. For weddings the bridal party is especially formal. The bride wears a long white gown, and her bridesmaids wear matching formal gowns. The men of the groom's party wear tuxedos, usually in matching pastel shades or in white edged with a dark color. The congregation wears formal Sunday clothes. At funerals men wear their Sunday suits, women wear black.

Both weddings and funerals have little in the way of music, and there is normally no choir. This absence is noteworthy and symbolizes the special nature of these services. Weddings and funerals involve unique communities of relatives and friends which rarely, if ever, coincide with the full church community. The choir represents and works for the church community, not indiscriminately for any group that wishes to use the church.

Thanksgiving and Christmas services are special services for the regular church community. They take place on the eves of the respective holidays and are narrowly focused on their particular concerns. They are slightly shorter than regular services and have the following order:

Prelude	Organist
First Hymn	All
Prayer	Pastor
Welcome	Pastor
Second Hymn	All
Special Music	Choir
Message	Pastor
Third Hymn	All
Benediction	Church member
Postlude	Organist

At the Thanksgiving service in the observation year the hymns were both topical and popular. They were "We Gather Together" (# 492), "Come, Ye Thankful People, Come" (# 490), and "Count Your Blessings" (# 318). The special music was a choral arrangement of "Bless This House" which is always sung in Tidewater at the Thanksgiving service.

For the message the pastor recounted the story of the Pilgrim Fathers and was especially interested in the five grains of corn placed at each plate at the first Thanksgiving. He then said that we can count five blessings of our own:

#1 American flag
#2 Advanced medical technology
#3 Free enterprise
#4 Bible
#5 Jesus

He elaborated briefly on each theme in turn.

On Christmas Eve the order of service is the same as for Thanksgiving. The hymns are traditionally "O Little Town of Bethlehem" (# 75), "Silent Night, Holy Night" (# 72), and "Joy to the World" (# 65). The special music is a solo or duet plus chorus rendition of "O Holy Night." The message is directed toward the Nativity.

Holy Communion is sometimes celebrated on Sunday as an addition to the regular service, sometimes held in a special service. In either case it takes place after the second hymn. The special music is dispensed with and the sermon slightly truncated so that the proceedings can fit within the normal sixty minutes of service. Communion is normally held every three months, and even though it could be held more often, the congregation is adamant that its comparative rarity helps keep it special. The church clerk summarized local sentiment on the point:

> Catholics believe in communion every Sunday, I guess because in the Bible Christ said, "As often as you do this you do it in remembrance of me." Now we had one minister here who had it once a month. But I've heard a lot of people in the church argue that when you have it every week it just gets to be an old everyday thing, you see, that it's not as effective as if you don't have it as often.

A standing committee of women is responsible for preparing the basic accouterments of the service, glasses, dishes, and table linen as well as the bread and "wine." Before the service begins the women of the committee lay the communion table with a clean white linen cloth. In the center they place a silver jug and goblet, to one side four silver plates containing small cubes of white bread and to the other side four trays of small glasses filled with grape juice. Then they cover everything with white linen napkins.

At the point in the service when communion is about to begin, that is, during the last verse of the second hymn, the deacons come forward and sit in the front pew. The chairman and vice-chairman of the deacons remove the napkins from the table and set them aside, and when all is set the preacher comes down from the pulpit and sits at the table. The chairman of the deacons then sits beside him.

The preacher reads 1 Corinthians 11:23b–26, which describes the basic elements of the communion. He follows this reading with a short prayer asking that the bread and wine "be set apart from normal use." Four of the deacons take the plates of bread and pass them round the congregation, then to the other deacons, and finally to the preacher. When everyone is served, they all eat the bread together and spend a few moments in quiet meditation. The "wine" is distributed in like manner, and the whole is concluded by a short formulaic prayer from the preacher. Then the deacons and preacher resume their customary places. After the sermon, instead of a hymn of invitation all sing "Blest Be the Tie" (# 366).

Several aesthetic aspects of the communion service are worth noting. This is the only act of eating and drinking that takes place within the sanctuary. The aesthetics of taste involved are intentionally mini-

[151]

mal. The portions are tiny and the ingredients bland: white bread and nonalcoholic grape juice. But the act of tasting these "foods" is attenuated and given deep concentration by many participants. They close their eyes, keeping silent so there is no noise in the room, and swirl the bread and juice in their mouths, allowing the tastes to melt slowly away. Several said their moments of meditation are defined by the time it takes for the taste to evanesce. It is also significant that everyone eats and drinks at the same time. Several members explained it is an important act of unity. Although the act of eating and drinking is highly personal, it is a *shared* personal experience.

Church members also engage in a host of other activities away from the church building, and the great majority of them have food as a central item. Many are fund raisers, such as the annual chicken supper and the harvest sale (featuring a celebrated Brunswick stew), whereas others are purely for pleasure and entertainment, such as the summer picnic and the Christmas party. Many of these events involve the whole Tidewater community and not just church members.

The fund raisers were inaugurated in the 1950s when the church began its renovation and expansion program, and all rely heavily or exclusively on selling and sharing food. Some pastors have frowned on fund raising, arguing that if the members were tithed there would be ample money for all needs. The congregation for the most part feels that fund-raising events are a more effective means than tithing of establishing church unity. Furthermore, they argue, it is the members who donate items for sale and mostly the members who buy them back again. Consequently, such events are a veiled form of tithing. In addition, the members gain a lot of pleasure out of working together for a common purpose or sitting down at a meal together.

The aesthetic contrast between church services and fund raisers is marked. Apart from communion, the services do not involve the sensations of eating and drinking, and even at communion the act is minimal and highly controlled. The preacher in his sermons prior to the important feasts of Thanksgiving and Christmas lays stress on self-control and abstinence. His Thanksgiving sermon, for example, reminisced on the Pilgrims' sparse meals in their first winter in America and was structured around a symbolic meal of five grains of corn. Fund raisers are boisterous and lavish feasts. The meals prepared are the talk of the town for weeks before and after the event, with many conversations anticipating the delights to come or savoring them in retrospect. Jokes about gluttony and eating in grand manner are the order of the day.

The annual chicken supper is held in a clubhouse on the river bank because the church does not have its own hall for special activities. It is held in mid-May, when the tourist traffic has begun in earnest. Supper is served between 5 and 7 P.M. and consists of a quarter of fried chicken, potato salad, string beans, cornbread, pickles, and a slice of cake for dessert.

All of the food served comes from donations from members and prominent local people determined in advance by a special committee set up for the purpose. Donations are roughly as follows:

1.	Two 3 lb. chickens quartered	40 women
2.	Half-gallon of potato salad	30 women
3.	One pan of cornbread	20 women
4.	One cake	20 women
5.	$3 donation to buy sundries	30 men and women
6.	Assorted small contributions	10 men and women

The congregation feels that the chicken supper is a community event and that as many people as possible, both within and outside the church, should be encouraged to participate. Two categories, potato salad and three-dollar donations, are highly flexible. Many of the people in these categories are not church members or are not very active but might be more engaged if given a push. All of the tasks—installing cookers, preparing and cooking the chicken, preparing plates, and so on—are parceled out to reliable workers.

Just about every member of the church comes to the supper, and a take-out service supplies the housebound and those who must work during supper hours. On that night almost all adults in Tidewater eat one of the suppers. There is universal agreement that this meal is aesthetically very special. It has all of the hallmarks of a fine meal: good company, traditional recipes, home-cooked food, and loving care paid to everything served.

The harvest sale is the biggest event of the church calendar. Like the chicken supper, it involves the whole of Tidewater, not just the church community. It is held in mid-October, when the tourist traffic is still steady. The sale is an all-day affair with a country store selling general merchandise, a clothing store, a bake sale, a crafts table, a hotdog and hamburger stall, and children's games. But the major attraction, and the talk of the town, is a homemade Brunswick stew.

The preparation of the Brunswick stew spans three days, and many old members consider it to be the core event of the festival. On the Thursday before the sale selected women kill, pluck, draw, and joint twelve chickens and dice sixteen pounds of salt pork. On the Friday the crew of men who are to prepare the stew light a fire in the church yard and put a cauldron with a little water in it on to boil. When the water starts to simmer they put in the chicken and pork and add water so that the meat is just covered. The mixture simmers for about four hours, by which time the chicken is in shreds and the salt pork has all melted. Several men take turns to stir the mixture with the sawed-off remains of a poling oar, so that it does not stick or burn. Other men stop by from time to time to watch over the process and give advice or just visit. The women of the church laughingly refer to this process as "the men's idea of work." After four hours the men ladle the mixture into large pans and let it cool. When the pans are cool enough to handle, two or three women separate out the bones and divide up the meat to be refrigerated overnight.

On Saturday morning the men rekindle the fire and warm several gallons of water in the cauldron. When the pot is hot they return the boned chicken and pork mixture to it and then make up the stew with butter beans, corn, tomatoes, chopped onions, diced potatoes, and a strong seasoning of red pepper, black pepper, and salt. At the outset the stew is soupy, but after four or five hours of slow cooking it thickens considerably. Around noon the stew is ready to be served. Volunteers make up plates of stew, cornbread, and coleslaw.

The chicken supper and the harvest sale are the biggest fund-raising events of the year and have been established the longest. Smaller sales are held irregularly, but the efforts for these are not as concerted because they usually do not benefit the church as a whole.

For the two months in the middle of the summer when the tourist traffic is at its peak, the adult Sunday school classes take turns holding a bake sale. The proceeds of these sales go to the building fund. These sales rarely last longer than an hour. A table full of home-baked goods proves irresistible to passersby, and any holdups or traffic jams make business that much swifter.

Occasionally the youths of the church, under the guidance of an adult youth director, hold functions to sponsor outings. These are sporadic and directed toward a small, special segment of the church community, so they are unlikely to become part of the regular calendar. Once they held a fishfry in June, along much the same lines as the chicken supper. In August they sometimes sell homemade ice cream on Saturday afternoons.

The church also has two gatherings solely for entertainment, an afternoon picnic on Labor Day and a Christmas program. The picnic is held on the shore of the sound where baptisms take place and is an afternoon of simple fellowship. The Christmas program is organized by the youth of the church and includes carol singing, a nativity or Christmas play, and a visit from Santa Claus.

According to the rules of discipline of the church a business meeting must be held every quarter. Extraordinary meetings may also be held if pressing business needs to be discussed. For the most part these meetings are uneventful with barely a quorum—seven members— present. Matters discussed are generally uncontroversial and, even though a few members are noted for their ability to talk on any subject at length, there is little debate. Such matters include the dates for the chicken supper and revival, choice of preacher for the revival, and the like.

Issues that require planning or complex decisions are handed over to ad hoc or standing committees for investigation and implementation. In the case of an investigation the committee reports back to the full body for a final decision to be made. The standing committees also handle the day-to-day running of the church, such as maintaining the property, paying bills, and so forth. The bulk of the secular business of the church is handled in committee, and in reality most decisions are made there too, because in the great majority of cases the congregation accepts committee recommendations. This is not to say that all business meetings are pro forma. The church body may, in the end, accept the decisions of committees, but sometimes the precise wording of motions provokes lengthy debate. In all discussion strict parliamentary procedure is supposed to be followed, but there are lapses.

The meetings, which are usually held on a Wednesday evening at 8 P.M., open with a hymn or scripture reading, or both, followed by a short prayer. The hymns and readings are mostly concerned with unity, but now and again the pastor will read a passage of seasonal interest instead. One of the commonest hymns is the communion hymn "Blest Be the Tie" (# 366), the first verse of which is:

> Blest be the tie that binds
> Our hearts in Christian love;
> The fellowship of kindred minds
> Is like to that above.

The clerk reads the minutes of the previous meeting, which are amended if necessary and approved. The business of the day is then conducted, and the meeting closes with a prayer of dismissal. If nothing of any great moment is to be discussed, the whole meeting may be over in thirty minutes.

Dissension, wherever it starts, always comes to a head at business meetings and is resolved there. The church is not prone to dispute, but one problem arose several years ago which has considerable bearing on church aesthetics. It was on the matter of what kind of music the choir should sing.

The regular choir was founded in the 1950s by a trained musician who was a member of the family that had donated land for the church to be built on. (She was part of a small professional-class elite whose aesthetics derived from a mainstream, upper-middle-class, boarding school education. Her needlecrafts, for example, included embroidery and cutwork rather than quilting and sewing, and she played the organ rather than the piano.) She taught the choir to sing in a controlled manner, with particular emphasis on clear enunciation and on singing sweetly and softly. Some ten years later, however, she developed a serious illness that forced her to give up music for a long period. The congregation selected another director to act as a long-term substitute, without realizing that her musical tastes were quite different from the founding director's. In the past the new director had simply played the piano to fill in for the director and had had no role in choosing special music or rehearsing the choir. But the new director favored music of the camp meeting style, that is, songs with antiphonal verse and chorus structure, to be sung loudly and without attention to the canons of musical taste as established by the conservatory. At about the same time the members hired a new preacher who, unbeknown to them and by an odd quirk of fate, also preferred camp meeting–style music.

With a new preacher and a new music director working together, the music of the church over the course of a year was changed to camp meeting style. This change caused an undercurrent of dissent, although few complained openly. Older choir members gradually stopped singing in the choir, and volunteers who preferred the latest developments filled their places. Not coincidentally, the people who left the choir were members of old Tidewater families, and the people who took their places were relative newcomers in the community. After another year dissent had grown so strong, and become so open, that the preacher decided to preach a sermon on church music entitled "World Upside Down." He even printed up the text of the sermon and distributed it to all members, and had copies bound with the church history and meeting minutes. In the sermon he said:

The present lack of co-operation that is giving the Church much concern is that of the music program of our church. With all Godly and due respect to all persons of our Church, only lately have we had a leader for our music program who participates in the full program of our church. This is as it should be, but it seems that many of the choir members who co-operated at least half-heartedly before do not seem to want to co-operate at all now. It falls out that we have a relatively new choir of volunteers at this point. Praise the Lord for that! I don't see anyone "Taking over" the music program of the Church. I see a worker, working and inspiring others to take part in the wonderful ministry of singing the gospel.

Some do not like the style of the music used lately. Keep in mind, there are those who would not like mine or yours either. We all have individual tastes for music developed over the years. And this being true, we need to have respect for the styles of others as well as our own.

Some do not like the quality of the music presentation. There are those who desire and require "Note Perfect music" for our Church. Also a choir of "Trained Voices" to sing.

I'm sorry. This is not a Conservatory.

This is a CHURCH.

Psalm 66:1&2 reads: "Make a Joyful Noise unto God, all ye lands: Sing forth the honor of His name; make his praise Glorious".

Did the psalmist say: "All ye trained choirs". No. He said, "All ye lands".

As important as musical quality is (because shoddy music is not a good offering to the Lord) SPIRITUAL QUALITY is still and ever will be most important in the Church.

Then let the choir consist of those who are willing to make their "Joyful Noises unto the Lord". Let the choir consist of every one who prays earnestly to be used to sing the Gospel.

The best choir member is not necessarily the best trained voice but the *best trained Soul*, singing the very best he or she can.

In the course of the sermon the preacher referred to the missions of Paul and Barnabas. He suggested that the Jews, especially of Thessalonica, were outraged at Pauline teaching because it radically conflicted with the teachings of "their fathers." But, he suggested, Christians must be bound not by tradition but by what is morally right. He illustrated this point by referring to a part of the Tidewater church's covenant which states that members are not opposed to the temperate use of alcohol. He suggested the members were blindly following the lead of their fathers and not doing what was morally right. As such they were just like the Jews of Thessalonica. Adherence to tradition

[157]

was the cause of all of their troubles. They needed their world turned upside down, because in the end "upside down is right side up."

This sermon raised a general furor. Members do not like personal attacks of this sort, regardless of the provocation or justification. In this case the preacher's attack had injured the pride of the original choir director and the singers and musicians she had trained. He had also struck out at the families of the founder members, most of whom controlled the key offices—deacons, Sunday school director, clerk, and treasurer—and many of whom had sung in the old choir. This sermon made a public battle inevitable.

Perhaps because he felt the ground was stronger, the preacher shifted from a defense of the new choir to a vehement attack on the church's alcohol policy. He launched a crusade to change the wording of the covenant and preached (and distributed copies of) three sermons on the nature of covenants. His ultimate aim was to distribute a referendum form to all members asking whether they wished the covenant to remain the same or whether they wanted an amendment banning all use of alcohol. He planned to present the referendum issue at the next business meeting, and the sermons were designed to sway opinion. However, opinion in the church had already been polarized over the question of musical style, and the same sides remained drawn up over the alcohol policy. (Several years earlier the Southern Baptist Convention had asked all member churches to adopt a standard covenant and put aside their own formulations. Tidewater church voted against this move and retained its original wording.)

The preacher presented his draft for the referendum at the next regular business meeting. Heated debate followed. When it was clear the tide was turning against the preacher, members voted to table the motion in order to salvage some degree of unity. If discussion were allowed to continue, it was felt, irreparable damage would be done and a serious split in the membership would follow. The opponents of change thought that tabling the motion would quietly settle the issue. However, three months later at the next business meeting the preacher again brought the referendum to the floor, together with the question of who was to be permanent choir director (the original director was now well enough to continue her duties). Only fifteen members were present, none of whom was fully conversant with Robert's rules of order. By the end of the meeting two motions had passed. The first (9 aye, 6 nay) changed the wording of the covenant, and the second called for the reconstituting of the nominating committee to produce nominees for the post of choir director. But in the matter of the covenant parliamentary procedure was not followed rigorously. The change had been voted on without its first being removed from the table. Therefore, opponents argued, the vote was invalid, and a special meeting was called a week later to resolve the issue.

Before the extraordinary meeting was held opponents of change called and visited friends and relatives in order to pack the meeting. The first item on the agenda was the wording of the covenant, and this time, correctly, the first motion was a call to remove the matter from the table. The motion failed (16 aye, 20 nay). At this point the major proponents of change left the meeting, and subsequently most withdrew their membership from the church.

Next the nominating committee gave its recommendation that the original director be responsible for music and choir practice on the first and second Sundays in each month and that the substitute director be responsible for the third and fourth. A third organist would take care of fifth Sundays when they occurred. This recommendation was crafted on the assumption that the covenant issue would go against the preacher and was meant to be a healing compromise. The preacher's supporters having all left the meeting, however, many members felt that compromise was unnecessary. The husband of an organist trained by the original director moved that the committee's recommendation be set aside and that the church elect the original director to a new term of office. The motion passed unanimously.

Three months after this meeting the preacher resigned his post. The "row," as it is now called, was the culmination of many years of dissatisfaction with this preacher and his predecessors. In all cases of dissent the catalyst was a matter of church aesthetics, even though other issues were drawn in. But it is important to note that dissension began at about the time that new families were beginning to enter the community and settle down. In the "row," as in previous debates, the newcomers voted with the preacher and the old families voted against him. The power of the old families lay in tradition, and if new families were to rise in the hierarchy, they had to oppose tradition.

[7]

Aesthetics of Leisure

This chapter deals exclusively with leisure activities that take place away from home and are not associated with the church. Leisure at home is covered in Chapter 4, leisure connected with the church in Chapter 6. There are three other broad classes of leisure: hunting and fishing, informal associations, and formal associations. All three are male-oriented, and the aesthetics involved are frequently conducted with an air of privacy or secrecy.

Any local man who does not hunt or fish is considered an oddity. These leisure activities are the pride of Marsh County, and the area is nationally renowned for them. Although both hunting and fishing are immensely enjoyed, hunting involves more public display. Gun racks, decoys, wildfowl pictures, and trophies adorn many living rooms, whereas fishing tackle is relegated to the garage or the barn. Furthermore, the single most common sport for home exhibit is duck hunting, considered *the* traditional sport. All local men who are able will go "ducking" at some time during the season, and for many their passion borders on obsession. The aesthetics of this sport are subtle and potentially misleading to the outsider. What appears largely functional, such as the look of duck blinds and decoys, turns out to be more aesthetic than pragmatic.

By late October most talk among men in the community concerns the upcoming duck-hunting season: who is preparing blinds, where to get materials for blinds, new shot cartridges on the market, and so on. At the same time preparations are in full swing. Earliest attention is paid to blinds from which hunters shoot.

Local men distinguish four kinds of duck blind: bush, point, marsh, and float. The first three are built on much the same principles, differ-

Figure 58. Bush blind

ing only in location, the fourth is fundamentally different. A bush, point, or marsh blind is essentially a box six feet by three feet and four feet high, with a door in one of the long sides. The hunters drive four stout juniper poles into the mud to support the box about one foot above the waterline. The box is secured to these poles, and the whole construction is surrounded by cut pine saplings. Bush blinds are located in the sound in water about five feet deep (see Figure 58). In many cases the hunters build a boat blind adjacent to the box to hide the skiff they will use to get to the blind. The boat blind is a boat-shaped frame to support more saplings that will surround and conceal the boat.

Marsh blinds are located on the edge of marsh ponds. A boat may

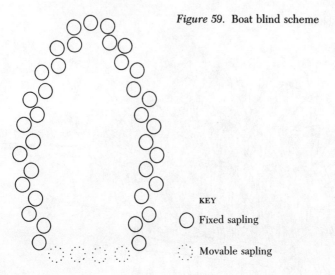

Figure 59. Boat blind scheme

KEY

◯ Fixed sapling

⦂⦂⦂ Movable sapling

still be needed to get to them, but stowed at a distance from the box—in this case the boat blind is simply a hedge of saplings stuck in the mud. Such blinds may also be used in lieu of a box, to hunt from. In this instance the boat itself serves as shooting platform (see Figures 59 and 60). Point blinds are built on the points of the shoreline and may have either an adjacent boat blind or one located at a distance, depending on the ease of walking on the shore.

A float blind is nothing more than a skiff with a temporary frame to hold small saplings attached to the washboards. The hunter drives the skiff to a suitable location and anchors. Then he pushes pine saplings into holes in the frame to surround and conceal the boat. Hunting is done from the boat itself and is carried out in parts of the sound where the water is too deep for a bush blind (Figure 61).

The term "bush blind" strictly refers only to blinds built in the open water of the sound, but all of the blinds described above are "bushed," that is, camouflaged with pine bushes. This choice of materials is noteworthy because the effect, to the outside eye, is decidedly odd. The marshes in mid-November are mostly pale brown where the grasses have turned color. A marsh blind bushed with green pine boughs is visible from a great distance. But the hunters as they bush their blinds seem oblivious to this observation and constantly assess their handiwork, visually checking with each other on the naturalness of the look of the bushes. Their greatest concern is to hide the "human look" of the box, which by their lights means right angles, straight

Figure 60. Boat blind

edges, and raw cut wood. These all look unnatural, whereas pine boughs, regardless of their location, look natural. Because of the normal reluctance of the waterman to fool around with the natural environment, this process struck me as odd at the time and led to conclusions concerning the aesthetic nature of ducking. I return to those conclusions after considering another aesthetic aspect of the hunting environment: decoys.

Having repaired or built and bushed his blind the hunter turns his attention to his rig of decoys. No one in the area makes decoys now, but most hunters still use hand-carved wooden decoys made at the turn of the century by market hunters. The aesthetics of the decoy itself is of considerable importance in understanding the general aesthetics of duck hunting.

All hunters will admit they do not think a decoy has to be lifelike. The following statement is typical: "You could paint every one of them a grayish black, every one of them a grayish black, and not put no other color on 'em, and I swear stuff'd come to 'em just as good. Doesn't make no difference. I've took cow manure—it was cold and dry—in the winter time, and set 'em out on the edge of the ice, and had just as good shooting as I ever had in my life." Other older hunters

Figure 61. Float blind

spoke of the practice of "turfing out," that is, wedging lumps of sod in cleft sticks as rough decoys. And modern hunters make snow goose decoys by filling white trash pail liners with dirt. Even so, contemporary hunters keep their wooden decoys freshly painted to resemble various species of ducks. They are also very particular about having their rafts of decoys resemble as closely as possible a raft of feeding ducks. At the outset, then, it is fair to speculate that the decoys serve primarily an aesthetic function.

Most local carvers took some care to make their decoys resemble ducks, and some were quite remarkable craftsmen. But as the market

[164]

hunters had to keep a raft of between four and five hundred decoys in working order, the carver could not take too long on any one decoy. One hunter described a turn-of-the-century carver: "He made the roughest, outlandish decoys there was made in Marsh County, I believe. But ducks would come to 'em. He could kill ducks with 'em. He just knocked the corners off a block of wood and rounded up a little bit, and nailed a head on it. And it didn't make any difference what size head it was." Even though "ducks would come to 'em," this hunter added: "I've got a few of his decoys here and I expect to work 'em over with a spokeshave and make 'em a decent decoy." A "decent decoy," in other words, is one that looks good to the hunter, not one that is noted for attracting ducks.

Almost all of the wooden decoys still in use are painted to resemble one of three species: canvasback, redhead, and widgeon. During the market gunning days canvasback and redhead were prime ducks, fetching up to seven dollars a pair. It takes little artistry to paint a decoy to resemble a canvasback or redhead, and the broad splash of white on the back makes the decoys show up well. Market hunters so depleted the flocks of canvasbacks and redheads that it is now illegal to shoot them, but, nonetheless, hunters still use the decoys. The widgeon decoy was made more for sportsmen than for market hunters. The complexity of its markings shows how much of a part the hunter's aesthetic preferences play. To paint a redhead is simplicity itself (Figure 62), and touchup at the beginning of the season requires little effort. By comparison the widgeon is complicated to paint and difficult to maintain (Figure 63). For this reason it did not find favor with the market hunters. Some widgeon decoys are even more elaborately painted than the one in Figure 63, with white bellies or a patch of black on the wings. All of this decoration is done even though the hunter knows that a lump of grey wood will do the same job.

Market and early sport gunners did not use goose decoys because they were cumbersome and the long neck was easily broken. Modern hunters on the sound use a small raft of goose decoys in conjunction with their duck decoys. They say the whole scene looks more peaceful and inviting. Most of these decoys, made in the 1940s and 1950s, are of wire-frame and canvas construction (Figures 64 and 65). The decoy maker begins with an elliptical wooden base and attaches a series of wire hoops to it, over which he stretches the canvas body. Finally he carves a head and neck from juniper and nails it on. The whole may be painted to resemble a Canada goose or a swan. These frame decoys are lighter to handle than solid wooden ones. Again, the decision to use

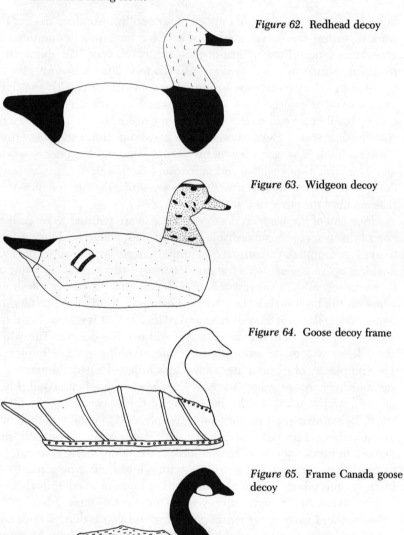

Figure 62. Redhead decoy

Figure 63. Widgeon decoy

Figure 64. Goose decoy frame

Figure 65. Frame Canada goose decoy

goose decoys at all is primarily an aesthetic one. The hunters feel that goose decoys give the raft a natural look, yet they also claim the wildfowl cannot identify the species of a decoy until they are within firing range.

Most modern hunters have some plastic decoys in their collections.

Hunters who wish to hunt the marshes buy a few mallard and ringneck decoys for use there. Canvasbacks and redheads do not frequent marsh ponds, and hunters feel that rafts of this type of decoy in a marsh setting would look unnatural. Market hunters had no use for marsh duck decoys because they hunted exclusively in the sound, where the high-priced ducks flew. As a consequence there are no wooden marsh duck decoys for modern hunters to use. Modern hunters have no objections to plastic or rubber decoys, which are light, do not need painting, and look realistic.

A few weeks before the season opens the hunter makes sure he has a sufficient number of decoys in working order. He touches up worn paint and replaces frayed weight lines. He may need only twenty to thirty decoys per location, but if he hunts in both the marshes and the sound he may need as many as fifty duck decoys plus some geese so he will have sufficient numbers of the species appropriate to the different locations. He also needs a few spares, because he will not have time for running repairs once the season is under way.

The day before the season starts sees the most energetic preparations. Decoys must be sorted and stacked in the hunting skiff's bows, where they will be stored when not in use all season. Guns are given a final check to make sure they are clean and in good working order, and shells are packed in ammunition boxes. The younger men can hardly suppress their excitement as they make ready, whereas older hunters affect a casual air. The next day, first day of the season, is often the best day's hunting all year. The ducks will not have learned to be wary and can be expected to come to blinds easily. As the season progresses they are harder to deceive, and daily bags are slimmer.

The hunting party sets out for the blind at about thirty minutes before sunrise, so as to be set up and ready at sunrise, the legal start of the day's shooting. Upon reaching the blind the hunters throw out their decoys. Each hunter has his own theories about the positioning of the decoys in rafts, but most end up bunching them in loose rafts directly in front of the shooting platform of the blind, with goose decoys, if used, rafted upwind from the ducks. For a float rig, the geese are rafted at the bow and the ducks at the stern. Most hunters are aware of more "scientific" placements of the decoys, such as the one in Figure 66, but few bother with them (several men owned the book and showed this diagram to me). It takes a good deal of time to place the decoys in this manner, which also demands that the decoys be stored separately in a way that is impracticable in a small skiff. What is more, these placements do not mirror natural rafting behavior

Figure 66. "Scientific" decoy placement (after Walsh 1971:12)

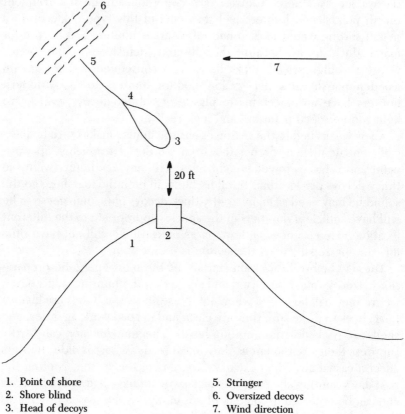

1. Point of shore
2. Shore blind
3. Head of decoys
4. Tail of decoys
5. Stringer
6. Oversized decoys
7. Wind direction

so that, whether they work or not, they do not look right to the hunter.

With decoys set up and boat stowed, the hunters prepare themselves. Normally two men hunt together, although most blinds can comfortably accommodate three. Men who hunt together are old friends who enjoy each other's company as much as the hunting itself. During slack times they exchange hunting stories, discuss current conditions, and so on. Even when nothing is flying about they still keep their eyes on the horizon. Their ability to spot and identify ducks at a great distance is an important skill.

To a novice glancing through a manual on field identification, it may seem an easy matter to tell species of ducks apart. With a few exceptions the coloration of drakes is distinctive and, one might imagine, makes identification on the wing a simple matter. But in fact, until a duck comes within short firing range its colors barely show. The observer may catch a glimpse of white on back or wing, but usually he must rely on more subtle signs.

The three keys to field identification are silhouette, flock pattern, and flight pattern. Some examples of this kind of identification show the visual acuity necessary. Canvasbacks travel in lines or Vs when migrating and in compact flocks when flying over feeding grounds. They fly very fast with a rapid wing beat. They have a large, plump body, flattish neck, and long beak. Widgeons fly in open flocks, constantly twisting and turning. Their bodies are medium-size and slender, and they have short beaks. All mergansers fly in straight lines low over the water. They have long necks, which they stretch out straight in front of their bodies when flying. In Marsh Sound the gunner will see all three species but is interested only in the widgeon. It is illegal to shoot canvasbacks, and locals consider all fish-eating ducks, such as mergansers, inedible.

When the hunter has identified a small flock as legal and edible he may use calls to lure it closer. Whether to use calls is a subject of some controversy, and the general feeling in Tidewater is that one should either be an expert with a call or use none at all. The sight of a tourist hunter at the local stores with a duck call hanging from the zipper of his hunting jacket usually calls up a knowing smile from residents. Tidewater men will feel that such a "foreigner" probably frightens more birds with his call than he attracts. The duck call is supposed to complete the illusion that the decoys are a peaceful raft of ducks feeding contentedly, but in the wrong hands it can destroy the whole deception.

If a flock looks as if it is getting ready to "decoy," the hunter gives a few greeting calls: a loud qu-a-a-quack-quack-quack, followed by a feeding noise: a low k-k-k-k-k-k-k. (Some hunters do not use calls but produce an array of honking and quacking sounds using their voices.) When the ducks come within range the hunters stand and fire. If the ducks do not decoy, particularly if they veer away at the last minute, the hunters discuss the cause of this behavior. Discussion almost always turns on what in the scene does not look natural enough.

A neophyte might be forgiven for thinking that these men believe that a lifelike scene around their blinds is what attracts ducks. Certainly they are at pains to create what they consider to be a natural setting. But there is another, less mysterious, reason why ducks come

[169]

to the blinds: they are baited with corn. This practice is illegal. A baited blind attracts large numbers of ducks regularly, as every hunter knows, but most hunters are afraid that without bait they will have no ducks. It is difficult to avoid the conclusion that decoys, calls, and so on are part of an elaborate staging for the hunters' benefit.

It could be inferred from this elaborate seeming hoax that hunters have found a way to indulge aesthetic fancies without appearing to do so. They can claim publicly, with some authority, that all of their blind making, decoy painting, and quacking serves a practical function, yet on the sly they will not hesitate to reveal how unfunctional it all is. As an aesthetic form the act of hunting is multisensory, involving the sight of the natural environment, wildfowl, blinds, and decoys; the sound of real and imitation ducks and geese and the powerful explosions from shotguns; the feel of cold blasts of winter air, icy rain, and sleet; the fetid smell of the marshes and the acrid smell of gunpowder; and the anticipation in long narratives of the taste of duck. Such an aesthetic performance might well be the subject of men's passions.

Duck hunters *never* hunt alone. Passionate or not, the hunter who cannot find a partner for the day will not go out. If duck hunting is a performance, it is one that requires an audience. The lone hunter has no audience, and in consequence the pleasure and meaning of the act are absent. In addition it is de rigueur to recount the day's events at the general store in the evening, and it is considered immodest to tell of one's own fortune's (although one may recount mishaps). It is the task of the partner to extol one's skills.

Locals consider all other forms of hunting to be second-rate in comparison with ducking. These forms tend to be relegated to boys and "foreigners" or are indulged half-heartedly when duck season is out. None of these secondary forms of hunting has the aesthetic accouterments of duck hunting, nor do they carry the prestige and weight of tradition. Furthermore, their goals are pragmatic: they supply meat. Each of these sports attracts men and boys who like the taste of the game they hunt. No aesthetic elaboration obscures this relationship.

The basic idea behind deer hunting is simple. Before the season opens in mid-October the hunters watch the woodlands beside bean fields at dusk to see where deer are feeding. They also keep an eye out by day for spoor, rubbed bark, and other signs of the presence of deer. When the season opens, and having gained the requisite permission from the landowner, a band of hunters hunts a stretch of woods. If the woods are completely on dry land the hunters position themselves individually around the woods in concealed spots that offer a wide field of vision. When all are ready one member of the gang takes five or six deerhounds into the woods and turns them loose when they pick up a fresh scent.

A good deerhound remains silent while searching for a scent and when he finds one sets up an intermittent bark. If he catches up to a deer and pursues it, he will howl continuously. The hunters on their stands strain constantly to hear the hounds and to determine what they are doing and in what direction they are traveling. Most commonly the dogs run for an hour or two, barking on occasion as they catch a scent but ultimately failing to flush anything from cover. In this case the dog handler rounds up the dogs, and they move to a new set of woods to begin again.

When a deer is shot it is tagged and registered. Next the carcass is hung from a tree limb and skinned, gutted, and butchered. This operation is carried out with great excitement, most of the banter focusing on how each hunter will cook his allotted portion (all members of a hunting party share in the kill). The flesh is butchered very much like a carcass of beef but with fewer divisions. Shank, rump, and round are taken as one cut, as are rib and plate, and chuck and brisket. The hounds get the offal as a reward and to reinforce the taste and smell of deer. Someone may take the heart and liver to make a hunter's stew, but this practice is now rare.

At the end of butchering the hunters divide the meat. The hunter who actually made the kill gets first choice. He takes either the sirloin or one of the rump/round roasts. Next a choice piece is set aside for the owner of the land on which the kill was made. Then those who made special contributions to the hunt, such as providing dogs or transportation, make their choices. The remaining hunters then choose from what is left. Preferences generally are for hindquarter cuts first, then forequarter, then ribs.

No one goes deer hunting who does not enjoy the taste of deer meat. The final pleasure of the hunt is to sit down to a supper of roast, broiled, or barbecued venison. Younger men and boys often reserve a whole carcass for an outdoor barbecue party. In this case they open-roast the meat on a rack above a slow flame in much the same way that a hog is cooked at a pig picking in other parts of the South. The roast meat is served with a hot barbecue sauce and appropriate trimmings, such as potatoes and coleslaw.

When the duck season provides poor hunting, or between seasons, some men take to field hunting. Animals hunted include dove, squirrel, rabbit, raccoon, and quail. These kinds of hunting have few devotees, mostly boys and a few newcomers to town.

To hunt dove a group of men (any number) sit singly along a known flyway in a corn or bean field. They fire as doves fly within range. Although the hunters are in solo positions, they are not isolated like deer hunters. Each can see all of the others at all times and observe the overall pattern of the hunt and the activities of the birds. Doves may be hunted from noon to sunset, but most hunters do not care to stay out longer than an hour or two. At the end of the hunt the hunters compare bags. Those with one or two give them to those with larger bags to form "messes," that is, enough for a family meal.

Squirrel hunting is definitely a boy's sport, and men consider it to be important training in marksmanship. Hunters despise poor marksmen for a variety of reasons, but perhaps the most important is that the "sorry shooter" cripples many animals that then crawl away and die in hiding. Men prefer to kill an animal with the first shot or not shoot at all. They also hate to see animals suffer or to loose cripples.

Squirrels are hunted by single hunters or by pairs. The hunter quietly positions himself in a wood where he has seen squirrel activity and waits for a shot. This kind of hunting teaches boys to be patient and quiet, to select only good shots by properly gauging distance and angle, and to judge their own skills. Squirrel hunters use .22 caliber rifles, considering anything larger to be unsportsmanlike. Raccoon hunting is similar except that it is done at night with the aid of lights, because raccoons are nocturnal.

Rabbit and quail hunting reach peaks of considerable sophistication and cooperation between man and dog in many parts of the South, but in Tidewater the sports are haphazard and largely confined to newcomers. The simplest way to hunt quail and rabbit, often at the same time, is to send a flushing dog into thickets and brier patches on the margins of arable fields. Sooner or later something will fly up or out and provide a shot for the hunter. Local men consider this very poor sport and hardly worth the effort.

In spring and summer Tidewater men devote their leisure energies to fishing. For many fishing is the ideal way to spend as little or as much time and effort as one wishes. Men may go out into the sound if they have enough time, but many are content to fish in ditches or on the river bank. Freshwater fishing is universally popular, but most men make one or two expeditions to the beach each year for some surf casting. In both cases the pleasure resides in a good battle with the fish. Largemouth bass provide the best freshwater sport, bluefish in saltwater. The primary difference between freshwater and saltwater fishing is that the former produces little in the way of "edible" fish whereas all saltwater fish are considered edible.

Local freshwater fishermen toss back bass (too strong), pike (too bony), and panfish (too small). The only fish they routinely keep are "rock," that is, striped bass, because they are highly prized by local cooks. The joy of freshwater fishing resides in being out of doors near water and putting up a challenge to nature. Many consider the challenge especially satisfying because no permanent harm is done to the fish. They also despise and ridicule out-of-town fishermen who keep (and eat) everything they catch.

Surf fishing is less common because it requires time and energy to get to the beach and get set up. However, the culinary rewards make the effort acceptable from time to time. All saltwater fish are considered edible: drum, flounder, croaker, spot, and bluefish. But the bluefish alone provides the sport that justifies catching other varieties of fish. One local compared catching a flounder to landing a dishrag, but a bluefish is a different story. It may bite the line, jerk up and down, run up to the beach and shake violently, in fact do almost anything to free itself. This kind of challenge provides the main reward for fishing at the beach.

For many men in Tidewater the day's sporting activities are not complete without a trip to the general store to give an account of adventures and mishaps and to hear the same from others. Two quite distinct groups meet at the stores: youths and retired men. As younger men get married and have children they drift away from the "store crowd." Their time is taken up with family matters, and many work both days and evenings. But when a man retires he finds he has time on his hands, and slowly, reluctantly at first, he returns to the store. At the beginning of my observation year a well-respected, hard-working man retired from a city job he had held for thirty years. Throughout the year he was ambivalent about retiring and would periodically take on small jobs from his old employer. At the same time he began to get moderately involved in gill net fishing and was seen more and more frequently hanging around at the store. His kin were surprised to see him at the store because he is stubborn, and joining the store crowd is an open admission of old age. By the end of the year he was a regular at the store, and at the same time he bought the materials to make eel pots. This final act severed him completely from employment, because eel pots need daily tending.

The meeting of youths and old men at the store is a microcosm of a much greater unity between the two. Youths and old men share much of the same work and leisure habits and have similar outlooks on the world. Both regularly hunt and fish for pleasure and take only intermittent employment. They enjoy informal associations such as the store crowd and prefer to come and go as they please. Both groups are often characterized as "roosters" or "pistols," meaning that they are generally unbridled. However, the older men have a different status from the youths.

A senior adult may buy a few gill nets or crab pots to earn a small supplement to his other sources of income, and he may take on a youth, especially a family member, to help. But because he owns the equipment, and because he has a great deal of experience, the senior adult is definitely in charge. At the store the senior adults are the raconteurs, and the youths sit and listen or provide prompts for the older men to continue storytelling in a certain vein. Although older men return to the activities of their youth, activities they had to forego in their middle years, they assume a higher status when they return.

Men hang around the store all day, but it is after supper that the most active sessions occur. Generally by seven o'clock three or four men are present with a handful of boys, and talk wanders across topics of general interest. Whenever a known storyteller shows up the general flow of conversation slackens, and he is given the opportunity to amuse the crowd. A good storyteller is generally allowed to proceed at his own pace, without interruption, and to tell as many stories as he likes. But if two happen to meet, they may trade stories with everybody else looking on.

Samples of stories and exchanges give a broad sense of the ethos of storytelling and "shooting the bull" at the store. The first story is, like most, a segment of local history, and I have chosen it for extended review for several reasons. First, and perhaps most important, I have two versions of the tale told by the same man, which allows careful comparative checking of conclusions concerning narrative structure and performance style (the second version appears as Appendix B). Second, the tale contains many narrative and performance elements that are common to all local tales.

Following leads from the literature on ethnopoetics (Bright 1980; Hymes 1976, 1977; Tedlock 1971, 1977), I have transcribed the tale in a way that makes manifest some basic elements of narrative and performance structure. A complete list of my transcription conventions appears in Appendix B, but they boil down to a simple rule of thumb: an untabbed line break or a conventional punctuation symbol indicates pauses in the narration. I have ordered the lines so that each begins with a particle, usually "and," because repeated listening to the tapes has convinced me that they mark segments of the narrative structure. The narrator commonly paused at the end of a thought or flow of ideas, said "and," often paused again, then added a new element to the narrative. Comparison of the two versions shows that similar narrative elements are framed by particles and pauses in both and confirms the general validity of this approach. I have also divided the lines defined by particles into couplets, again because analysis of the two versions appears to warrant it. The units of meaning in the couplets seem to belong together. But I have not been completely reductive in this regard. Some segments cannot be paired into couplets and so have been put into suitably longer or shorter units. Nor do I make any assertion that this narrative is poetry, nor adopt the theoretical perspectives of ethnopoeticists wholesale. Such claims are outside the bounds of the present work.

And, I . . . was a fellah buried on Tate's Point that was . . . died in
    eighteen, and forty eight
And his name was Wallace Tyler—he had a son named . . . Harry—
    Harry Tyler   (1)

And of course when the old man died he left the place, there
And was six thousand acres of that property   (2)

And was all timber was good timber
And this was a point of land, with a creek in back of it, two miles
    long—in another county it is now   (3)

And he used to make sailing vessels
And trade with the West Indies [*]   (4)

And he had a hundred slaves on Tate's Point—he couldn't always said
    he couldn't keep a hundred—this is things I've heard—he couldn't
    keep a hundred just as soon as he got a hundred one of them would
    die or something would happen to one of them
And he never could keep quite a hundred slaves.   (5)

And, he built ships up that creek
And I did know the name of—three he had three—   (6)

And, what the way I understand it this is . . . fact with maybe some
    fiction into it or maybe some . . . warping of the truth
But the way I've got it from . . . three generations back, that, Wallace

Tyler was in Baltimore harbor, about the turn of the seventeenth century—not the eighteenth century but the seventeenth; he was in Baltimore harbor about . . . seventeen, and four—somewhere around seventeen and four.   (7)

And there come what they call a Baltimore . . . waterfront fire; it wiped out . . . the docks, with a hard north . . . west wind, from what I've understood.
And it would just sweep right down . . . the waterfront—it was cleaning the houses out.   (8)

But he had a schooner tied up to the dock.
And they just moved his schooner back they traded in them days . . . in gold and silver—paper paper money was nothing
And, all these traders
And, Baltimore harbor was always a trading center—they just moved this schooner down . . . the docks . . . as the fire forced them to   (9)

And took their safes
And strongboxes they had their silver in and their gold;   (10)

And took it and put it aboard this schooner,
And moved along—take the next one take the next one;   (11)

And when he got loaded . . . with strongboxes—the wind was to the west'ard—he just pushed off from the dock and set sail—it was at night—
And set sail down the Chesapeake and he had a fair wind,
And perhaps a strong one,
And when it come daylight he was gone.   (12)

And, of course he came . . . on . . . down the Chesapeake and come on out the Chesapeake—mouth of the Chesapeake
And the first inlet . . . that you could get in south of the Chesapeake, in them days, was possibly . . . Cooper's Inlet, which was about three . . . three to four miles north from Tate's Point Creek   (13)

And I . . . from what I understand he run in that inlet with this boat
And went in that creek and up in a place called Gum Cove with about six feet of water—six to eight feet of water and mud—he got afraid the revenuers would run him down—he dumped all these safes overboard, strongboxes and stuff overboard in—in . . . Tate's Point Creek.   (14)

And, he stayed around, see what was going to happen and nobody didn't bother him

[176]

And so he got—took these safes up—went overboard and dove them
up or whatever he can, may be some of them in there yet.   (15)

And, of course he had money then
And he bought this . . . property—six thousand acres of it.   (16)

And this . . . point of the land known as Tate's Point is . . . in that . . .
six thousand acres—this creek is in that six thousand acres, Tate's
Creek's two miles long,
And he carried on a trade with the West Indies.   (17)

And the war come in; he died; his son took over—you could still have
slaves—so he took over his daddy's slaves
And got more   (18)

And Harry—not Harry but . . . Hyram . . . not Hyram, Harry's
child—Harry is the one—he took over from his dad
And, run the place, till the war come on between the states;   (19)

And when . . . he could see that the war was coming on between the
states, he got his three vessels . . . in . . . inside . . . from the West
Indies [*]
And got them in and got them in Tate's Point Creek   (20)

And he had a railway there for pulling them out and
And, cleaning them—cleaning them and painting them   (21)

And I've seen the railway—it was still . . . visible when I . . . lived
there
And, when the war come on, he had all his vessels in there   (22)

Well, Burnside come up, from Hatteras, from inside and started to
clean up . . . the sounds and clean up the boats [+]
And . . . take over this section of country   (23)
And, when he come up there to Harry's Harry knew he was coming—
he had a boatload of nails, bound for the West Indies
But he couldn't get her out   (24)

So he run her out out of the creek
And tried to . . . run her into Whiskey Creek which is on the other
side of the sound, about four miles   (25)

And take the masts out of her—with the intention of taking the masts
out of her
And covering her with . . . trees up that creek to keep the Yankees
from burning her up   (26)

[177]

But they caught him in the middle of the sound
And burnt him up (27)

Course he weren't aboard if his captains were
Then they went ashore at Tate's Point (28)

And he had took his gold and silver
And supposedly put it down a well, at Tate's Point, in brass boxes he
    had had it in brass boxes—put it down the well; (29)

And when the Yankees come there to get him they knew he had gold
    and they knew he had silver—cause he was a trader
And, they beat him nearly 'bout to death to try to get him to tell where
    it was [*] (30)

And he wouldn't
And he didn't (31)

And that was around eighteen and sixty . . . three,
And he . . . I've never been to look at his tombstone (32)

But I don't think he lived more than four or five years after it I think
    they beat him up so bad—he didn't live long
And, that's where all the Tylers down at the south end of this—Marsh
    County—this peninsula down here—that's where all the Tylers
    come from—that's where the name Tyler came from there's lots of
    Tylers down there—not a hell of a lot now 'cause a lot of them
    moved away (33)

But, Tate Tate's Point Creek and Tate's Point has always been a a—
    well I think he had fifty acres cleared up on there—fifty or seventy-
    five acres at one time or more
But it's always been a little bit mysterious—mystery about it. (34)

And, I'm sure, it wouldn't be any use to go look I know where that well
    is or I think I know—there was two wells when I moved there in
    nineteen hundred
And, my daddy lived there in nineteen three (35)

And I was born in nineteen two
And I stayed there till I was till I was thirteen years old (36)

But, I knew where the well was in the old house that we moved in
    when we went there and poppa tore that down and built a new one
And of course he plugged the well up (37)

And I know where the other well was terracotta well, where it was
    within . . . ten feet of it; we took that well up—pulled the ter-
    racotta—the well out of the ground . . . in sections and put it to
    another place—it was it wasn't too good a water
But I know where them two places is   (38)

But I don't think you would find anything if you was to give it a
    thorough search
Because, he lived for five . . . years or more I'd go look at his
    tombstone and find out   (39)

But I haven't looked at it in a many a day
And I forget—I don't think he lived too long after that   (40)

And
But he lived long enough to tell somebody or go get that money . . .
    after—I don't think you'd find anything in either place   (41)

But I—I knew a fellah
And his daddy . . . was one of the captains on his ships—that was Ted
    Midgett—his daddy . . . was captain . . . of one of his ships . . .
    that went to the West Indies.   (42)

And, he told me his daddy told him, he lived to be eighty-five he's
    been dead about ten fifteen years . . . years—about fifteen years
And he told me that his daddy told him these things—that this was put
    in—it was in—put in brass boxes down in the bottom of that well (43)

But that—that's a . . . story that there's some truth in
But you can't tell . . . how much truth there is in it; you can't tell how
    much truth there is in it   (44)
But it ain't all fiction—it's not all fiction
And it's not made up by me—it come to me in pieces, as I was a young
    fellah   (45)

And as I remember it
And I put the dates and stuff I put them together myself—I could be
    wrong it could have been before . . . eighteen and four but it was
    around that time somewhere, maybe a few years before that or a few
    years after; what I date that on is . . . he lived to be—he was
    buried . . . in eighteen . . . and forty eight—see, he was . . .
    maybe fifty sixty seventy years old I could look on his tombstone and
    see   (46)

But I never bothered to look—just to—date he was—I didn't—didn't
    know the day he was born—it's—it's on there I'm sure

But, I never remember it didn't remember ever looking   (47)

And
But the date of his death—eighteen forty eight—I thought for many
   years it's eighteen forty seven   (48)

But, the last time I visited that tombstone, somebody had rubbed that
   off with acid—that date—that last figure
And it was a eight instead of a . . . seven—somebody before me had
   rubbed that . . . over with acid, made it come up bright—him and
   his wife are buried side by side over there   (49)

And they're the only white people . . . was buried on Tate's Point
But there was a . . . lot of . . . negroes buried over there   (50)

This narrative has two action elements, Wallace Tyler and the Baltimore waterfront fire (7b–17) and Harry Tyler's meeting with Burnside (18–31), plus a coda in the form of personal ruminations on the wells (32–43). The whole is also elaborately framed in several ways, including a prologue containing snippets of the main stories and establishing the general truth of what is to follow (1–7a), and an epilogue recapitulating the claims of truth, citing authorities and methods of reconstruction.

The narrator spends considerable time at the beginning and end of the tale giving the audience tools for interpreting what the story contains and his role in its construction and telling. He warns that the story is "fact with maybe some fiction into it or maybe some warping of the truth" (7a); at the beginning and at the end he says, "You can't tell how much truth there is in it" (44b). He also includes at start and finish a statement concerning his sources. At first he merely reports that he "got it from three generations back" (7b); he elaborates on this statement at some length at the end (42–43), with a more detailed summary of sources. At the end he also makes strong claims for the truth of at least part of the story, including the reduplicated statement "it ain't all fiction—it's not all fiction" (45a), as well as a personal disclaimer: "it's not made up by me" (45b). But although he did not make up the story in the sense that it is not all fiction, he did make it up in the sense that he put all of the pieces together (45b) and through detective work added dates to the sequence of events (46). The tale is, in consequence, as much his story as it is history. What is more, it is his story because the location is personally significant and the themes associated with it are affective for him, which is why he researched the details in the first place.

The tales of Wallace and his son Harry contain many parallels and oppositions that unite the two into one structure. Wallace escapes from Yankee fire (Baltimore is Yankee country to the people of Tidewater) and becomes rich as a result, whereas Harry is trapped by Yankee fire and loses his means of trading as a result. In both cases the fire is spoken of as a cleansing element: the waterfront fire "was cleaning the houses out" (8b), and Burnside (of all names) "started to clean up the sounds and clean up the boats" (23a). This symmetry of treacherous action born in fire and retribution visited on the son in the form of fire is patent in the second version of the tale, where the burning of the vessel marks the end of a narrative section. The themes of illgotten wealth avenged with fire also reflect classic sentiments concerning the punishments of hell and, as the fire is of Yankee origin, casts these outsiders as devil-like.

The elemental flavor of the tale continues. Water is a means of escape from the dangers of land for Wallace, but Harry fails to escape when he flees to a safe haven via water. For both men, however, water serves to keep wealth safe. Wallace tosses his gold and silver into a shallow creek, Harry puts his down a well. Thus for both water can be used to bury things (in the old sense of the word *bury*, meaning to keep safe), and this ethos is reinforced by the association of the water in question with earth. Gum Cove is "six to eight feet of water and mud" (14b), and a well is drilled in the earth.

Even air can be brought in to complete the elemental symmetry. Wallace "had a fair wind" (12b) and so was able to make his escape, but the wind could not help Harry. In addition, note that for Wallace the ship's masts represent safety—they carry the sails that use the fair wind—but for Harry they represent danger. The overall structure is neat. In the first half of the story fire is associated with land and is dangerous whereas masts and sea bring safety. In the second half fire is associated with the sea and is dangerous whereas lack of masts and land bring safety. In all of this activity the wind plays a dual role. The wind that is fair for Wallace is foul for the waterfront because it spreads the fire rapidly (8a), and the wind that is fair for Burnside is foul for Harry.

These oppositions and symmetries suggest that what seem to be two related actions are really one unified story, and that what look like two characters are really one metonymic (father/son) composite. The narrative begins "was a fellah buried on Tate's Point" (1a) and ends "him and his wife are buried side by side over there" (49). The son's name is not clear (19), his death date is unknown (47), and his burial place is not mentioned. Two graves and two death dates would imply two people.

Significant also is a concern with timber and wood, which may be either helpful or harmful. On the one hand timber represents wealth. Wallace uses gold and silver to buy six thousand acres of land covered with "good timber" (3a) and uses it "to make sailing vessels" (4a). He uses these vessels, as does Harry, for trading, which in turn makes more gold and silver. Furthermore Harry tries to use trees to cover up his vessel in order to save her from the Yankees. But, of course, wood also burns: the fires that are central to the story consist of burning wood.

At the end of the tale the narrator indicates hesitantly that he is beguiled by the fact that Tate's Point has "always been a little bit mysterious." He seems reluctant to spell out this conclusion and falters in getting to it (34a). Indeed, in the second version he starts to make this point and then changes tack (21a). The revelation that Tate's Point is mysterious pulls all of the sections together in one grand mystery. What is truth and what is fiction? Which well was the money hidden in? Is there some treasure still hidden in the well? Why couldn't Tyler keep quite a hundred slaves? Why did someone rub the tombstone with acid? Why did the date on the tombstone appear to change from 1848 to 1847? When did Harry (or Hyram) die?

Part of the mystery stems from the fact that this is a story about treasure, wealth, and trading. Money is a taboo subject in normal conversation, and the act of trading has a distinctly "foreign" and distasteful air to it. Take, for example, the ethos of the general store that is the stage for most storytelling. Most local people keep accounts at the store and rarely carry or exchange money when they visit. Furthermore, the purchase of goods appears minor compared to the general social visiting that takes place at the store. Some men visit the store at night for several hours and in the process buy at most a pack of cigarettes or a soda. Foreign visitors are easily spotted: they walk into the store, select items, pay cash money on the spot, and leave with barely a word spoken. I have more to say about the conflicts between these lifestyles in the next chapter.

Because the fascination with buried treasure is taboo the narrator hedges about it while at the same time being irresistibly drawn to it. For several minutes he goes back and forth between suspecting that the treasure is still in the well and believing that it was all taken out (38–41), while also making it clear that he has never looked (although he had the opportunity). At the same time he gets vague about dates that previously he has been proud to have researched. He cannot remember how long after the incident Harry lived, cannot remember looking at his tombstone, and, if he did, cannot remember the date of his death.

The fate of the family and the property is appropriate. The sons continue their transactional heritage: they go off to a city to be new-style traders. The land continues its associations as primarily of wealth value: it is bought for investment purposes by a Yankee who seldom visits (see Appendix B).

Comparison of the two versions of the tale reveals much about the mechanics of narrative structure and its relationship to performance style. It is clear that the particle "and" drives the narrative along and defines story elements. Point-by-point comparison of the two versions shows many identical or near-identical phrases following the particle. For example, compare the following pairs. In each case the first comes from version one.

And there come what they call a Baltimore waterfront fire   (8a)
And there come what they call a Baltimore waterfront fire   (3a)

But they caught him in the middle of the sound
And burnt him up   (27)

But they caught him on the way over
And burnt him up   (19)

Not only do these similarities help confirm that story elements defined by particles are critical narrative units, they also confirm the significance of fire. These are fixed verbal formulae that anchor the narrative.

Special particles—well, but, because, course—mark special elements. The pairs cited above begin with "but," marking the couplet as central to the action. Generally the action moves forward under a constant stream of "ands," so that other particles either create dramatic pauses initiating an element of particular significance (25a, 34a and b) or break the rhythm in more reflective passages (37–46).

At places in both versions the teller also conflates and temporarily confuses chronology or the flow of the story. Compare, for example:

And the war come in; he died; his son took over   (18a)

And when the war come on with the . . . he died in eigh . . . teen . . .
   and forty eight
But he had a grown son that took over   (13b–14a)

[183]

In both cases the teller, anxious to join the main action tales together, temporarily forgets to tell the audience that Wallace dies in the interim, and so he has to break the beginning of the second part to insert this information. The effect of this dovetailing is to further confuse the histories of father and son, making the unity of the whole with its symmetries and oppositions more evident. It also makes it seem as if Wallace and Harry are a single character or a single unit of some sort. Certainly as father and son they would be a single social entity in the minds of a Tidewater audience.

The teller seems to conflate story elements at points where he is trying to move action along. In both versions he has to halt the action about placing the strongboxes on the schooner to add the context element that "they dealt in gold and silver then" (version 1,9; version 2,3–4). In both versions two separable couplets are inextricably wound together in the tumbling forward of the action. The teller may also be trying to avoid explicit reference to wealth because of local taboos.

In general he prefers to move the action along and add the explanatory content parenthetically:

And, all these traders
And, Baltimore harbor was always a trading center   (9)

And he had took his gold and silver
And supposedly put it down a well, at Tate's Point, in brass boxes he
    had had it in brass boxes   (29)

This technique suggests that in the narrator's worldview the existential conditions are assumed and well-known and that it is action plus motivation (both the hero's and the narrator's) which lie at the core of the tale.

The delivery style is rather slow and deliberate, as marked pauses in the transcription attest. Sometimes the story hangs suspended while the teller gives careful thought to a particular element, especially dates, which, as he says, are a major contribution of his to the story (see, for example, 7b, 46b, and 48b). He may also realize that he has a tendency to mistake dates, as in his mistaking the century at the beginning of the first version (7b).

In conspicuous contrast to this slow, attenuated rhythm are occasional spurts of energy in the delivery where, lack of breath notwithstanding, he is determined to get one segment out intact. For example:

[184]

I knew where the well was in the old house that we moved in when we
    went there and poppa tore that down and built a new one   (37a)

he couldn't keep a hundred just as soon as he got a hundred one of
    them would die or something would happen to one of them   (5a)

These phrases are delivered without a pause and dramatically change
the slow rhythm of the narrative. It is perhaps not surprising that
these long phrases are associated with mysterious aspects of the story
or mid-points of action.

The teller also marks key points in action with various forms of
direct or incremental repetition, that is, repetition that involves small
changes. To indicate the steady loading of Wallace's schooner he says:

And moved along—take the next one take the next one   (11)

Harry's brutal interrogation by the Yankees is marked by two incremental repetitions:

And when the Yankees come there to get him *they knew he had gold*
    and they knew he had silver—cause he was a trader
And, they beat him nearly 'bout to death to try to get him to tell where
    it was

And he wouldn't
And he didn't   (30–31)

The story also helps illuminate the general character of the narrative
and the joint sympathies of narrator and audience. The tale has direct
appeal because it is about the sea and boats, and audience and performer are watermen. Even though the tale involves treachery and
retribution the narrator relies on the audience being on the side of the
Tylers and against the Yankees. Tylers, whatever their origins, are
local people now: neighbors and friends. Yankees are the devil incar-
nate. In the second version these sentiments carry over to the Yankee
who ultimately bought the property for investment purposes. In many
ways she represents the incursion of newcomers into the vicinity and
the changes involved.

It is not necessary to repeat such detailed analysis for all the tales I
recorded, but it is important to sample a range of narratives. What
follows is a selection of styles and narrative structures. As in the first I
have punctuated the transcriptions to follow the narrator's pauses, but

I present each tale more like a straight prose account to make it immediately readable.

It is common for tales to move from the generally historic to the personal and to terminate with a funny tag, even if the tag is not the main thrust of the story:

The best moonshine stills there was in the world was in the Bull's Creek section of country. I've always claimed it was so much sought after because it was made out of what they call "juniper water." That was juniper timber down there, and the water was red from juniper roots. It was rainwater, and they used that rainwater, which was saturated with tannic acid from the roots of junipers. And it was a pure water. You could drink it right out of the river. You go up the river there five miles, and you could take a dipper from right overboard and drink it. You needn't worry about it. And they used that in making their mash. It was the most sought after whiskey there was in the bootleg days, was Bull's Creek liquor. It was the best. And they run it at a hundred proof. Most whiskey you get in a bottle now is ninety, eighty-five, eighty-seven. Some went down to eighty-three, I think. Ninety proof is pretty stiff. Now, Bull's Creek rye was a hundred proof. I used to drink that Bull's Creek rye. I didn't drink a whole lot of it but it was my whiskey. I don't drink any whiskey now and I never was much of a whiskey drinker. I never did like the taste of whiskey. Everything I always put in my mouth I want it to taste good, and whiskey never tasted good to me. You can mix it any way you want to. You mix it up in a Manhattan or anything you want to, and it don't make no difference to me. It just got whiskey in it. It don't taste right. Always when I put anything in my mouth I want it to taste good. That's the reason why I can't stand false teeth. They don't taste good.

Some stories end on a proverbial note, and their emphasis is on building up to a peroration on that proverb or saying:

They never used much oak [to build boats]. The oak around here, and the oak you could get—there's so many different kinds of oak. There's a white oak, and red oak and chestnut oak and swamp oak and ditch bank oak, and it won't last. But a white oak—upland oak—way away from here. If you've got logs from it, you could tell the difference when you're looking at it. But the oak all through this section is no good for boatbuilding. It'll rot in two good moonshiny nights. Two damp nights and it's rotten. But you can take real white oak, and if it'll last seven years, it'll last seventy. If it don't rot in seven years, it won't rot in seventy. That's what they always said.

Joke telling is quite uncommon, but funny stories are well-loved, especially if they turn on the teller's own misfortunes or mistakes:

I had a job once putting up four ninety-foot poles, and I wanted to take a picture of it with the crane holding it up. I only had a forty-five-foot boom, so I was handling everything I could handle. I was overloading everything to do the job and I wanted to take a picture of it. When he got that thing straight up to set it on top of that other piling to bolt it for overhead cable, I snapped the picture. I had a camera and I went back on the other end of the barge—it was on the water—and went back to the other end of the barge and snapped a picture of the whole thing, and I got it just so. I got the piling all in there, the pole and everything. Snapped it with a Brownie. But I was looking the wrong way through the hole, and took a picture of my face. My face filled the whole camera and my cap was sitting sideways and my nose was crooked the other way. And that was the funniest-looking thing. You could look at it for about ten seconds 'fore you realized what it was. But I did take another picture. I took two or three, and the other ones I had the camera turned around right. I never knew 'till the negatives come back that I had that camera turned. It was looking right at me. You could look through either way. I snapped the picture. I got the picture right here. My son saw it and he looked at it and looked at it, and by and by he commenced to laugh and he laughed. Poppa's face filled the whole picture. Says, "That was a hell of a looking thing." My cap was sitting one way, my nose the other.

This kind of storytelling is a deeply established way of life, but it does not meet with universal approval. Telling tales is occasionally referred to as "lying," and even though the majority of tales are not lies in either the common or the folklorist's sense, the practice carries a connotation of confusing truth and fiction in a deceptive way. Note that in both versions of the first story given above the main action is framed by statements about the confusion of truth and fiction in local stories. Sitting at the store is also called "shooting the bull," "bullshitting," or "shooting the breeze," all of which carry the meanings "to lie deliberately" and "to tell stories for amusement." This local belief may also explain why "storified" sermons are frowned upon: preaching should not be confused with shooting the bull, nor should preachers be associated with those who do. As it happens, I was sitting outside the store one afternoon with a group of men when the preacher walked past, affecting not to notice us even though he was passing within a few feet and knew most of us well. But one of the more raucous men in the bunch called out to him that he should come over and get to know some of the liars sitting on the bench, because they were never likely to get to church. At this the preacher paused in his track, replied "I don't recall seeing you too often either," and walked on.

Yet there are some similarities between preaching and storytelling style, and it may be the potential confusion in the aesthetic forms of two supposedly very different acts which leads to problems with preachers who tell too many stories. Good storytellers (and preachers) are judged on the basis of certain elements of style, particularly vocal quality. Early in my fieldwork several men in the store crowd advised me that I must certainly get to hear Ben or Roy because they have the "knack to tell a story," following this suggestion with an imitation of the vocal manner of one of them. All men identified as good story-tellers had strong voices that they modulated dramatically. They also (like preachers) emphasized critical points in a tale with marked gestures. Given such similarities in mode of delivery, it seems natural that the congregation would prefer a distinct difference in narrative type between sermons and store tales.

In addition to being tagged "liars" the store crowd have a bad reputation because historically, and still to a limited extent, such men's groups planned and carried out illicit activities. In prohibition days, for example, the store was the scene of sale and consumption of bootleg whiskey. In consequence there were fights and other frowned-upon behavior.

The general sense of the store as a place for "rooster" behavior is kept current by the youths. From an early age they can surreptitiously sample the sensual pleasures of whiskey, cigarettes, and chewing tobacco provided by other youths or the older men. They also have a passion of their own not shared by the older men: their cars and trucks.

Although the cars and trucks of the youths have day-to-day functions, they are sported and displayed as objects of aesthetic pleasure to the virtual exclusion of other considerations (with the possible exception of speed, which also has important aesthetic components). Exteriors are kept polished and shiny, and interiors are fitted with ornaments, decorative gadgets, and fine upholstery. Many engines and mufflers are fixed to provide bursts of loud noise, which are accentuated by gravel-throwing, tire-squealing maneuvers in the store parking lot. Such performances inevitably cause great delight among onlookers. These public displays of roosterhood are the prelude to private drag races that take place on a straight stretch of swamp road very late at night, after the state troopers have gone off duty. For most youths the combination of liquor, tobacco, and speed is an irresistible (though occasionally fatal) affective attraction.

These cars and trucks are also important for the youths' amorous adventures, much of their courting depending on possession of a vehicle in which to get away to some isolated spot. Young men often begin a night out with a girlfriend at the store, deliberately running the gauntlet of sly remarks by friends and older men for the sake of making it known that they are "otherwise occupied" for the evening. As a rule, though, the sexual activity of youths is taken for granted and is not the source of much comment. It is firmly expected that marriage and raising a family will calm these "dark passions." Thus those who remain single, or in some other way call attention to their continuing status as sexually available, are marked in ordinary conversation as unusually passionate.

The two major formal associations in Tidewater, Freemasons and American Legion, in large part take the place of informal associations for middle-aged adults, although the ethos differs from one to the other and from that of the store. Many adult men in the median age range belong to one or the other group, the choice depending on their personal philosophies, friendship and kinship ties, and facts of personal background. Belonging to a formal association symbolizes one's place in the community. The Masons are respectable and respected, the Legionnaires are held in low esteem.

The Legion hut is thought of as little more than a bar, even though the American Legion is a formal club with strict rules of membership, policies, meetings, and so forth. It bears all the hallmarks of disrepute: liquor, pool tables, and "uncivilized" behavior. A clear symbol of the "outlaw" status of the Legion is the evening meal served there. The fact that an evening meal is served at all is socially disruptive because it lures men away from their customary place at night, namely, at the family table. Moreover, the food served sometimes cuts across the canons of taste of the community and is deliberately advertised by members as such. In hunting season, for example, the Legion may serve barbecued raccoon, a meat considered inedible by all female cooks in town. Not only will the Legionnaires eat raccoon, but they will talk expectantly about the feast for days beforehand, adding to help confirm their social status that "coon only tastes good with whiskey."

The status of the Legion hut as a bar is accentuated by the general architecture of the building. It was formerly one of the older period 1 houses, but additions front and back have radically altered internal and external appearances. These additions, coupled with the removal of all of the ground-floor partition walls, have created one large square room, the main gathering space. It is furnished with tables and chairs,

[189]

a pool table, and a large bar. The general ethos of the club as bar is completed by the fact that the new front and back additions have no windows, so that the room is quite dark and requires artificial light regardless of conditions outside.

Superficially the social characteristics of the store resemble those of the Legion hut, but the differences are fundamental. Most important, the membership of the Legion is made up heavily of the men of the newer families in the community, whereas the store crowd is predominantly drawn from old families. Although an outsider might consider both Legion members and the store crowd "roosters" or "pistols," the terms are used of the latter only. Such expressions embody general ambivalences that can be thought of as incorporative, that is, a man might be a pistol but he is one of "us," and we can privately joke about his scandalous behavior. When it is said that a man is "down the hut every night," there is no ambivalence involved. Finally, the Legion hut is a new institution, the present hut having been established eight years before the time of fieldwork, and represents a move on the part of newcomers to satisfy social needs. Meeting at the store, by comparison, is believed to be as old as the community itself.

The Freemasons, in complete contrast to the Legionnaires, carry with them an air of genteel respectability. Although their rituals are secret, their general comportment is socially approved. The officers make a point of attending the local churches as formal visitors several times during the year, they give to charitable organizations as well as performing good works of their own, and they are traditionally associated with Christianity.

The nature of the organization makes it inappropriate to discuss the aesthetics of the meetings and ritual in detail. What can be said, though, is that meetings are highly structured and theatrical, with a primary emphasis on obedience and loyalty to God and to the fellowship. The core of Masonry, the three degrees of the Craft, are extensive rites of passage. The rituals of these degrees are all concerned with acceptance and instruction of new members, and all formal business is focused on brotherhood and enlightenment. These rituals require special clothing, very elaborate staging, and a complex prescribed text that must be learned.

Once more this complex aesthetic behavior of men is veiled in secrecy and withdrawn from the public eye; in this case they are perhaps at their most aesthetic and their most secretive. I believe a detailed account of the rituals would be improper, but some general references to the rite of initiation to Master Mason give a feeling for the aesthetic intricacy of the institution. The climax of the ritual in-volves the theatrical enactment of the murder of the legendary archi-tect of Solomon's temple, with the initiate playing the part of the victim and the officers of the lodge playing Solomon, the murderers, and other essential characters. The lodgeroom itself is turned into a stage for the drama, with specially made furnishings positioned to create different scenes inside and outside the temple. The play also requires appropriate props and costumes. At the end of the enactment the master of the lodge lectures the initiate on the meaning of the ritual, particularly emphasizing the nature of beauty and its relation-ship to the many aspects of Masonry. Indeed, the question of the nature of beauty, a paramount aesthetic question, lies at the heart of masonic teachings. The Tidewater man normally assumes an anti-aesthetic public posture, and it is little wonder that such activities are conducted in secret.

Despite their private nature the Masons hold regular public func-tions to which they invite respected members of the larger commu-nity. The installation of a master, for example, is generally cause for public celebration, and wives and dignitaries are in conspicuous atten-dance. These parties, consonant with the company and the image members wish to project, are sumptuous but sober. They are pro-duced according to local canons of good taste.

Part of the distinction between Masons and Legionnaires rests on the history of the two groups, both locally and nationally. The Masons are a venerable institution with a putative history leading back into antiquity, whereas the Legion is a relatively modern invention. To complement this distinction the Masons are well established in Tide-water, the Legion hut is quite recent. Thus the Masons draw their members primarily from the older families, and the Legion consists in large part of men from newer families. It is, therefore, not surprising that the Masons should embody the traditional values of the commu-nity and the Legion should work against them. The tensions between insiders and outsiders are once again manifest.

[8]

Synthesis

It would be premature to begin building theories of the interaction of aesthetic forms and the role of aesthetics in daily life on the basis of a single ethnography. Clearly this kind of study needs to be multiplied many times before generalization can become meaningful. Nonetheless, I shall attempt some conclusions that remain faithful to the data gathered in Tidewater. These conclusions may point the way for continued investigation and broader theory.

My analysis at the outset shares views with established theory in anthropology, and these commonalities are noted where appropriate. My indebtedness, in particular, to semiotic and semiological perspectives should be evident. But symbolic approaches to aesthetics cannot be the end-point of analysis, even though their methods may prove useful in the process of interpretation. Not all that is aesthetic is symbolic, and not all that is symbolic is aesthetic, although the areas of overlap are considerable and the analysis of the one can often be applied fruitfully to the other. But ultimately I must confine myself to the issue of why aesthetic forms are particularly suited to do what they do, whether they function symbolically or not. I return to the issues I raised in dealing with the definition of aesthetic form, namely, that aesthetic forms are sensual, affecting, matters of taste that may be appreciated disinterestedly. In this context I consider aesthetic forms not as systems of expression, communication, or symbolizing but as forms with properties that must be understood in terms of aesthetics.

I also hope to make it clear that my analysis rests on the local understanding of Tidewater's social world even though the terms used are strictly my own. Much of what follows picks up threads from different chapters and weaves them together. As occasion arises, I repeat pertinent aspects of the field data to demonstrate the foundation of the analysis on elicited or observed materials, and I also add new data. These tidbits stand primarily to refresh the memory and recall lengthier disquisitions and descriptions in earlier chapters; they are not meant to substitute for them. My aim here is to reintegrate data pulled apart in the previous four chapters, in the process ascending to a higher level of abstraction. In Chapter 1, I showed how aesthetic forms were related on a personal level; now I shall do so on a theoretical level.

Extended analysis of the complex and dynamic opposition between "inside" and "outside" as it pertains to a variety of social spheres makes it possible to understand a great deal about the functioning of the aesthetic realm in Tidewater. This opposition applies both spatially and culturally, and in both domains its applications are complex. The opposition is also positively correlated with others, such as female/male, controlled/uncontrolled, civilized/uncivilized, bounded/unbounded, that together help define social relations in Tidewater. My method for the creation of these complementary oppositional categories derives in general from the seminal work in structuralism by Claude Lévi-Strauss (1963, and commentary in Leach 1976) and in particular from the essays in *Right and Left* edited by Rodney Needham (1973), notably those by T. O. Beidelman, Clark Cunningham, John Middleton, and Needham himself.

The simplest inside/outside opposition is that between inside and outside the home. Inside the home is the woman's domain and outside, the man's. Aesthetic control of the interior of the house is the prerogative of the woman and that of the outside of the man. The interior space of the house, the woman's realm, is highly bounded, ordered, structured, controlled, and artifactual. The house itself is clearly defined by external walls, and spaces within the structure are rigidly marked. Decoration, furnishing, and appointments announce the respective functions of the rooms. Each room has a clear purpose, and when one wishes to change tasks a necessary movement follows from one room to another.

A good-looking house interior is clean and orderly. Even though the space is carefully divided according to function, the whole has a clear unity. Some aspect of the owner's personality is stamped on the space, making it evident that the place is not some neutral ground but the home of a particular individual. Those aspects and areas of the home which are open to scrutiny from the outside are especially ordered and controlled. Public rooms must be kept orderly at all times, so they are

[193]

the first and most fastidiously cleaned. Quilts for guest beds are highly ordered in comparison with the quilts for the private use of the house-holders. The former are regular, symmetrical, repetitive, and labor-intensive—displays of the appropriate skills of the woman at home.

I conclude that even inside the home there is an inside and an outside dimension. That is, some spaces and artifacts are for insiders, others for outsiders. Kitchen, sitting room, work room, and guest bedrooms and bathrooms are set up for public view, whereas the occupants' bedrooms and bathroom are not. A great portion of the house, therefore, is to be defined not exclusively in its own terms but in relation to the outside world. It projects an image to the outside and is judged in terms of its capacity to affect people from outside.

The exterior sections of the home, the man's domain, are less bounded, controlled, and confined than the interior. On the outside there are few rigid boundaries. There are no fences in the entire town, so one property blends with those adjacent. Because the land is so flat, and no landscaping or use of plantings creates separate spaces, all parts of the yard can be seen from all others. Different parts of the yard, it is true, serve different functions—lawn, garden, work space— but they are not neatly delineated, and some of the functions can overlap. The functions of spaces in the yard are determined and ex-pressed by cultivated plants rather than artifacts (as is the case inside the house). Order resides in the careful domestication and control of natural products.

Whereas the walls of the home rigidly define the woman's domain, the man's appears to extend ever outward. The choice to stay at home or to venture beyond it for work and leisure involves a concomitant choice among aesthetic domains. Work inside the home bears many of the hallmarks of the home itself. Stores, for example, are located in the storekeepers' homes. The internal space is highly bounded and organized. Shelves and aisles delineate spaces for specific functions: one area for food, another for laundry products. Within these spaces items are further divided and subdivided in bureaucratic order. But also as in the home, a space is set aside for "visiting." A trip to the store or to a house often has an underlying purpose, but it is rude to transact business without the graces of visiting. Because services are dispensed from homes, in a homelike ethos, it is appropriate for women to have a hand in their operation. At one store the woman takes care of transactions inside, such as purchase of groceries, and the man handles transactions outside, such as oil and gasoline sales. When the owners want time off they hire a woman to work inside, a man to work outside.

Farming is the work equivalent of gardening. Fields and spaces on farmlands are not demarked by tangible barriers or boundaries, even though they are distinct. Areas are defined in terms of domesticated plants, such as a cornfield or a beanfield. Farm fields are near the homes of the farmers. They are in many ways like extensions of the garden space, and their aesthetic dimensions are quite similar.

A yet larger dimension of the work space may be characterized by the inside/outside opposition, and it is one of fundamental importance for understanding many kinds of social relations in Tidewater. The distinction is between inside and outside the town (yet still within the traditional boundaries of the "section" or community, that is, not beyond the traditional fringes of work space). This distinction sets up the important opposition of land workers and water workers. The water work space is the least bounded, least cultivated, least controlled environment of all. Tidewater Sound is deemed uncontrolled and uncontrollable, and its attraction lies therein. In recent years the state has sponsored several pilot projects to alter the composition or nature of the sound. One involves an attempt to salinate the sound, thereby providing more productive fisheries for local watermen. Another is the investigation of ways to reduce or eliminate the milfoil that chokes the waters and fouls propellers and motor intakes. Watermen never hide their scorn of these projects, not because they do not see their benefits but because they do not believe it possible or proper to change the sound.

The sound is self-governing and self-regulating. Watermen enter this domain with due respect and understand the consequences of failure to take adequate precautions. The necessary skills are those of knowledge, not of mastery. One learns the ways of the sound to protect oneself from it, not to dominate it. Such knowledge requires attunement with the elements. Unlike other spaces, the sound is superficially undifferentiated. No location is designated as suitable for a particular function. Fish and crustaceans wander under the surface, and the waterman must follow them. He cannot organize and demark the submarine life, nor in any way bureaucratically delimit and structure it. As a consequence of becoming attuned to his environment the waterman sheds many of the attributes of the landsman's world. He strips off his clothes when he wishes, he urinates and defecates where he pleases. The waterman is a freebooter, and the aesthetics of the world that draws him are as wild and unpredictable as he. This opposition of land and water, landsman and waterman, is the foundation for much social interaction in Tidewater.

One further outside domain lies at the greatest cultural distance from home, the world completely outside the community. Before the main road was put through the town the "outside world" was a place for cautious and rare visits. In a sense, everything beyond the bounds of the community was foreign and everyone from that world was labeled a "foreigner," whether he or she came from the next county or across the country. Ventures into that world were viewed with suspicion, distrust, and distaste, as the following anecdote clearly shows: "They had an exposition in Philadelphia and my grandfather left home to attend that exposition—eighteen and seventy-eight I think it was, or seventy-seven. He was thirty days making his trip with sailboats and steam transportation up to Baltimore, and then a train from Baltimore up to Philadelphia. He was thirty days making the round trip. When he came back home after making this trip some of 'em said to him, says, 'Well Captain, what'd you gain out of your trip,' to kinda throw up on him." The coming of the road made the outside world more readily accessible for regular visits, but, more important, it made it possible for the men of Tidewater to find jobs beyond the traditional frontiers of the community. Such a change required a degree of resilience in the men who undertook it. Foreigners are beyond the bounds of traditional tastes, and their world is incomprehensible and uncivilized.

Characteristically, men now work outside the community in their middle years, when the necessities of raising a family force them to seek a regular income. None of these men wishes to work outside the community, and they have little intercourse with the world beyond except in connection with their employment. In the towns and cities outside they are called "hicks," and their ways are labeled "country." Their customary dress, verbal style, and outward manners all serve to identify them to others, and to themselves, as away from home.

Because of the possibility, and often the necessity, of taking outside employment a man's working life is often cyclical. As a youth he may work sporadically with a kinsman as a waterman, often taking on the least rewarding jobs because of his low status and lack of equipment. He may guide hunting and fishing parties for an older relative, he may assist in haul seine fishing, or he may fish a small number of pots and gill nets. None of these occupations brings in a steady wage, and because he is essentially extra help, in times of thin profits his labor is sacrificed first. Still, most youths are content with this position. They are usually not married and live at home. Their cash needs are limited, and when no money comes in they can still survive.

Youths and young men may begin to work more steadily as they

[196]

progress in the fishing world and as they inherit equipment or earn enough to buy more gear for themselves. Indeed, they may rise considerably up the ladder outlined in Chapter 5. But no matter how far they climb, the fishing business cannot support them if they choose to take on the responsibilities of a family. A very small number opt out of marriage and are thereby able to maintain their freewheeling lifestyle. Most choose marriage and children. At first the married waterman tries to preserve his ties to the water. But soon he realizes that the two worlds are inimicable, and most water-based activities cease.

On retirement the Tidewater man can return to the water. At this stage in his career, however, he occupies a different position from when he first began. Chances are that his older relatives have died or become infirm, so that their gear, the unaffordably expensive components, are now his to use. Thus he takes on the position of benefactor to his own junior kin. He can enter limited partnerships with youths, adopting again their outlook on life, which he set aside on marriage.

The cycle of work has attendant cycles in the realm of leisure and the church, although several different paths exist. All male youths and young men enjoy the pleasures of hunting, fishing, and hanging around with the store crowd. Most boys begin fishing and hunting as soon as they are physically capable of using the equipment, and in appropriate sports they learn basic skills. A ten-year-old boy can take a .22 caliber rifle into the woodlands at any spare moment to hunt squirrels. He needs no other equipment, not even transportation. In the woods he learns patience and marksmanship. As he matures he can progress to hunting doves, which provide more of a challenge than squirrels because they fly, swoop, and dip in the air to avoid being shot, and because they must be hunted with a shotgun, a far more ponderous firearm than a .22 rifle. Eventually a relative will take him duck hunting, the supreme sport, where he can put together all that he has learned in the field with the additional skills taught him in the blind. If he is fortunate, he may inherit the use of a blind from a family member when he is old enough to accept the responsibility. If so, he may use the blind for pleasure only or, more likely, will combine pleasure with guiding to help finance the costs of hunting equipment.

At night boys and young men are anxious to hang out at the store, which provides them with many opportunities. They can listen to the tales of the older men and in the process learn local lore and acquire knowledge that may be useful, as well as simply be entertained. They may also strike deals with older men about working relationships. In the informal atmosphere of bull sessions the older men test out the verbal skills and mettle of the younger. An older man looking for a partner wants someone he can get along with. He wants a quick learner and someone he feels comfortable talking to. At nightly sessions at the store the older men are able to create tentative relationships that can later be put to the test.

Boys also have their own group business to transact at the store, so they spend as much time away from the bull sessions as in them. They frequently meet girls at the store and use walks and dark corners in the environs for their courting. They may also experiment as a group with taboo or illegal activities such as drinking beer and whiskey or chewing tobacco. The older men watch these experiments with benign amusement.

When a man takes up employment outside the community he gives up not only paid water activities but most or all of the attendant life. Hunting requires much of the same gear as other water activities, such as a skiff and motor, and it is not practical to keep these things if they are not making money. Furthermore, hunting takes great amounts of time away from home which most family men cannot spare. Similarly, hanging around at the store at night becomes a burden on spare time, and the store associations and the deals struck there have less importance.

For leisure the man in his middle years has several choices. Some choose home activities, such as working in the garden, woodworking, or general house maintenance. But many decide to ally themselves with one of the town's formal associations. Many join the Masons once they have organized themselves sufficiently to be able to set aside the necessary time. The lodge demands a degree of loyalty and time away from the family, but it is time that is circumscribed and rigidly delimited. The Masons also organize events that involve wives and children, so that a man may be an active member yet still fulfill obligations to family. The officers and general membership of the Masons are predominantly men in the middle years who have regular outside employment. As men reach retirement age they fall away from the strictures of the society, although they maintain some ties, and return to more informal associations and activities.

The American Legion is open only to men who have performed military service, so the choice to join is not entirely open. But not all men who have been in the military join. The act of joining is in many ways a signal quite opposite to that of joining the Masons. The bar is open every night and all weekend, so that participation in the group is unstructured and potentially unlimited during leisure time. An evening meal is served also, so that a man may absent himself from the family circle for the most important meal of the day. Many women liken the Legion to the store crowd and do not hide their disdain for men who are "down at the hut every night." As in Masonry, so in the American Legion the most active men are in their middle years, but there is less falling away as the men approach retirement. However, the Legion does not draw its members in large numbers from the old families of Tidewater. Legionnaires are mostly from new families in town and from families in surrounding towns. As such the Legion is less of an "inside" institution than the others discussed. I explore the tension between outsiders and insiders within the community later.

On retirement men return to the leisure activities of their youth. They begin to hunt and fish as they see fit because they have both the time and the equipment. An older man may take a younger work partner with him if he enjoys his company and, if they are kin, may eventually bestow a blind location on him. Older men also form the core of the storytellers at the store.

Finally, the man's participation in church has similar cyclical qualities. Most boys in the community attend Sunday school for a few years. Some stop attending at a relatively early age, in their early teens; a small percentage continue into their late teens before finally dropping out. Those who stay on past sixteen come forward at revival time and are baptized. But sooner or later, baptized or not, boys leave the church and take up other associations. Hanging out at the store and going to church do not mix as far as youths are concerned.

Few men in their middle years attend church. Any man who does is marked as being especially devout and an oddity. A man is expected to have a few roustabout, godless years as a young man. The church sees its main mission as wooing men back to the fold after those years are over. But the transition is not immediate or certain. Married men find their energies in great demand, and time is precious. Services on Sunday take up half a day's free time, and many men feel that this commitment is too great. They may, however, flirt with attendance from time to time. They may be seen with their wives on one or two nights of the revival or at special services, such as those at Easter and Christmas.

Those men who return to the church begin serious, regular attendance as their retirement approaches or upon retirement. Most attend church for several years before they take any steps to commit themselves. They join the men's bible class and sit at the back with the men during regular services. But at some point they make an active decision and come forward during the invitation at a regular service or a revival. Those who have not been baptized become members and go through the rite, and those who have, rededicate their lives to the church. In either case the metaphor of "coming home" is applicable. The hymn of invitation pleads with them:

Come home, come home,
Ye who are weary come home;
Earnestly, tenderly, Jesus is calling,
Calling, O sinner, come home!

Jesus is tenderly calling thee home,
Calling today, calling today;
Why from the sunshine of love wilt thou
    roam
Farther and farther away?

Or the retiree may sing:

Coming home, coming home,
Never more to roam,
Open wide Thine arms of love
Lord I'm coming home.

The preacher too will admonish him that he has wandered away from God and must come home. The related metaphors of wandering far and coming home are the mainstays of the invitations and emphasize that the man has indeed spent much of his life away from home, outside the community, in a strange and unaccepting world—an unsatisfying, unrewarding, unaesthetic world of labor:

I've wandered far away from God,
Now I'm coming home;
The paths of sin too long I've trod,
Lord I'm coming home.

The man who comes home has a safe and secure place in the church. Soon he will take up one of the offices held in his family—deacon, treasurer, Sunday school director—and he will have a solid position of power and prestige.

Traditionally, then, the man is an "outside" person. He works and plays outside the home, and as life progresses he moves farther and farther away from home. But at the point when his ties to the inside are at their most attenuated, he returns home. The full complexity of this return can be understood more fully by examining the aesthetics of the home and the church, and the roles that women play in both.

The woman's life is not cyclical like the man's. A girl remains bonded to her mother and mother's home as long as her mother is living. In growing up she helps her mother with household tasks, and even after marriage she spends a considerable portion of the day with her mother preparing the evening meal. The woman does not wander far away from home, nor does she wander far from the church. Girls are baptized at about sixteen years of age, and they continue their association with the church throughout their lives. A few girls fall away temporarily in their late teens prior to marriage, in a manner similar to but shorter than a boy's rooster years. This period is followed by marriage and establishment in a house in the community, however, not by taking employment out of town. The inexorable move away from home of the young man is not replicated by the young woman. As women marry and have children they may have periods of sparse attendance because of home needs, but the church is prepared to meet every eventuality. During Sunday school a nursery is provided for babies, and from preschool upward an appropriate peer group exists for children of every age. Thus a woman is encouraged to bring her children to church as soon as she feels able, so that after a brief hiatus she becomes a staunch member.

In her middle years a woman begins to take on responsibilities in the church. The commonest jobs are teaching children's Sunday school and assisting in the food preparation involved with fund raising. Some women, who get tagged as particularly active, develop formal and informal youth organizations and activities. The Baptist church sponsors many youth auxiliary organizations, such as the Sunbeams, Girls' Auxiliary, and Royal Ambassadors, which may have local chapters if a local woman is prepared to take on the job of organizing them. Generally a mother with children of the appropriate age volunteers. In similar fashion mothers run the youth choir, youth fund raisers, and the youth Christmas play. It is at this point also that some women become members of the choir.

As her mother becomes infirm the woman must increasingly take on the duties of the head cook. An aging mother may continue to supervise household operations, but her daughter slowly takes greater command. If, as is common, her mother is a widow at this stage in life, a woman may move her family into the old home place, which allows her to direct her attention to the care of her mother without ignoring her family in the process. On the death of her mother she becomes the head cook.

Once a woman has reached the status of senior generation in her family, she takes up new roles in the church. She will, at some point, cease her teaching jobs and join the women's Bible class. She will also take on committee posts and may assume an officership if a suitable one, such as church secretary or music director, is available. Eventually she will also succeed to one of the directorships of fund-raising activities, because as a head cook she now has the experience needed to direct and supervise others.

Thus whereas men hold many significant offices in the church, women dominate its management and development because of their lifelong dedication, and there are many more women's auxiliary groups than men's. Women run the choir, youth groups, and Missionary Union, they plan and coordinate all fund-raising activities, and they have a leading hand in church aesthetics. They also form a simple and very large majority of the church membership and attend services more frequently than men, and with more evident interest in the proceedings. Older women sit at the front of the congregation and are lovingly called the "angels" of the church, whereas the older men sit at the back in what is sarcastically labeled "amen corner."

Whether because women control the organization of the church or because of broader religious principles, church aesthetics are akin to those of the home. Spaces are clearly and rigidly defined, and the whole is thematically unified. Each room has a special function, and each clearly defined peer group has its own room (except, significantly, the men's group, which uses the sanctuary as its meeting room). Group business is closed off and isolated from that of others. There are also public and private spaces. The sanctuary is a public space where all are welcomed, the choir room and Sunday school rooms are private and not for general view. Just as at home, these two kinds of spaces are decorated and kept differently. The public space is kept fastidiously clean and orderly, with everything in its proper place. The private rooms vary in orderliness and reflect the personal tastes and creativity of the occupants. Decoration varies according to the peer group, but much is ephemeral, creations of one week's lessons.

Yet in some ways the church is even more highly structured than the home. Proceedings are carefully orchestrated and demarked by aesthetic forms. The space is delineated by static aesthetic objects, such as the architecture and the furniture, and time is delineated by temporal or lively aesthetic forms. The service starts and ends with choral formulae that mark the interval as a highly structured sacred time but also indicate appropriate behavior and its consequences:

> The Lord is in His holy temple;
> Let all the earth keep silence before Him.
> (Call to Worship)

> Grace, love, and peace abide, now, with you:
> Through Jesus Christ our dear Redeemer.
> (Benediction Response)

Business meetings, similarly, are marked with a temporal aesthetic form that indicates appropriate mien:

> Blest be the tie that binds
> Our hearts in Christian love;
> The fellowship of kindred minds
> Is like to that above.

Once the aesthetic markers have established the sacred time at regular service, the order of events is rigidly controlled. As the overall structure of the service is controlled, so are the individual elements that compose it. That is, the order of service is printed ahead of time and distributed to the congregation, so that all follow a prescribed and unchanging structure. But just as important, the aesthetic forms that are part of the structure are highly controlled. The choral music is marked by well-rehearsed singing with clear enunciation and practiced restraint. Freedom and individual expression are not called for. When a preacher and music director introduced antiphonal, uncontrolled music into the services the result was an inevitable schism in the church body. This music was believed to promote spontaneous and emotional responses from the congregation, which was entirely at odds with the traditional aesthetic of calm and order.

The sermon should also be aesthetically in keeping with the other aesthetic forms in the sacred time and space. It should not be over-emotional or delivered in a manner suggestive of uncontrolled absorption in its message. It should be planned, structured, coherent. Vocally it should be well-modulated, but the modulation should be considered and stylized, not unrestrained and highly emotional.

Finally, the act of coming forward itself is not a spontaneous, emotional act but a controlled and considered one (although it may be initiated by an affective change). The preacher almost always knows when someone plans to come forward. Men and women discuss the act with him and with friends and relatives before proceeding. At the revival the youths were stirred to come forward on the Wednesday night by the direct and blatant appeals of the evangelist, but they did not come forward under those stirrings. They discussed the matter with parents and preacher and *then* came forward. One of these youths had come forward several years earlier and had been forbidden to proceed further with baptism by his parents. All acts of coming forward are considered and planned. They are acts that, although ostensibly concerned with spiritual conversion, are as much public displays of unity with the body of members, statements of intent to be on the inside, as they are acts of personal faith.

The ritual complex of coming forward and being baptized, described in Chapter 6, is of course the rite of passage par excellence of the Baptist church as its eponymous nature indicates. Thus I have taken broad hints on how to approach the subject matter from the general Durkheimian tradition concerning ritual and social solidarity (Durkheim 1915, Mauss 1924, Douglas 1966 and 1970) as well as studies aimed specifically at rites of passage (Van Gennep 1960, Turner 1969, Gluckman 1962).

The rites attendant on coming forward have a particular relationship to the aesthetics of space. I noted earlier that as one proceeds farther from home, spaces are less well-defined and structured. The most structured and controlled space (excepting the church) is the interior of the house, and structure and control decrease as one moves through gardens to farms and finally to the open water. Work and workers share the qualities of their respective environments in a homologous continuum: services are highly controlled, farming less so, and fishing least of all. The church's space is even more rigidly defined than that of the home: it is "home" aesthetics taken to extremes.

In the sanctuary each group has its own space. Men, older women, family groups, youths, and strangers all have their own special places to sit. Similarly, the choir and preacher have sections that denote their special functions. To be out of one's place has particular significance. Older couples who sit together are marked as unusually devoted. When the choir music was the subject of controversy, choir members began to sit in the congregation. And, of course, leaving one's seat to come forward is of central importance.

The nonmember who leaves his seat to be baptized leaves the space of his peers and enters the preacher's space. The preacher is an outsider; among other things he is a representative of the other world beyond the community, the world that entices men away from the community, the world that is full of material temptations. The rite continues with a farther removal from the structured, controlled space of the sanctuary to the most uncontrolled space within the community: the sound. The candidates are dressed in old, ragged clothes, as is the preacher. The congregation is disorganized and not formally dressed. They pay scant attention to the ceremony but talk and visit in separate groups. Attempts at orderly ritual, such as singing appropriate hymns ("Shall We Gather at the River"), have failed. Each candidate walks out into the water with the preacher/outsider, and the candidate *alone* is totally immersed in the uncontrollable element. After baptism candidates are reunited with their families and on the following Sunday return to their customary places in the church.

For men this rite has particular significance, because it mirrors their passage through life: the journey away from home to the outside world and their subsequent return and reacceptance. But the symbolic rite of baptism is also spiritually opposite to the journey to the outside world. The journey to the world outside is defiling and full of cares. The baptismal journey to the sound is cleansing and relieving of cares. The sound and all in it are natural products, made by God. Though wild and uncontrollable it is a natural world, and it is inside the community. The world beyond the community is not natural, it is a human artifact. Its disorder and uncontrollable ethos are the products of human artifice.

The preacher occupies a powerful position because he may play the roles of insider *and* outsider. His outsider status is clearly marked. He occupies a special, solitary space at services, a space separated by a considerable gap from other people in the church, and he has a raised platform to speak from. Simple comparison of his use of space with that of the Sunday school director is instructive. The director stands on a level with the congregation, and people fill the pews up to the front row. The director is an insider. In matters of management and governance the preacher has no control, as is evident from a tale narrated by the church clerk: "We had some problems when we put the air conditioning in. The contractor, he made such a mess of it. And he came here to be paid, and several of the members told me not to pay him until he got it right. So he came and he got so mad with me because I wouldn't pay him. He said 'Well, I'll go see the preacher.' I said 'Go right ahead. He's got no authority whatsoever.'" The preacher does not serve as a member of committees but may choose to sit in as a nonvoting observer. Suggestions that he makes in committee or general meetings are usually considered interferences. A regular member of the church can speak at length on any issue and will at worst be called long-winded. Preachers who attempt to talk at length are privately condemned.

Yet the preacher also has some of the rights and privileges of an insider. He is a registered member of the church, duly elected, and conventionally he belongs to the men's Bible class and attends as a regular member. He has the right to vote on any matter coequal with other members. Despite his ambiguous position, however, he is decidedly more outsider than insider.

It is in the best interests of the church to have an outsider as preacher, because he can then act as a scapegoat when problems arise. A local-born preacher cannot be expelled from the community, but an outsider can be sent on his way when there is discord in the church. By firing the preacher the church symbolically purges itself of bad, that is, outside, influences and is made whole and unified again. Also, a local preacher would have kin ties in the community. Should he be at odds with parts of the congregation, his kin would be bound to stand behind him. Such a schism could not be healed by firing him; indeed, firing him would certainly make matters worse.

Three of the last five preachers have resigned under pressure, and it is reasonable to wonder whether there is so much bad influence in the church that it needs constant purging. Rather, do unresolved and long-term problems plague the church? It may be that, paradoxically, the events that led to the establishment of a full-time preacher's position are also responsible for the constant dissatisfaction with the men that fill the role, so that a cycle of rebellion and repose is now built into the system. The general analysis of social unity in the face of deep conflict was explored by Max Gluckman and his students, so that their case studies and theoretical position can be compared with the analysis that follows (Gluckman 1954, 1955, and 1963, and Turner 1957).

Until the modern road system was put in the church was not large enough to support a full-time preacher. The roads brought a gradual influx of people from outside, and many of these outsiders joined the church. By settling in the community and becoming members of the church they did not, however, become fully integrated. Outsiders usually rented property from the old families in town and had no kin ties with the old families. But landholding and kinship are the foundations of power and prestige in the community. They provide individ-

Table 8. Insider/outsider oppositions

	Insiders	Outsiders
Church fabric	oak pews plain walls	white pews white walls
Music	controlled voices	uncontrolled voices
Covenant	old law Robert's rules temperance	new law rule of thumb abstinence
Politics	major offices	minor offices
Members	kin ties landholders	no kin ties landless

uals with an identity, with employment, with important offices, with a place in the world. The old family that donated the land for the church is a major force to this day. The eldest scion is church treasurer, his wife is the clerk, and his cousin is president of the women's Bible class.

The main oppositions between outsiders and insiders in the church are summarized in Table 8. The organizing principles may not be obvious in these oppositions, but they are very important. Superficially the oppositions might be put down to different approaches to Protestantism. The outsiders appear to favor a more spontaneous and emotional religion where the judgment of what is right comes from the heart. The insiders favor control and reflection. This superficial reaction makes sense of the division that lines up conservatory singing and Robert's rules on one side and camp meeting–style singing and rule-of-thumb democracy on the other.

But at a deeper level the division is a split between the forces of conservatism and those of change. The insiders seek to maintain the status quo, the outsiders seek to change it. It is politically and socially easy to understand part of the reason for these positions. The insiders hold their positions of power and prestige by virtue of long-standing traditions of inheritance and have nothing to gain from changing things. The outsiders are shut out of these positions and so have nothing to lose, and possibly a lot to gain, by opposing the established order.

For the insiders plain walls, oak pews, and temperance all represented continuity with the past, and parliamentary procedures would ensure the preservation of these links with the past because old families hold a simple majority of the church membership. Old families control the key political offices, so there can never be an effective direct frontal challenge to their position. The officers can be trusted to see that parliamentary procedures are strictly enforced.

To counterattack the outsiders have adopted a beguiling approach: they try to be better Baptists than the insiders. They invoke the spirit of revival with all of its attendant desires to throw over complacency and tradition and replace them with moral fervor. The preachers are their natural allies and leaders for two reasons. First, the preachers are outsiders themselves and gain a measure of power by being in the vanguard of this moral faction. Second, they are generally fresh from the seminary and so filled with zeal to convert the world. The battle of revival versus tradition is a natural one for them to take up. All of the sermons preached on the old covenant and abstinence in the battle over church music and alcohol policy pitted what was "right" against "tradition."

Theologically the moral stance adopted by the outsiders is difficult to challenge, and the insiders do not attempt to marshal arguments against it. Nor do they attempt to vote on points of religious principle. Instead, they use their numbers to block debate, so that complicated issues, when they come up for discussion, are either tabled or sent to committee. This avoidance of conflict is, in turn, symptomatic of more general relations between insiders and outsiders in Tidewater and reflects tensions in the larger community.

It is possible to divide social relations into two styles or modalities: aesthetic-incorporative and material-transactional. (Although these categories and their use are mine, some of their attributes are to be found in previous scholarship. See, for example, Sorokin 1957, Geertz 1957, Parsons 1951, Tönnies 1887, Redfield 1941, 1947, 1956, Peacock 1968, 1975, and Douglas 1970). Aesthetic-incorporative relations are those which operate primarily in the aesthetic sphere; their ethos is one of cohesion and cooperation. Material-transactional relationships are based on the material worth of items or services exchanged and are founded on the rule of strict reciprocity. This opposition is by no means clear-cut, nor are its poles mutually exclusive. It is best seen as two ends of a continuum of types of social interaction. I draw the distinction at this stage primarily for heuristic purposes.

Cases considered in previous chapters serve to show that the people of Tidewater traditionally prefer aesthetic-incorporative relationships to material-transactional ones. The annual chicken supper at the church is supposedly a fund-raising event, but as such it is not particularly efficient. Basic computation plus observation shows that the women and men of the church contribute the materials and labor to make the meals, which they then buy back at suppertime. The church takes as profit the five dollars per head charged for the meals, but the members have contributed more than that. They have spent money making cakes, cornbread, and potato salad or buying chickens as well as the five dollars they each pay for a meal. Some local cynics occasionally argue that it would be cheaper and quicker to pay five dollars to the building fund. Indeed, my calculations over one year show that an annual contribution of twenty dollars by each member would raise as much as all the special events combined. But the members adamantly oppose such ideas when they are raised periodically by preachers who oppose fund-raising events. The majority argue that there is no substitute for the fellowship of a church supper and that the financial rewards are a distinctly secondary consideration. Fund raising, an obvious candidate for material-transactional relations, is deliberately placed in the aesthetic-incorporative sphere.

Since Tidewater's founding food production has been at the core of the local economy, and food sharing has been a major force in the creation and maintenance of social relations. The traditional occupations for men are fishing and farming. In addition, older men have kitchen gardens, and sport fishing and hunting are regular leisure activities. Thus it is an everyday occurrence for men to give food to kin and friends. Before the advent of modern roads all that was eaten was caught or raised locally, and for many contemporary families this is still the case. The distribution and redistribution of food follows predictable paths because of the character of meals as social institutions. The people of Tidewater live in nuclear family households. The oldest woman in the matriline cooks for her daughters and their husbands and children. Meals are not planned for a fixed number of participants but are flexible within generous limits. Friends of the family are always welcome, and a stranger in the house at mealtime is expected to stay to eat.

When a man has meat, fish, or vegetables to share he takes it in its raw, unprepared state to a family cook, usually kin. It is her job to prepare the food in some way, and then she is at liberty to redistribute it to her family (at the table) and to other family cooks if there is enough to share. Between the food producers and the food preparers the town is united in a complex food-sharing network, a web of aesthetic-incorporative relations.

In recent times this aesthetic-incorporative ethos has been challenged by supermarkets whose material-transactional nature undermines traditional values. Modern roads foster these innovations in two ways. They give access to wage labor jobs in far towns for men, who in turn do not have time to grow their own vegetables. The roads also provide women with access to supermarkets in other towns where they trade using the wages earned outside the community. But the whole orientation of supermarkets does not suit the needs of Tidewater cooks. Supermarket foods are prepackaged in small quantities designed for nuclear family–sized meals. It is difficult and expensive to buy the quantities once grown for distribution throughout the community.

All women in town dislike supermarket shopping because of its ethos of impersonal, strict reciprocity. To lighten this necessary burden they shop in groups of three or more. In this way they may inject some aesthetic-incorporative feelings into a generally alienating experience. When men retire they take up food production as fishermen and gardeners in order to relieve the necessity of using supermarkets and to preserve as much as possible of the traditional networks of food sharing.

Whereas the out-of-town supermarkets cut across traditional behavior, the in-town general stores preserve their old-fashioned character. Of all the social spheres in the community the general store could most easily fall into material-transactional ways, but it remains, even in modern times, aesthetic-incorporative. In the past the general store was a vital link in the economic lives of all families in Tidewater, because it provided credit. A commercial duck hunter could buy essential supplies, such as powder and shot, from the store on credit and then settle up with the storekeeper when he was reimbursed by poultry buyers at the end of the season. Farmers and fishermen filled their seasonal needs in the same fashion. Even though there is less need for credit in the contemporary world, local families keep accounts at the stores and use these accounts to buy items even when they have enough cash to pay for them outright. Such behavior is anomalous when viewed in material-transactional terms. The reliance on credit unnecessary from a purely monetary standpoint secures the relationship between buyer and seller. The transactional is transformed into the incorporative, and other activities involved in trading reinforce the socially cohesive nature of the act.

No one conducts business hastily if he or she can avoid it. Most men sit at one of the benches provided and chat for at least a few minutes. It is also polite to sit before purchasing goods, which gives the appearance of coming to visit and then buying something as a secondary matter. What is more, at night the store is the scene of as much socializing as purchasing. Many men come to talk and leave without buying anything. Even though the store is a commercial enterprise, its ethos is fundamentally aesthetic-incorporative.

These examples could be multiplied, but they establish the points that aesthetic-incorporative relations are preferred over material-transactional ones, and that material-transactional relations, where they encroach, come from outside influences. What we have is the seed of an explanation of much of the social interaction, particularly conflict, in Tidewater. The old order is changing because of the outward movement of men in search of work and the influx of foreigners bringing new lifestyles with them. The old families are trying to preserve their status in the community by holding on to the old ways, but the new families are beginning to challenge the power of the old families. At heart it amounts to a clash between aesthetic-incorporative and material-transactional philosophies. The next issue to explore, then, is why the old families deal in aesthetic-incorporative terms, that is, what aesthetic-incorporative relations have done for them in the past and why they continue to rely on them.

Even though times are changing, virtually all power within the community still resides with the old families, each of which is governed by a senior generation. Power resides in three broad socioeconomic categories: landownership, inherited titles, and inherited offices. The senior generation controls all three spheres.

Almost all of the land in Tidewater is owned by the members of three or four families. The significance of this single fact cannot be underestimated when considering lines of power and authority in the community. First, identification with the land is extremely strong. The old house is occupied by successive generations who add their own character to it by slow accretion in structure and furnishings. When it becomes too dilapidated to be habitable the house is vacated, not torn down, and a new house is built in its shadow. Somewhere on the land is the family burying ground, so that in death the family remains united on the land. Second, the land provides employment or access to employment. Each family has a farm that provides work for one or two men. But landownership also includes control of water access for fishing and other water-based jobs. Third, family land titles include juniper swamp, woodland, and saltmarsh, which are prime hunting grounds for waterfowl and deer. And, of course, arable fields may be hunted for quail and dove. Also, the swamps and woodlands provide timber for house- and boatbuilding and other necessary equipment, such as oars. In sum, key activities are closely tied to landownership.

New families in town do not have rights over land, and they are beholden to the old families. They rent houses and occasionally farm land from the old families. New families pay for docking privileges at water-access points, otherwise they must drive miles to public access locations, loading and unloading their boats each day. They may also rent or exchange services for hunting grounds. Thus new families have set up basic material-transactional relations with the old ones. The young members of the old families are equally beholden to the old members, but they do not establish material-transactional relations with them: their relations are aesthetic-incorporative.

Older men take on younger male kin as limited partners, not as wage-earning employees. A commercial fisherman, for example, takes on two partners who share in the proceeds of the catch. The owner takes half of the income—one quarter share for him and one quarter for the equipment—and the boys take a quarter share each. Young married couples are given the use of a house on family property or land on which to build or place a house trailer. They do not rent property from the older generation. All family members, young and old, have use of hunting grounds and water access. Younger families eat at night with the older generation and are not expected to contribute money in return for a meal. What is required is that younger women assist in food preparation and keep the family cook company. Younger men keep the company of their older relatives and their friends at the store at night.

Although young men must succumb to the authority of the older generation, they can confidently expect to rise to positions of prestige in the community over time. Members of the new families do not have the same expectations, and in consequence their lifecycle differs from the traditional one.

A complete understanding of the difference between old and new family workstyles requires us to review the most important occupations in the community, those that are water-based (see Table 7, p. 105).

The young man starts out somewhere near the bottom of the ladder, and his goal is to rise as quickly as he can. But such ambitions do not make clear sense from a purely material or pragmatic point of view. Guiding for hunters and fishermen provides a steady, reliable income. Foreigners pay between thirty and forty dollars per day plus tips. The chief outlay is gasoline. Crabbers may gross more, and sometimes their day's haul is considerably more, but in the course of a season they may not make profits much in excess of the fishing guide's. The main difference is that guiding jobs are onerously transactional. The guides complain that they spend all day arguing with their charges to behave properly. Some fishermen treat the guides as paid servants and expect them to bait hooks, release fish, and other menial tasks. The relationship between guide and guided is a subject of constant negotiation. At the end of the day the guide is paid and tipped in accordance with his capacity to negotiate an agreeable relationship.

Guiding involves constant dealing with outsiders and is, therefore, material-transactional, whereas fishing and trapping, which are individual or small-group activities by insiders in an aesthetically pleasing environment, are in some measure aesthetic-incorporative. (All water activities have a material-transactional aspect, discussed below.) It is highly desirable to get away from material-transactional jobs with outsiders, but to climb the hierarchy requires more equipment. It is not financially possible to buy new all of the gear needed to be independent of outsiders. A man must inherit some or all of his equipment from older relatives. But usually before he inherits, other circumstances arise that worsen his position vis-à-vis the outside world and material-transactional relationships. He takes a factory job that pays a standard hourly wage, though he can be confident that this exile in the outside world will end.

When the retired man from an old family "comes home" he can to a considerable extent withdraw from material-transactional relations. He does not have to guide because he has the equipment to fish. He may join the church as public display of his new status. He has left the world of sin, that is, the outside world of money and exchange, and returned to the cohesive, nontransactional little community. The church, with all of its aesthetic elaboration and emphasis on salvation through grace alone, is the epitome of the aesthetic-incorporative. By coming forward the retired man reaffirms his commitment to the aesthetic-incorporative. But this decision emphatically does not entail his becoming "holy" or "spiritual." He is affirming his faith in the community and its values, not in the theological doctrines of the church. He sits with other such men in "amen corner" and quietly assents to the proceedings. These men do not become great proselytizers and evangelists, because what they have attained is not freely available through evangelism.

Men and women from new families live, whether by choice or force of circumstances, predominantly in the material-transactional realm. They work at wage labor and shop at supermarkets. They do not keep accounts at the general stores, nor do they stop to chat when they buy items. They rent homes as individual family units and take their evening meals as nuclear families. Everything they require must be bought, they have no land or gear to bestow or inherit. In the three areas of traditional power—land, traditional occupations, and key offices—they are permanently disenfranchised. As the old families hold such power, however, it remains to be understood why these newcomers pose a threat to the old aesthetic-incorporative order.

The old families could force their will in all community and family affairs on a strictly financial basis. For example, it is no secret that the Sunday school director keeps the church solvent. Whenever there is a monthly or annual shortfall, he makes up the difference out of his own pocket. At times when the preachers have become argumentative he could simply have withdrawn his support, which among other things provides the preacher's salary, and conflict would have ended abruptly. An unruly young man could be refused fishing partnerships or access to water activities. Troublesome newcomers could have their leases revoked. But the members of the old families never behave in this fashion, they never invoke their material-transactional powers to get their way. They avoid material-transactional power for two main reasons. First, the Protestant ethic is a powerful force opposing the material-transactional; second, material-transactional relations are used by outsiders and so to use them is to identify with the wrong people.

The Protestant work ethic is clearly one of the dominant themes in Tidewater life. Examples of its effects are legion. One woman confessed she had taken only one bank loan in her life. She hated the thought of paying interest because someone was getting "something for nothing." She could hardly sleep nights at the thought of the burden of the loan and was driven to take paid jobs sixteen hours a day, seven days a week, until the loan was repaid. An older man condemned television as "the worst vice in the world. It takes your time from you and gives you nothing in return." One young farm worker was chided by other men in the town for being lazy because he worked from ten in the morning until eight at night instead of the customary eight to eight.

The nub of the whole matter is that the Protestant sees material wealth as the *result* of a good life, not the *cause* of it. The Protestant leads a good, hardworking life for its own sake, and prosperity comes as a natural corollary. It is quite inappropriate, even sinful, to see money as powerful or as an ingredient in happiness, and this message is reinforced from the pulpit (see Weber 1958 and Peacock 1971). Therefore, it is not possible to fight battles or live life in the material-transactional arena, because to do so is to admit that money does indeed have power in its own right. A father wishes his son to be loyal and obedient simply because it is good to be so, not because the father can take away the son's livelihood. A fisherman shares his catch because it is good to share, not because he will get something in return. To resort to material power to get one's way is to admit defeat.

In addition, when the people of Tidewater are forced to enter the material-transactional sphere they generally lose. In particular, farmers and fishermen sell their products to dealers, mostly from the North. When selling these products they are almost entirely at the mercy of external forces. Farmers must take the price they are given for corn and soybeans and have no personal power to change it. That power resides at the commodities exchange, which is driven by national and international politics and economics that the local farmer scarcely understands. Fishermen sell their catches to buyers from Northern cities, and prices fluctuate wildly from catch to catch. Big hauls cause an immediate lowering of prices, and arguments usually result in the buyer refusing to buy. Such brutal transactional relations cause divisions among the fishermen which are considered distasteful but unavoidable. Pot fishermen keep quiet about catches and placement of their lines, and net fishermen race each other to market to get the best prices. The transactional nature of the buyers encourages "bad" behavior among the fishermen.

Fishermen know that such behavior is not necessary. Before the modern roads came buyers did not journey to the South to buy the watermen's catches. The watermen salted down fish, crabs, wild game, and so on, and sent it up North in barrels made in a barrel factory in Tidewater itself. The Northern buyers published seasonal price lists and settled up with each waterman according to the same rates, either monthly or at the end of the season. There was no need to race to market or to compete in a cutthroat way. But when the roads came, the buyers came too. It was easy to draw the conclusion that the buyers had imported these disruptive material-transactional ways.

A general survey of the dealings of the people of Tidewater with the outside world leads to the ineluctable conclusion that in these proceedings they lose power or have none. They work as wage laborers for, or sell their goods to, capitalists who hold the upper hand. Lobbying by the local church at the state legislature to prevent passage of liquor by the drink laws failed. Lobbying at the Southern Baptist Convention concerning the racial composition of congregations failed. In the latter case Tidewater's own delegate, the preacher, betrayed them. He was sent with a specific mandate from the congregation but nonetheless voted with his (outsider) conscience and against their wishes. Although the locals are drawn to the outside world for financial or ideological reasons, the frequent result is defeat and subsequent withdrawal back into the comforts of the aesthetic-incorporative little community.

Because the outside world represents material-transactional relations and, thereby, defeat and loss of power, the influx of outsiders into the community is deeply troubling. Tidewater was always a place to withdraw to, a safe haven. With outsiders coming in and staying, the town's status as haven is diminishing. These outsiders must be resisted as much as possible. But they cannot be resisted by material-transactional means, even though the old families would most likely win if they used these methods. The locals are caught in a bind created by the Protestant ethic. If they use material-transactional methods they lose in a double sense, even though they might technically win. Their aim is to keep the material-transactional out of the community, and so it is illogical to use material-transactional power to do so. By adopting material-transactional methods, moreover, they would be asserting the power of that which they wish to deny has power. But by relying on the aesthetic-incorporative they run the risk of losing out to the material-transactional, because in their dealings with outsiders they have tended to lose.

There is no better example of the insider/outsider clash than the "row" over church music and the covenant, and the way it was handled is now understandable. The battle started over church music, but the preacher shifted the ground to abstinence and the church covenant. His supporters were members of the new families and his opponents, the old families. The three sermons he preached on covenants were strictly transactional arguments. A covenant, after all, is a binding contract between two parties who come to mutually agreeable terms. The preacher's arguments were taken from the contractual segments of Mosaic law. Even the framework he used was highly legalistic. His aim was to apply arguments and logic to turn the tide in his direction and ultimately to win a referendum, as if one's position in these matters were subject to change by debate and verbal transactions. The response of the old families was a refusal to debate or transact on the issue at all. Their most decisive action was a move to *table* discussion. The issue was not subject to transaction; if they had entered the fray using those tactics, they might have won the battle but lost the war. Instead, they avoided all action in the material-transactional realm, and the last act of the night was to vote unanimously to restore the music director to her old position. This was a clear signal for the preacher to resign, which he did one month later.

By firing the preacher the church and the town are purged of outside influences. New families continue to arrive each year, however, and the old and the new are beginning to intermarry and confuse the boundaries between them. It is difficult to know whether the aesthetic-incorporative little community will survive the onslaught. The preacher claimed he was turning their "world upside down," but really he was drawing the "outside world in." Periodic purges may stem the tide temporarily, but the aesthetic-incorporative may ultimately fall victim.

In essence, then, for the people of Tidewater aesthetics define and maintain the inside world or, perhaps, a number of inside worlds. Tidewater could be defined as an aesthetic community—a community that shares aesthetic forms and values. This sharing has a double sense because the values are held in common and the forms often are freely exchanged. That is, aesthetic-incorporative relations are so named because they are mediated by aesthetic forms that are shared and represent shared values. But Tidewater is also an aesthetic community in that, regardless of individual aesthetic judgments, the people hold being aesthetic as a value in and of itself. Their relationships are aesthetic-incorporative because they actively choose them to be so.

This analysis suggests the existence of at least two kinds of aesthetic community. In the first kind the people's aesthetic judgments are unified or informed by similar cultural values. In such cases the aesthetic world is a unifying factor, but it may not have primacy in human interaction. It may be one among many shared attributes or one among many ways of defining the community. In the second kind the people give primacy to aesthetic value, perhaps above economic, social, and political values, even though individual judgments may differ. That is, they see the aesthetic realm as the appropriate place in which to hold human interaction whatever particular form it may take. A community might satisfy both defining criteria, and I believe Tidewater does. The locals share aesthetic values and agree on the fundamental importance of the aesthetic in daily life.

What remains to be reviewed is the issue of why aesthetic forms should act in the ways described. To do so it is necessary to return to the attributes of aesthetic forms outlined in Chapter 2. In particular I focus on the sensual and affecting qualities of aesthetic forms, but in the process I also consider issues related to critical tastes and disinterested contemplation.

The basic sensual and physical character of aesthetic forms is of critical importance to how those forms operate and are manipulated in Tidewater. Nowhere can this point be seen more clearly than in the architectural construction and reconstruction of space. The church building has two distinct aesthetic aspects: the new brick-veneered outside and the old wood-paneled inside. Perhaps easy to overlook in the search for grand theory is the fact that this inside/outside distinction is made possible by the physical nature of the way that the people of Tidewater define sacred space, namely, with a permanent structure.

There is no absolutely compelling reason for defining sacred or any other space either visually or permanently. The smell of incense, heat of a fire, or sound of a musical instrument could define a space used for religious purposes. But the inside/outside qualities of these forms are fundamentally different from those of a building. They are ephemeral and need constant effort to maintain them: incense or fire must be fed, an instrument must be played. When the effort ceases so does the space that is being defined. Also, these forms define space by pervading, as opposed to surrounding, it. They fill up the space rather than making a perimeter around it. Smells and sounds, being airborne, flow around and into the participants in the space so defined. Finally, the margins of space defined by these forms are unclear and difficult to control. Smells and sounds drift with the wind and taper gradually to nothing over great distances.

Thus while sounds, smells, feels, and so on can be used to define space, they do so in ways that are critically different from those of a permanent visible structure. For these forms being inside or outside the defined space is marked by a simple binary feature, that is, the sensation of the form is absent or present. But the inside/outside dimensions of a visible structure are more complex. Being outside the building does not simply involve the absence of the sights of the inside. The sights of the outside can be, and in the case of the Tidewater church are, aesthetically different from those of the inside, so that people both inside and outside a building have a visual aesthetic experience of the building. In the case of a space defined by, say, smell, only those inside the space have the relevant olfactory experience, or, rather, the production of a smell in a space does not produce one sensation for those inside and simultaneously produce another, different one for those outside.

Whereas forms involving touch, smell, and hearing cannot easily be controlled over space, a few can be controlled over time and can be used to mark time. This is especially true of sounds, whose controlled manipulation over time produces music and the modulated vocal qualities of oratory. Smells and feels are less controllable over time than sounds, although some manipulation of degree of intensity is possible. Starting up or shutting down the source of a smell or heat does not effect an immediate change in sensation, nor are small changes in intensity perceptible.

From these generalizations about the sensual and physical characteristics of different aesthetic forms it is easy to conclude that it is efficient to define sacred space with a permanent, visible structure and to define sacred time with sounds. This is, of course, precisely how services work in the Tidewater church. People congregate inside the building and behave in a subdued, somewhat orderly fashion consonant with the surroundings. But their behavior becomes completely orchestrated during the service, whose beginning and end is marked by music. The space is always sacred, but certain times, marked by temporal forms, are special. Within the temporal boundaries marked by music, regulated sounds—hymns, special music, doxology, sermon, and so on—structure the time, and because they function in this way it is no surprise that they occupy a critically important political position in the church, as the "row" over music indicates.

The relationship between architecture and sounds is not simply one of intersection between spatial and temporal variables. The physical natures of these forms interact. The building acts as a container and resonator for sounds, allowing them to be controlled and manipulated. Because walls and ceiling keep the air inside the building relatively still and reflect sounds back into the space, a greater modulation of sound is possible inside than outside. A preacher can range from low tones to loud admonitions, and musical instruments can vary in loudness.

When the people of the church moved the choir from the side to the center of the sanctuary, the change had a visual aspect, but the results were also, and perhaps more significantly, acoustic. When the choir was located to the side their voices reflected back to them from the other side wall and were only weakly transmitted to the body of the room. From a central position the sounds now radiate directly out into the sanctuary, with strengthening acoustic effects from the back alcove, ceiling, and side walls. The choir stalls are banked so that each voice projects out, without interference from the body of the singer in front and to take added advantage of the reflective qualities of the ceiling. The organ's speaker is centrally placed behind and above the choir so that its sound flows directly outward, and the preacher's position on a platform directly in front of the choir allows his voice similar scope. Both use the back alcove as a resonator.

Compare the sound and space associations of worship service with those of Sunday school. In the latter a piano placed to the side where the choir used to sit leads the music, and the director stands directly in front of the congregation. Both positions mute the sound qualities of their respective sources. The director at ground level stands far from the resonating effects of ceiling and back alcove. Much of the piano's music is swallowed up by the corner where it stands, and it is usually played with top and front closed. In other words, to say that the aesthetic forms of the regular service are "expansive" and those of the Sunday school are not is to make a direct statement about the physical and sensual qualities of those forms rather than about what they signify, symbolize, or refer to.

It is enlightening to view a regular service in the church using the sensorium as a frame of reference, to see how forms acting on each of the senses are controlled and how they influence each other. This analysis forms the basis for comparative investigation of aesthetic complexes in other arenas in Tidewater.

Several hours before the service begins the preacher goes into the church and regulates the heating or cooling system so that by the time services begin, the internal temperature will have stabilized. These systems effectively maintain an even temperature throughout the service and in consequence neutralize the skin sensations associated with heating and cooling. These sensations may be stimulated on first arrival if internal and external temperatures differ markedly, but they soon become quiescent. The heating and cooling systems use forced air that is filtered and recirculated, thus minimizing internal smells; the olfactory system is easily fatigued if new smells do not arise to provoke it. On entering the building there is usually no smell detectable, unless the flower displays are unusually large. Even in the latter case the floral aroma is indistinct and soon subsides as the nose grows accustomed to it.

The systems that regulate air temperature and smells work in conjunction with the building structure. Careful control of heat and smell is possible because the building acts as a container for the air, thus creating a marked difference between internal and external air qualities. What might otherwise be vagrant and uncertain sensations are held rigidly in check and eliminated from consciousness for the duration of the service.

Regular worship services do not involve taste at all. (Holy Communion is a special case.) Chewing even the smallest item, such as a piece of candy, is highly uncommon, and other oral stimulants, such as tobacco, are strictly prohibited within the sanctuary. Addicted smokers linger outside until the start of the service, taking one last puff, and leave quickly at the end of proceedings to light up in front of the building. For them the denial of the service is framed by indulgence.

When the preacher turns the heating or cooling on he usually turns on the interior lighting also. These lights—incandescent bulbs in frosted glass mantles—shed an even yellow light that makes the interior woodwork glow in rich, honeyed, amber hues. Sunlight filtered through the colored glass windows makes little difference to the interior light unless the sky is exceptionally bright or cloudy. Thus during the service the basic visual aspects of the sanctuary, smells, tastes, and most touch sensations are all kept stable. Marked differences in sights, tastes, smells, and skin sensations occur on entry to and exit from the sanctuary only, making the actual moment of transition from outside to inside a multisensory experience.

Within the stable sensual environment of the sanctuary sounds are controlled with considerable sophistication. A summary of the range of these forms indicates their diversity. The full range of loudness is employed, from total silence (silent meditation), to very soft (prelude), to soft (morning prayer), to moderately loud (special music), to loud (hymns). And, of course, the preacher uses this entire compass in his sermons, making the preacher's performance in many ways a microcosm of the entire sound range of church aesthetic performance. Some of these forms are strictly predictable—hymns and readings are taken from written texts. Some are moderately predictable because of conventional patterns and formulae—morning prayers use standard formats but change according to contemporary circumstances. And some are barely predictable—the sermons are extemporized with varying formats. Some forms involve one performer, some a select group, and some the entire congregation. Some are in unison, others involve harmony, antiphony, or counterpoint. These variations in number of performers and modes of performance produce ranges of timbre and tone quality.

Some idea of the value of the manipulation of sounds in a sacred context can be gleaned by examining the physical and sensual qualities of the sounds. Normally it is difficult to shut sounds out, and attempts to block the ears mute rather than extinguish sounds completely. Furthermore, in an enclosed space sounds are omnidirectional, so that turning the head does not appreciably diminish intensity or quality. Hearing is critically different from sight in these two respects; closing the eyes or turning the head efficiently blocks or changes sights.

It is, perhaps, these properties of hearing that associate it in English and other languages with notions of obedience. As Julian Jaynes notes (1976:97) "obey" comes from a composite Latin verb *oboedire,* which literally translated means "to hear facing." An etymological digression reveals a possible root connexion between hearing and aesthetics. The Greek verb *aisthanomai* (to perceive), which gives rise to the adjective *aisthetikos,* may derive from the verb *aio* (to hear). Without question the Greeks understood hearing to be a deeply influential sense, as Plato's railings in *Republic* against certain kinds of music, drama, and spoken poetry attest. Children, he argues, obey the sounds of aesthetic forms too willingly and without sufficient critical judgment.

Sounds are richly layered in several ways. In the church service they are often composites of many voices—human and instrumental—and they can have both musical and linguistic aspects. Communal singing produces unity out of diversity. Bass and soprano, loud and soft, coarse and mellifluous, all blend to form a whole that can be heard and appreciated as an integral unit. All participants can attend to that unity, or to their own individual contributions, through direct feedback, creating an alternating sense of whole and self.

In sum, the sounds in the church service are strictly controlled, they call for obedience, and they create unity out of diversity. All of these aspects of the sounds of the service are basic to a cultural understanding of religious behavior in Tidewater: religion involves control and obedience; it requires unity. But this analysis comes from a direct understanding of the physical and sensual nature of sounds, not from a symbolic analysis. Control, obedience, and unity are physical and sensual aspects of the sounds themselves rather than what they refer to or signify.

Even aspects of the music which have referential or symbolic meaning do not signify in an unambiguous way. Much of the music has words sung to it and, as already noted, the semantic import of these words is often related to expected action. But the curious thing about sung words is that they can be, and frequently are, treated disinterestedly, that is, they can be sung or heard without conscious attention to what they would mean if spoken in a nonmusical or nonaesthetic context. This phenomenon is well attested in the ethnomusicological literature (see, for example, Merriam 1964:187–208, Tracey 1954, and Devereux and LaBarre 1961), and most Westerners know the experience of suddenly attending to the words of a favorite song, seemingly hearing them as words with literal meanings for the first time. The music director in Tidewater occasionally asked the choir to "listen to the words" of the special music to assist in interpretation, the admonition indicating that otherwise they might not listen. Sung words, therefore, give the singer and listener a choice as to how to attend to them: cognitively or affectively.

This ambiguous quality of sung words is complemented by the often subtle relationships between words and music. Take, for example, the classic hymn "All People That on Earth Do Dwell" (# 13). Here words denoting the call to be blissfully content and to sing cheerfully—"Sing to the Lord with cheerful voice" and "Come ye before Him and rejoice"—are paired with a slow, heavy tune. Or consider the old favorite "We're Marching to Zion" (# 308), which, despite its constant allusions to marching, is not a march. Such contrasts allow singer and listener some latitude in attention and interpretation: giving concern to one or other aspect, shifting between the two, or taking in the complex whole at once.

Sung words also have poetic form by themselves, so that they may be viewed affectively or cognitively irrespective of the music. This component of the words can be subsumed under musical analysis in part, because many poetic qualities, such as meter, pace, and tone, have analogues in the music. For example, most of the church music is syllabic, meaning that each syllable in the text has its own note in the music. Therefore, the meter of the music is necessarily the meter of the words. But many qualities, such as rhyme, word order, and diction, do not rely on the music. These poetic aspects of the words are distinguishable from, and may contrast with, the literal meanings.

The church service at Tidewater depends very heavily on the aesthetic qualities of sounds. These sounds have various layers of complexity which complement the values inherent in the service. The layers also interact with one another to produce composite, textured wholes. But certain aesthetic forms are deliberately excluded, and to understand why this is so it is necessary to examine the sensual and physical qualities of these forms and their role in Tidewater social life.

The conspicuous absence of food and taste at most church services seems to me of particular importance, because food and taste are of overwhelming significance in other church activities and in all arenas of social life in Tidewater. Food occupies a central role in all spheres of everyday life. Men produce food at work from farming and fishing, at home in kitchen gardens, and in leisure hours through sport fishing and hunting. Women process and redistribute food in networks that reinforce ties of kinship and neighborliness, and the role of family cook is of special social significance. The church mobilizes all of its active members to prepare and participate in feasts that are designed to enhance ties of fellowship as well as make money. Food is exchanged and shared in daily acts of friendship and cooperation. These facts might suggest that food should occupy a key position in a church whose purpose is, among other things, to foster unity, sharing, and harmony. Yet contrary to these expectations, food plays no role in regular worship.

The sensual and physical qualities of food help explain why under some circumstances it may foster unity whereas under others it is forbidden. The foods of Tidewater run the gamut from dishes that contain many ingredients all boiled and mushed together to those in which components are kept strictly separate. For compactness of analysis I compare two meals prepared as part of church fund-raising events. These descriptions of food and cooking apply to home cooking as well and should not be thought of under a separate (nonexistent) rubric "church" cooking.

Brunswick stew contains meats and vegetables simmered to a disintegrated pap. Each bowlful, spoonful, or mouthful contains particles from all the original ingredients, and however the whole is divided, the parts all taste the same. The texture and temperature are homogeneous. Because of this sensual uniformity, eating the stew quickly leads to taste fatigue, which further reinforces the sameness of each bite. By contrast, the chicken supper served by the church consists of discrete units that have individual sensual qualities. The basic meal of fried chicken, boiled green beans, potato salad, and cornbread is almost a microcosm of Tidewater cooking styles. The three basic cooking methods and media—frying/oil (chicken), baking/air (cornbread), and boiling/water (beans)—are used. The textures include crisp, crumbly, chewy, and soft. The temperatures range from chicken straight from the fat, almost too hot to touch, to potato salad that has been refrigerated. The chicken coating is spicy, the beans are salty, the cornbread is sweet, and the potato salad is milky bland. Each plateful is composed of different quantities and types of components.

Each diner can make choices based on personal tastes: breast or leg meat, corner or middle piece of cornbread, and more or less of each of the vegetables. These components can be eaten in any order or combination, producing a range of individual taste sensations that prevent sensory fatigue and so highlight the variety in the meal.

The differences in sensual and physical qualities of these two meals, representative of extremes on a continuum, result from radically different styles of cooking and create different affective states. The preparation of fried chicken, cornbread, and potato salad is specialized and deeply personal. Each cook has her own special recipes, handed down from her mother, but to which she has added her own special touch. The complexities of frying chicken serve to illustrate the point. Every ingredient and action is considered crucial to the success of the final product. Do you soak the chicken before you flour it? Do you bread or batter it? What spices do you add to the coating? Do you shallow or deep fry? What fat do you use? What temperature do you fry at? How long do you fry? These and many other variables lead to end-products that are widely different and immediately recognizable as "Libby's chicken" or "Elsie's chicken." Each cook pays scrupulous attention to the proceedings because a false move at any stage can ruin the enterprise. One spice missing or a minute too long in the fryer often spells disaster.

Brunswick stew has no such critical variables. The ingredients can vary in type and quantity, and the cooking time and method are extremely flexible. There is no formal recipe, and only the most general rules of thumb apply. Yet no matter how freely a cook plays with the process, the end-product turns out just about the same every time. An hour more or less cooking or a quart more or less corn does not appreciably alter the final taste. Therefore one cook's stew is the same as another's, and this year's stew is the same as last year's.

What is intriguing is that both kinds of meals, seemingly at opposite ends of the culinary spectrum, have pride of place in the community. Both are the talk of the town for weeks before and after the church events at which they are served. From the structuralist's perspective this observation might appear odd. Lévi-Strauss's analysis of cooking methods (1965), for example, seems scarcely able to accommodate such facts. His distinction between cooking methods and what they represent is too general to apply to Tidewater cooking practices. For example, he classifies roasting as a wasteful process because meat juices are lost and boiling as economical because all of the juices are retained. Roasting is, therefore, aristocratic, prodigal, and suitable for

[225]

elaborate entertaining, whereas boiling is plebeian, thrifty, and suitable for humble family meals. But the people of Tidewater relish both boiled Brunswick stew and roast Thanksgiving turkey as festival dishes.

The idea of wasteful versus conservative cooking styles can be preserved, but not by classifying methods generally under one or the other rubric. Rather, I am inclined to believe that when women cook they tend to conserve, but men are wasteful. Men cook outside, and their commonest method is charcoal grilling. In this process the fat from the meat is rendered by the heat and falls on the hot coals to be converted to aromatic smoke that wafts away. As the preference in Tidewater is for very well-done grilled foods, a substantial amount of fat and juices escapes in this manner. And because it is customary to eat indoors even when the cooking is done outside, diners cannot even minimally appreciate the vagrant aromas of cooking. Women, on the other hand, conserve the rendered fat and cooking juices from direct dry-heat cooking methods. A drip pan collects the juices from roasting or broiling, and these are turned into gravies to be served with the meat. The smells of cooking that escape from the oven pervade the kitchen, where diners can savor them before sitting down to eat. Excess fats are stored in dripping cans for later use in gravies, bastes, or thickening roux. Equally, long slow boiling in the kitchen conserves juices and smells, with the latter being immortalized through slow incorporation into the fabric of the room, giving it a permanent seasoning.

Just as the church building controls sound by containing it and reflecting it back inward, so kitchens contain and magnify smells. The humidity, warmth, and stillness of the atmosphere intensify olfactory sensations. Because smells, like sound, are carried through air they can mix and harmonize into a complex whole, so that the individual components of a meal blend to form new aromas. Each night people entering the kitchen are greeted with a different aroma, even though certain elements, such as the smell of boiled greens, are constantly present.

Although intrinsically less controllable than sounds, the smells of the evening meal indicate the passage of time and change over time in controlled ways. An evening meal is prepared in stages so that items which take different lengths of time to cook will all be ready at the same moment. The skill to work in efficient manner so that, say, fried fish, boiled greens, boiled potatoes, corn dumplings, and hushpuppies are all hot and ready to be eaten at the same time marks the experienced cook. As each element in the meal begins to cook the complexity and intensity of the total aroma grows. When the meal is served up the general aroma starts to diminish because the sources of heat and humidity are eliminated. The unified aroma of cooking is replaced with the specific smells of individual items as they are passed around the table and sampled. At the end of the meal the smell of coffee marks a terminus and revives fatigued olfactory sensors with its sharp tang.

Such control of aromas is absent when men prepare the Brunswick stew for the church, because the cooking takes place outside. Certainly the slow simmering of the stew is a more conserving method than the customary outdoor grilling, but the slow buildup of complex aromas is completely absent and cannot serve to frame the meal. Moreover, there are surprisingly wasteful aspects in the cooking process. For a start the outdoor cooking causes any smells to disperse quickly. Also, the stew takes two days to cook in distinct stages, so the smells of one phase cannot blend with those of another. Even when the pot is full of finished stew and bubbling gently one has to lean over the top to catch the full deep scent, as some people do with evident satisfaction; the aroma does not pervade the outdoor space. As a final indication of the wastefulness of this cooking method in the hands of men, in the year I observed the process, on the first day when the men had finished stewing up the meats they dipped them out of the cauldron in order to separate out the bones and threw the cooking liquid away. When made at home by women this "pot liquor" forms the liquid base for the stew. (As an aside, it should be clear by this point that the relationship between inside and control and outside and lack of control is not simply a useful analytic tool that makes sense of the data. It is rooted in the sensual and physical nature of the aesthetic forms under discussion. Sounds and smells can be better manipulated when they are enclosed.)

Rather than look at cooking methods like a structuralist, I prefer to look to the sensual and physical qualities of specific dishes for an understanding of affective states associated with them. For example, in my experience in Tidewater such concoctions as Brunswick stew induce feelings of nostalgia, warmth, and unity among participants, and I believe that the sensual qualities of the stew are responsible for these feelings. Because the stew has a complex but homogeneous taste and texture, all diners of necessity share a basic common taste experience. (There is a potential philosophical problem here concerning the comparability of subjective states, but in practice it does not apply because it is clear that the people of Tidewater see the fundamental experience of taste as broadly similar from person to person. The discussion of good food, particularly that concerning good fish in Chapter 4, establishes this belief.) Each mouthful a person eats is the same as the next mouthful, the same as each mouthful for other people at the table, the same as mouthfuls eaten in previous years, and so on. A sensual, subjective link is created between all those present at the meal and between all those who took part in similar meals in earlier years. Thus the physical and sensual link between stew eaters is responsible for the feelings of nostalgia and unity.

This thesis is strengthened by examination of foods that are like and unlike Brunswick stew in their physical qualities. Haslet stew, which is a little less homogeneous than Brunswick stew but still basically all mushed together, evokes nostalgia and sentiments of fellowship. This comparison might lead one to believe that all old-fashioned foods evoke nostalgia, but the notion cannot be true except in a very general way, because fried chicken is considered a traditional dish yet it does not evoke the same sentiments. Fried chicken is highly variable, and the way a meal including it is composed is subject to individual tastes. It therefore creates individual subjective states and associations. Eating it is likely to elicit critical discussion and commentary about individual tastes, such as "This is better than the batch you made last week" or "What did you think of Mabel Jean's chicken?" or simply, "That was the best chicken I ever tasted." Similar discussions are held over the Thanksgiving turkey, so that even when the occasion or context might predispose diners toward nostalgia and fellowship, the food prompts critical discussion instead.

The sensual and physical qualities of fried chicken and Brunswick stew are consonant with the overall ethos of the church activities of which each is the centerpiece. The chicken supper takes place in spring, before the revival, and one of its principal functions is to attract new members to the church. In line with this function prospective members are encouraged to contribute and participate, and considerable effort is made to reach all members of the community. For example, a large contingent of volunteers take prepared dinners to households throughout the town. The October festival at which the Brunswick stew is served is a fall event, after the revival, and the weekend of the proceedings is designated as the church's homecoming. Contributions and help come from church members, and the occasion draws people to it. There is no delivery service.

The chicken supper, then, has an air of individuality about it, with prospective and old members getting to know one another. Matched with this ethos is the individual nature of the contributions: cornbread, potato salad, and cakes are made to individual recipes so that each can be identified as to its maker. Some women specifically ask to try "Janet's chocolate layer cake" or "Jeanette's cornbread." In this gently probing atmosphere critical tastes can be compared to see whether newcomers and old members coincide in expectations. Participation in the chicken supper involves critical discussion and appraisal.

By the fall of the year prospective members have either become actively involved in church affairs or quietly dropped away. All present at the October sale are committed to the church or are old members and kin returning to visit from far afield. It is a time for remembering old associations, strengthening fellowship, and drawing the church body together. To match this ethos the contributions to the stew are all tumbled in the pot together so that no individual item stands out or can be recognized. The warm, nostalgic affects produced by the meal are undisturbed by critical analysis. There is nothing to analyze: Brunswick stew is Brunswick stew.

Now we can contrast the aesthetic forms in two types of church activity, fund raising and worship service, and draw some conclusions about the roles of each. Smells and tastes are deliberately excluded from the worship service, but at fund-raising events they are star attractions. It is perfectly acceptable to draw new people to the church through the enticements of a pleasant meal, and members are unselfconsciously open about this motive, but once these people are involved the aesthetic foundations shift from taste to sound. An understanding of this shift lays bare much that is fundamental in Tidewater aesthetic values.

In simple terms a root difference exists between the affective and cognitive potential of sounds on the one hand and tastes and smells on the other. Sound is the basic channel of language and, as such, has the potential for all manner of symbolic, referential, and descriptive communication in addition to the affective states it may engender. Smells and tastes do not have such a split personality because their capacity to convey referential and descriptive meanings is extremely limited. What is more, the role of food is simple and direct: it satisfies a basic bodily need. Any elaboration of food beyond its status as human fuel is necessarily aesthetic and affecting. This basic contrast is exploited by church members in Tidewater.

It does not compromise basic religious values to invite nonmembers to partake of a pleasurable meal as the first step in integrating them into the church, but it would if the same meal were offered to those who come forward to be baptized. In the first case the offer is in line with the conventional value placed on food in all spheres of social activity. Food and fellowship are natural companions in Tidewater. Invitation to the family table is a normal, everyday sign of welcome and friendship. Even though the food can cause critical discussion bearing on aesthetic tastes, the food itself does not have in addition referential or descriptive qualities that require assent or discussion on the part of diners. Using food as an enticement beyond initial involvement in the church would create complications because of the meaning of the call to baptism.

The act of coming forward to be baptized is not simply an expression of willingness to join the church community; it is an act of faith stemming from a spiritual conversion. Conversion is a complicated, mysterious, subjective affair. Even so, the church body must endorse each conversion by a vote to accept the new convert as a full member of the church. To do so in good conscience each member must be sure the person who has come forward has had a genuine conversion experience. Generally the members are not given to questioning the validity of an individual's conversion experience, and such unquestioning faith is made possible by the context in which the conversion appears to take place. That is, it takes place following a direct appeal to do so which invokes linguistic and symbolic references to Baptist doctrine. It explicitly does not take place during a meal or when the senses of taste and smell are being stimulated.

Baptist doctrine, as interpreted by the preacher and Sunday school teachers of Tidewater, draws a basic distinction between the material and spiritual worlds. Favorite and often quoted biblical passages make it evident that this split locates concern about food squarely on the material side and conversion on the spiritual side. Some pertinent quotations include sections from the temptation of Jesus by the devil to turn stones into bread (Matthew 4:1–4, Luke 4:1–4), the miraculous feeding of the five thousand (Mark 6:30–44, Matthew 14:13–21, and Luke 9:10–17), Elijah at the brook (1 Kings 17), and sayings on care for the morrow (Matthew 6:25–33 and Luke 12:22–31). All of these passages assert that food satisfies the body and should not be a concern; God will provide enough for survival, as he does for the animals. What matters is the state of one's spiritual being.

Food, being material, feeds the material body, but sounds, being nonmaterial, feed the nonmaterial spirit. Sounds can feed the soul because they can be used to express spiritual concepts through a variety of linguistic modes, such as biblical readings, sermons, the words of hymns, and so on. But the crux of the matter is that plain language alone is insufficient to provoke spiritual conversion. Appeals to logic and cognition are of limited utility because some fundamental tenets of Christian doctrine are paradoxical—death is not death, God is one and three at the same time, Jesus was fully man and fully God. These are simple mysteries, and affirmation of them is an act of faith that arises as a consequence of conversion.

A direct appeal to affect might be a solution, but it carries problems too. First, men are wary of aesthetic forms that are openly and elaborately affecting. Second, an appeal to affect may be a moving experience, but without some information on what to do as a result it remains inchoate or unchanneled. Third, spiritual conversion as understood by Tidewater Baptists is not a monolithically affective experience. It has a rational component, as evidenced by the youths at the revival who consulted with parents and preacher before coming forward.

The various ambiguities and complexities of the sounds of the service resolve these dilemmas neatly. They contain symbolic, linguistic, cognitive aspects as well as aesthetic, affecting ones, so that they provide both direct information as a context for action and an affective foundation for it. Both jostle for attention so that neither has primacy, lest one or other aspect become dominant and disturb the sensibilities of the congregation. When the music of the service became too strongly affecting under an overzealous preacher, it had to be curbed. This dual aspect of the sounds of the service also gives participants a choice as to what they focus on or appear to be focusing on. The men, for example, need not appear to be concerned with aesthetic elaboration, and their failure to participate in the singing of hymns reinforces this appearance.

Some of the complexities of the sounds of the service help explain or exemplify the mysteries of Christian doctrine. Contradictory beliefs, such as "death is not death," may seem illogical when cast as simple cognitive statements, but nothing is apparently troublesome about singing a hymn such as "All People That on Earth Do Dwell" (# 13), which is solemn and joyous at the same time. In this case the musical and linguistic aspects of the hymn counterpoise. The three-in-one aspects of the Trinity can be interpreted by analogy with choral singing, where many voices create a unified sound. The whole is simultaneously both many and one.

[231]

Thus the setting for spiritual conversion is deliberately ambiguous, and the ambiguity exists because certain aesthetic forms are used and others are excluded. With both affect and cognition stimulated in a balanced manner, participants are free to construe their experiences in different ways. Those like the men, whose public posture only barely tolerates aesthetic experiences but whose private lives involve complex aesthetic forms such as Masonic ritual and decoy making, can appear to be stimulated by the simple message of the service while being privately moved by its affective qualities. Others, like many of the women, can take pleasure in creating and participating in aesthetic forms largely for their own sake. Were aesthetic forms that relied on taste to be employed, they would severely limit these ambiguities and the ranges of behavior they tolerate.

It is fitting to conclude with a brief discussion of the one church service where taste has a role: Holy Communion. In crucial ways the acts of this sacrament are like and unlike regular eating, and again the ambiguities involved are important if we are to understand the event. Eating and drinking routinely satiate hunger and thirst, but at communion the portions are so tiny that such considerations are virtually eliminated. Nonetheless, the morsels partaken of are real food—bread and juice bought from the store like regular groceries—with no indications beyond size of portion that they differ from items eaten at any meal. They are simultaneously food and not food.

The act of eating the sacramental foods is highly controlled and of particular importance. The bread and "wine" are distributed to all members, and all eat at precisely the same moment. The taste experience, which is minimal and in consequence transitory, is momentarily shared by all present. The taste experience is also the same as in past communions. In some ways the experience resembles eating Brunswick stew in that the affective feelings of warmth and unity derive from the uniformity of taste experiences between people past and present. But the level of control of the two taste experiences is diametrically opposite, as is to be expected from the different contexts. Sensually, then, communion links the affective qualities of worship services with those of communal meals sponsored by the church, unifying the aesthetic experiences of the church community.

This extended analysis of the aesthetics of the church barely scratches the surface of a complex world, but it sets an agenda for continued interpretation. Aesthetic analysis, it is clear, is a pursuit with its own framework, terms, and questions distinct from other established concerns in anthropology such as symbolic structures, kinship systems, economic models, and the like. But it should also be evident that aesthetic forms dynamically interact with these other concerns as well as with one another, so that they can no longer be relegated to secondary status or subsumed under other branches of inquiry. The aesthetic forms of everyday life are central to all human experience; their study should be central to any discipline with pretensions to understand our shared condition.

Appendix A

Outlines of Selected Sermons

Regular Sermon #1: "God of Adequacy"
Text: John 6:5–13   Miracle of the loaves and fishes.

God is a God of adequacy, he makes inadequate men adequate.

God's eye is on the sparrow.

People try to limit God, but he cannot be limited.

In a play about Truman a preacher wrote to Truman protesting his profanity. The preacher was going to pray that his language improved. Truman replied that he was sure that God had better things to think about. But God cares about everything. God is like a computer. He made the world by commands. When he made the world it was perfect. But humans are inadequate. They sinned and made the world imperfect.

Some people try to put God in a cage. They think that he lives in the church building only. They think that when they leave the building they leave God behind. But God does not dwell in a temple made with human hands.

The preacher's former church wanted to brick the exterior. Cost $4,000. They began fund raising. Soon the bricks arrived and work started. Eventually they had a note-burning ceremony. They thought they were inadequate but they achieved their goal.

The preacher was often in financial difficulties as a seminary student. One day went to school with a dime in his pocket. A professor called him into his office and asked about his finances, and asked him how he was going to eat. He replied "I don't know." Professor gave him $50.

Alcoholics say they can quit any time. But they need help. When they admit that they need help they have taken the first step. Becoming a Christian works the same way.

There was once a little girl who would always play the same discordant tune with two fingers on the piano. Once at a party her parents missed her. Found her playing the discordant tune and people laughing. A man came along and told them not to laugh. He sat down with her and created a beautiful symphony. God makes the inadequate, adequate.

Regular Sermon #2: "The Glory of Being Ordinary"
Text: John 1:35–42   Andrew calls Simon to meet Jesus

Andrew is usually thought of as Peter's brother. But Andrew was a charter member of the church. We are often thought of in relation to others. We are so and so's brother, sister, or husband.

There is a glory to being ordinary.

Jesus had an inner circle: Peter, James, and John. They were present on special occasions such as the transfiguration. No one knows why there was an inner circle, but Andrew, who was a charter member of the church, was not part of it. He could have caused trouble in the early church. He could have gone back to fishing. He did not.

We should realize the glory of being ordinary. In a football team one man crosses the goal line for a touchdown and gets the glory. But the tackles and linemen have done their jobs.

Some people think that they cannot do anything special, they are ordinary. Each person can contribute something. There are no small or big Christians. All are the same. Small Christians are those who make themselves that way.

An old preacher in London was told that he had to step down in favor of a younger man. He went to the graveyard and sat on a tombstone. A young man passed by and started talking to him. The young man became a great missionary because of the conversation.

Another young man was wandering the streets of London on a stormy night a hundred years ago. He stopped in a church because of the rain. A layman from the congregation was running the service because the preacher could not make it. That young man gave his life to Jesus that day. He set England alight with his preaching. An ordinary man converted him.

Jimmy Carter, a ginger-haired, freckle-faced boy with buck teeth, was converted by an ordinary preacher.

Andrew was special in many ways. He was the first missionary. He brought his brother to Jesus. You in the church are special, you are not ordinary.

In 1937 Alabama went to the Rose Bowl on a last-minute conversion. An unknown boy came on the field and kicked the conversion. He has never been heard of since.

Some of the preacher's class in seminary are in charge of big churches. He is just ordinary.

Regular Sermon #3: "Nobodies"
Text: 1 Kings 14:1–7   Jeroboam's wife disguises herself
Even the unknown are known to God.

The fifty churches in the Southern Baptist Convention who contribute most are printed in the *Biblical Recorder*. Top this year was the First Baptist in Hendersonville. Contributions amounted to hundreds of thousands of dollars. But the Convention cannot function without the contributions of the small churches.

The preacher once attended a revival where only one small boy came forward. One man said, "The revival was a failure." But the boy became a great preacher.

A woman who wrote biographies of great people was asked who was the greatest person she had met. She replied, "The nobodies."

Once the preacher was in care of a church that had a paraplegic in the congregation. He was the kind of man who did not need cheering up: he cheered you up. When President Kennedy was shot he was at this man's cabin. He said to the preacher, "Who will remember us when we die." The preacher replied, "nobody." The paraplegic died shortly after. Hundreds attended his funeral.

How great we are in the world is measured by the length of our obituary. Most of us will get a one-inch column in the local paper.

God knows what we have done in life. When we come to the bar of the judgment seat he will know what we did and did not do in life. We are not nobodies to God.

It is impossible to predict what people will do in life. Our young people may become famous doctors or lawyers.

Regular Sermon #4: "Bearing Your Burdens."
Text: 1 Kings 17   Elijah at the Brook
God sent Elijah to the brook. He drank from the brook and was fed by ravens. Eventually the brook dried up. Elijah may have thought that he was forsaken by God.

When Jesus was on the cross he said, "My God, My God, why hast thou forsaken me?"

Sometimes we think we are forsaken by God. Many people think that troubles are punishments sent by God. God does not bring troubles to punish us, but to shake us out of complacency.

There is nothing that we can do to change God's love. There is not one iota, not one jot or tittle that he does not notice.

God's eye is on the sparrow. How much more important to Him are we than the sparrow. God's love is unchanging, there is nothing that we can do to make Him love us more or less.

A man left prison to attend his father's funeral. His father had disinherited him. He was dejected and wept. He went to a preacher. Preacher said, "God never disowns you."

During Elijah's stay at the brook there was famine in Israel. There had been a drought for three years, just like the drought we are experiencing in Marsh County. When the brook dries up some people do not have the initiative to go and seek water.

We need water. One of our members is sick right now. The doctor said he was dehydrated and had to go to hospital.

When the preacher was in the seminary there were times when he did not have enough food. Unknown people supplied funds for him to get by on.

Elijah had a vision in the temple. He could not see king Ahab.

Sometimes we are blinded and cannot see God.

When the brook dried up God told Elijah to leave. Told him to go to a woman who had just enough meal and oil to make one cake for herself and her son. After that was gone she was going to lay down and die. Elijah said, "Make me a cake first." She made the cake, and her meal and oil did not dry up throughout the famine.

Elijah challenged the priests of Baal. He even poured water on his wood pile to make things difficult. He lit a fire and burnt his sacrifice.

Sometimes our burdens are heavy. Jesus prayed that if there was any other way besides the cross that he might take it. Jesus asks us to take up our burden daily. Sometimes it is light.

A man had a grandfather clock that had run for three generations. The man said to the clock, "You have worked faithfully for three generations. I am going to take off your weights." He took the weights off and said to the clock, "Your burden is lifted." The clock said, "Put the weights back, they make me go."

Regular Sermon #5: "Hang In There"
Text: John 1:12   Children of God

Preacher once saw a calendar in an office with a picture of a cat on it hanging upside down by its claws on a tree limb. The caption was "Hang in there, baby!"

We all have a hand to hang in there with. The hand has four fingers:

First finger—New chance

There was a theologian in the Jewish church called Nicodemus who was very knowledgeable in the law. He asked Jesus how he could be saved. Jesus said that he must be born again. When Jimmy Carter was campaigning for the White House a lot was made of the fact that he was born again.

Second finger—New status

Jesus was in Samaria and went to the well to get a drink. A woman came down and he asked her to draw water for him. She said, "Why do you, a Jew, ask me, a Samaritan, such a thing." Jesus said, "These differences no longer matter."

Third finger—New power

In old Israel there was only one man who could talk to God. This was the High Priest, and once a year he entered the Holy of Holies to talk to God. One man talked for all of Israel. Our God is not like that. When Jesus died on the cross the veil of the temple was rent apart. Our God is a personal God.

Fourth finger—New security

When the preacher was a boy in Tennessee he very seldom made trips to the big town. They only went on special occasions, such as to get a haircut. At the barber shop men would tell him about his father, and what a good man he was. His father died the day before he was born. But he has a new father. God is his father. Jesus gave us the power to be sons of God. Having a father means security.

The preacher had a professor who was very thin. When he was a small boy he wanted to cross a railway bridge over a river. The ties were widely spaced and he could see the river between them. He was afraid to cross because he thought he would fall between the ties. His father took his hand and he felt secure to cross.

We are always secure if our father takes our hand.

We do not take God's hand, he takes ours. The preacher takes his daughter's hand when they walk near traffic. If she held him she could let go at any time and run into danger. If he holds her she is always safe.

Our hand to hang in with has a thumb. The thumb allows us to grip firmly. A man's thumb can be severed and sewn back on. Monkeys do not have thumbs. They cannot grip firmly. The thumb is faith. With this hand we do not "hang in," we are secure.

Regular Sermon #6: "The Plumbline Has Fallen"
Text: Amos 7:7–9, 8:1–3   Amos and the plumbline

God showed Amos a plumbline and said, "What do you see, Amos?" Amos said, "A plumbline." God said, "I will set a plumbline in the midst of my people Israel: I will not again pass by them any more."

Sometimes a prophet's words are too harsh. A young preacher was starting a new job, and he called to see the senior deacon to ask if he had any advice on sermons. The deacon said that a lot of local politicians came to church so it would be unwise to talk about politics. There were several distilleries in town and a lot of the workers came to church, so he shouldn't discuss alcohol. The main cash crop of the area was tobacco, so he should refrain from comments on cigarettes and smoking. Finally the young preacher asked what it would be safe to preach on. The senior deacon said that the threat of Chinese Communists would be safe, since there were none of them in town.

Many seats are empty in church these days because the plumbline has fallen. The words are too harsh for many people to listen to.

Amos was an unlettered shepherd and a tender of sycamore trees. The trees have to be pruned for the fruit to grow. It is tasteless but a staple food. Despite being unlettered he went to Bethel to prophesy before the great theologians there. He condemned all the countries around Israel. He condemned Damascus, and the people praised him. He condemned Gaza, Moab, and Tyre, and the people praised him. Then he said, "For three transgressions of Israel, and for four, I will not turn the punishment away thereof." Everyone cursed him for speaking harshly of Israel. They told him to go preach for bread in Judah. Some prophets preached for money and they mistook him for one of them. He said that he did not preach for money but because God had sent him.

Daniel Webster did not go to church in Washington D.C. but in New England. He said that in Washington they preach to Webster the senator, but in New England they preach to Webster the sinner.

Today we have situational ethics. Morality is dependent on the situation. God laid down commandments, but they are too hard to bear. More and more people indulge in extramarital sex, and pornography is rampant. The courts can no longer define obscenity.

Amos accused the women of Israel of decadence. He called them "kine of Bashan." They sat on ivory couches and oppressed the poor. Civilizations do not fall from outside pressure but from internal corruption. Amos accused Israel of corruption. He predicted the destruction of the temple at Bethel. He said that jackals would howl there. If you go to Bethel today you will find the temple in ruins. Archaeologists pick over the remains. We have internal corruption in the U.S. A senator has been convicted of fraud, but he can still serve in government. There should be equality in the law.

God also showed Amos a basket of summer fruit. It was very ripe. God said, "The end is come upon my people Israel; I will not again pass by them any more." It is time for the fruit to be picked.

God is going to put down a plumbline and see if your wall is straight. If it is crooked he will tear it down.

Kraft, the founder of Kraft cheese products, was a good Christian. He was once asked to go to Alcatraz to take part in a rehabilitation program. As he walked through a door a man said, "You're clean." He had used an X-ray machine to check for weapons. Later Kraft said, "How much more will God see in you at the judgment."

Regular Sermon #7: "The Devil and His Works"
Texts: Job 1:6–8, 2 Corinthians 2:10–11, 1 Peter 2:8   Satan's works

God made hell for the devil and his angels. Satan was an angel who fell from heaven. God does not put men in hell, men put men in hell.

The devil is walking in the world, the world is his province.

This dominion will be taken away from him eventually. The devil knows that ultimately he will be destroyed, and quakes in fear.

The devil tricks you and makes sin attractive. The devil makes people follow false religions. He made nine hundred people take poison in Jonestown, Guyana. He made people kill their children in Guyana.

He makes people follow the Rev. Moon. Moon's followers are brainwashed and have to be deprogrammed.

The devil tells you that you know enough about the Bible. He will tell you not to attend January Bible study classes because you already know enough. The preacher once quoted the Bible to a friend when he was a seminary student. The friend said that he must really know the Bible. Preacher replied that he hardly knew anything. We all know the famous quotations, but we do not know everything.

The devil will tell you not to give to the building fund. He will tell you that the church has enough money. He will tell you not to give to the Lottie Moon Christmas offering.

The devil persuades you not to come to church. Some people are at home today nursing hangovers. If it were advertised in the papers that the church had to be closed there would be an outcry. The outcry would come from the people who never come to church.

The devil is in control.

Special Sermon: Thanksgiving

The Thanksgiving story is well-known. In the winter of 1623 the new colony had very little food. They expected a supply ship any day. When a ship arrived it carried twenty-three more pilgrims and no supplies. These pilgrims came to have religious freedom.

In the first winter Governor Bradford went to the seed store and gave each member of the community five grains of corn per meal.

That winter there were more crosses in the cemetery than people in the community. In the spring the game returned, fish returned, and they planted crops. They had help in survival from the Indians. Next fall they had a bountiful harvest. They held a big feast to give thanks. Bradford put five grains of corn at each place. He said that each grain was a blessing.

We can count five blessings of our own:

#1 American flag

The flag stands for freedom and democracy. The right to vote is very important. Some people do not vote because they do not think that their vote is important. We may have only one vote each, but sometimes that makes a difference. Remember countries that have no free elections.

#2 Medical technology

Preacher did the rounds of the hospitals today. There is suffering there. Medical science has made great advances.

Preacher's father died of blood poisoning. At the time the doctors shook their heads because there was nothing they could do. Now the cure for blood poisoning is routine. Polio, chicken pox, and pneumonia are no longer feared.

Missionaries work in primitive villages where there are no doctors or nurses. All they have are witch doctors.

#3 Free enterprise

In America anyone can start a business. This morning the preacher's son worked on a school assignment to design a letterhead. Used "Greg's Optical Service" for the letterhead. One day this may be a reality. He can be an optician is he wishes. In Russia people are assigned jobs according to aptitude tests.

#4 The Bible

Two weeks ago the preacher was in a motel room in Raleigh. On the bedside table there was a Bible open to Isaiah 40: "Comfort ye, comfort ye, my people, saith your God." Gideon's Bibles have a note in them saying "if you want a Bible take this one."

#5 Jesus Christ

Jesus died for our sins. He took on his burden even when the world rejected him.

These are our five blessings. Count your blessings.

Special Sermon: Christmas

Texts: Isaiah 53, Micah 5:2 Prophecy of a Messiah

Isaiah is the greatest of the prophets. He foretold the coming of Jesus.

Imagine the desert in Arizona or Death Valley. There is no water to sustain life. Yet Isaiah said that out of the desert would come a shoot. That was to be the Messiah.

The Jews do not believe that the Messiah has come. Sometimes their theologians gather to predict when the Messiah will come.

Some time ago they gathered in Jerusalem to wait for him.

Jews get involved in Christmas but they say "Merry Xmas" X means "unknown." But the Messiah is known. He has already come.

The prophet Micah predicted that Bethlehem would be the place where the Messiah would come from. The verse "But you, O Bethlehem Ephratha, who are little to be among the clans of Judah, from you shall come forth for me one who is to be ruler in Israel" is the preacher's favorite verse in the Bible.

Bethlehem is like Tidewater. It is too small to be on the map.

Tidewater is not on most maps. The preacher had friends come to visit who called from the next town because they could not find Tidewater on the map.

Isaiah says "Comfort ye, comfort ye, my people." This passage predicts the suffering of Christ.

There has never been a time when God and Jesus did not exist.

They existed before time as we know it existed. We should not say that the Son was created, but simply, "He was."

Jesus was born of Mary. Mary went down the road and was met by an angel who told her she would bear the Son of God. She said that she was not worthy. When she was heavy with child she visited her cousin Elizabeth who was also pregnant. The child leapt for joy in Elizabeth's womb.

The coming of John the Baptist had been foretold by Isaiah: "A voice crying in the wilderness, make straight the paths of the Lord." John baptized Jesus in the Jordan. He said that Jesus should have baptized him.

When Jesus was born he was laid in a cattle stall. The angels chose to tell humble shepherds the good news. Shepherds were of a low caste despised by the Pharisees. The Pharisees said they should be killed.

Wise men came with gifts, gold, frankincense, and myrrh. The tradition of giving gifts has continued but now it is too commercial. Too much time is spent on material things and not enough on the central message of Christmas.

Revival Sermon #1

Texts: Exodus 14:10–13; Philippians 4:10   Revival and salvation

The preacher always wanted to be a pastor, not an evangelist or a missionary. When he was in high school he came forward and took the preacher's hand and said that he wanted to be a pastor.

It is not his purpose to go back to Tennessee and say that he has brought twenty-five people in Tidewater to Christ. The revival is for Tidewater Baptist church. It should be the purpose of everyone in church tonight to get everyone in Tidewater to the church.

Tidewater is not insignificant. People open hamburger stands on roads that have less traffic than the one that passes Tidewater Baptist church.

The preacher wants people to come to Christ. Once knew an old colonel who did not know Christ. He often went to his house and told him he wanted him to come to Christ. One day he said to his wife, "Pray for me because I'm going to save the colonel." He went to the colonel's house and asked his wife where he was. She said, "In the garden." He took her by the shoulders and looked into her eyes and said, "Stay in the house." He went to the colonel and said, "I love you." He said, "I am not here to talk trivia to you, I want to know if you love Jesus." The colonel said "Yes." The preacher asked him to confess his sins before Jesus. The bible says we must confess our sins out loud. As the colonel confessed his sins a tear fell on the preacher's sleeve.

Preacher took out a New Testament from his left jacket pocket.

He had written the names of all of the people he loved but who did not know Christ in the fly leaf. He read the names. He challenged everyone in the congregation to write three names in their Bibles.

A man in deep despair went on a world cruise. He stayed in his cabin all of the time. No one saw him except the people who brought him his meals. One night a cry echoed through the ship: "Man overboard." He went up on deck. All was confusion. He went down to his cabin, picked up a flashlight, and thrust his arm out of the porthole. The light fell on the man overboard.

That was not chance. It is not chance that people are born and brought up in Tidewater.

Life was hard when the West was opening up. A family in North Dakota had a son who one day felt a sharp pain in his abdomen. They took him to a pharmacist, the nearest medical aid. He said, "Keep going, the boy has appendicitis." They traveled by wagon until they reached a doctor. By that time the appendix had ruptured, and he was several weeks in hospital. The doctor said that he would be a long time recovering and may never be strong.

While he was recovering he went into the attic of his father's barn and found something his father had brought from the old country: an accordion. He pushed and pulled on the accordion until eventually sweet sounds came from the barn. That was Lawrence Welk. God has designs for all of us.

In 1970 Apollo 13 was spinning toward the moon. Suddenly they radioed to earth, "We are in trouble." Earth radioed to them, "Look out of the window and find a star." You are never lost if you fix your sight on God's creation.

Joe Frazier has always loved the Lord. He always said it was his mother's influence. In 1964 his great goal was the Olympic gold medal. The night before the gold medal fight he broke the thumb on his left hand. His main weapon was his left. That night he prayed using the phrase, "All things are possible through Christ."

He asked his trainer to strap his left thumb in his palm. The trainer told him that when he used the left he would pass out with pain. He told him to do it anyway. All through the fight he kept his left by his side. His German opponent was told to stay away from Frazier's left, so he never had to use it and won by three rounds.

Revival Sermon #2
Text: Acts 9:26–31   Paul's preaching tour

While in the military the preacher found a circular sent to some of the soldiers. It said, "Take the lock off your preacher's door and put bars on it. Cancel his membership at the country club. Cancel his engagements in local politics. Visit him in his cell and bring him food. Ask him, 'Is there any word from God?' If he does not look haggard from praying and reading the Bible, leave him. Return the next day and ask him, 'Is there any word from God?' If he looks haggard and says 'yes' he has done what he should." Every preacher should have time to be by himself to study. He carries a briefcase loaded with books to study wherever he goes.

Jeremiah's name if it is translated from Hebrew means "God shoots." Jeremiah was born into a holy priestly family. They lived in a special priestly village just outside of Jerusalem.

One day when Jeremiah was walking God called to him and told him he was to be a prophet. Jeremiah, like all of us, began to make excuses. God asked him to look down and tell him what he saw. He said, "An almond shoot." God said, "I ordain when that grows. I send rain and fertilize it. The same is with you. I ordained that you would be a prophet while you were still in the womb."

He walked a little farther and God said, "What do you see?" Jeremiah said, "A boiling cauldron tipped over from the north." God said, "That symbolizes the nations that will invade Israel from the north. I am going to send you out to prophesy to them. Do not prepare speeches. I will tell you what to say. If you do not say what I tell you I will confound you."

Jeremiah means "God shoots." God shot Jeremiah like a bullet from a gun. We must be fired from God's pistol.

From around A.D. 100 to 300 there was a spirit of evangelism in the new Christian church. People went through the Mediterranean world preaching the gospel. Between A.D. 300 and 600 there was a spirit of missionary zeal. Churches were being set up throughout the known world. Between A.D. 700 and 900 the church almost died. It became like a flickering wick in a wind. The trouble was that Christianity had become respectable. Christians were offered good responsible jobs, and conflicts grew up between their jobs and the church. They had to put so much time into their jobs that they could not attend church. The church almost died. The same thing is happening today.

During World War II three airmen crashed into the Pacific. They inflated their liferaft and took stock. The pilot took out his map and said that they were ten miles from an island, but it was infected with headhunters. They had no other choice but to head for the island. When they arrived they pulled their boat ashore and covered it with sand and leaves. They went into the jungle until they came to a cliff. The first man climbed the cliff, looked around, and jumped for joy. The captain yelled for him to keep a low profile. The second man climbed up and he too stood up fearlessly. By this time the captain was quaking in his boots, so he climbed up as quickly as possible. He looked around and saw a church. Then he knew that he was safe. We always know that we are safe when we see a church.

A few years ago there was a series of robberies in Ann Arbor, Michigan. All the robberies took place within four blocks. No money, jewelry, or valuables were stolen. The only things that were stolen were bread, milk, and canned goods. The robberies all took place when people were out to the movies or a show. The police staked out the area, and one night saw a shadowy figure leave a house. They followed the figure to the back door of a church where he entered and disappeared. They heard a noise in the steeple so they went up. There was a Chinese boy sitting in the corner surrounded by empty tins, bread wrappers, and milk cartons. He had come to this country but was lost and didn't know what to do. He was in the church but was lost. Many of us are in the church but lost.

Appendix B

Tale of Wallace Tyler, Version # 2

In this version of the tale, and the one in the main text, I use the following notations:

1. /—/ indicates a pause at the end of a phrase which is followed by an additional related phrase or an interruption into the phrase as in a parenthetical or augmentative interjection.
2. / . . ./ indicates a pause in the midst of a phrase which would ordinarily be written in prose as a single unbroken segment.
3. /;/ indicates a pause at the end of an effectively completed phrase which is followed by the beginning of a new thought.
4. /,/ indicates a pause which falls in such a way that in conventional orthography a comma would serve to mark off the phrase from what follows (grammatically more smooth than the phrases marked off by /—/).
5. /untabbed line break/ indicates a pause followed by a marker of narrative structural segment such as "and," "but."
6. /tabbed line break/ indicates a continuation without pause or segment break.
7. /[+]/ indicates that the line break does not coincide with a pause because the particle marker has been tacked onto the end of the breath-phrase instead of beginning the following breath-phrase.
8. /[*]/ indicates that the line break does not coincide with a pause because the breath-phrase contains two segments marked by a particle.
9. /(numeral)/ numbers each couplet consecutively.

   A lot of people could tell—tell stories and tell jokes—a lot of truth in
      some of them and a lot of . . . fiction . . . in some of them; there's a
      lot of things told around this section of country

I—I—one—one story in particular . . . that . . . is concerning a place
called Tate's Point—it's in the south end—was in the south end of
this county it's in another county now   (1)

And I lived there at one time
And the story I picked up . . . from conversation with older people
that older people had told them—it seemed like . . . the names is
right—Tyler—Wallace Tyler was in Baltimore harbor . . . in about
eighteen and four—possibly before that—with a schooner   (2)

And there come what they call a Baltimore waterfront fire
And they moved his vessel . . . down the wharf   (3)

And all the strongboxes they dealt in gold and silver then—traded in
gold and silver
And they put all their strongboxes in his boat to keep the fire from
getting them it was sweeping the waterfront
And of course they didn't have much fire department in those days
And, when they got his boat loaded, wind was in the northwest and
blowing hard
And he just put sail on to her and took off with all of those safes
And when daylight come, he was down the Chesapeake out of sight   (4)

And the first place he came after he come out of Chesapeake Bay the
first inlet was . . . what was known as . . . Cooper's inlet; he went
in that inlet . . . with his schooner
And went up Tate's Point creek   (5)

And he got afraid that the revenuers would get ahold of him
And he dumped all those safes overboard, in what was known as Gum
Cove   (6)

And, course he stayed there . . . for quite a while till he found out the
revenuers were not gonna get him
And he fished up those safes so this is the story I've heard   (7)

And I've . . . heard it from good authority . . . that he got gold and
silver from that [+]
And he bought . . . property down there [+]   (8)

And he owned six thousand acres—tracts of timber down there [+]
And this creek and along Tate's Point   (9)

And he had a hundred slaves at one time
And he farmed and he built three vessels . . . in that creek that sailed
to the West Indies [+]   (10)

[248]

And, brought back salt or whatever rum or whatever they had [+]
And, carried nails down to them [+]   (11)

And, run a general—general trading with the West Indies
And, Martinique, Bermuda [+]   (12)

And, those different islands down there
And when the war came on with the . . . he died in eigh . . . teen . . .
   and forty eight   (13)

But he had a grown son that took over—his name was . . . Hyram—
   Hyram Tyler
And he had a hundred slaves they had a hundred slaves there   (14)

And of course he'd sail these . . . boats to the West Indies from there
   and he had the captains that lived along the shore there—they had
   their homes
And he built those boats in that creek, from that—from that timber   (15)

And when the war come on between the states, he got his three boats
   in Oregon Inlet or Hatteras Inlet
And got 'em up this creek—wanted to save 'em [+]   (16)

But, this old Burnside come up there [+]
And, cleaned things up, for the Yankees—he took one of these was
   loaded with nails   (17)

And tried to run her up—run her up Whiskey Creek . . . to save
   her—run her up there and take the masts out of her and cover her
   over with bushes
And, maybe save her   (18)

But they caught him on the way over
And burnt him up—came with fire and burnt him up   (19)

And that was the end of her
[. . .]   (20)

But, Tate's Point has always been—I lived there from the time I was
   four years old till I was thirteen
And, it's always been a mystery to me how much of this is fiction and
   how much is the truth—there's a whole lot of truth in it   (21)

But, they say that when the Yankees come there they—to capture the
   place—they put his gold—he had two boxes two brass boxes, that
   he kept his money in—they put 'em down in the bottom of a well

[249]

And, after they were gone, course he fished it up I imagine they did—
   I've never heard they did fish it up   (22)

But, it was supposed to have been put down in the bottom of the
   wells—of a well
And, he was very wealthy till—till he died; of course he lost all of his
   slaves—they freed the slaves and they took off   (23)

And his sons he had three sons—I can't remember their names—
   they're all dead now
But they went to Kinston and started different—wholesale and retail
   places in Kinston—they had sufficient money   (24)

And they sold this property to a—a—Mildred Miles from Asbury Park
   New Jersey
And my dad went there as keeper of that property, to look out for
   the . . . place and she'd visit there maybe twice a year   (25)

And, they had—they had the first power boats in this section not
   maybe the first
But, among the first   (26)

And, we had a boat there, built in nineteen and six, it would . . .
   log . . . eleven-and-three-quarters miles an hour easy—in other
   words, pappa always . . . logged her at eleven-and-three-quarters
But she'd do fifteen—she'd do fifteen when he put the throttle on her (27)

And that was a gasoline engine that run her
And that was awfully high speed in them days—boat run . . . twelve
   miles an hour . . . back in nineteen and six was so fast it took two
   people to see her   (28)

Course it's different now—any little outboard'll run that speed
But we had the fastest boat there was in this section of country for
   years   (29)

References

Alland, Alexander Jr. 1977. *The Artistic Animal: An Inquiry into the Biological Roots of Art.* Garden City, N.Y.

——. 1983. *Playing with Form: Children Draw in Six Countries.* New York.

Armstrong, Robert P. 1971. *The Affecting Presence: An Essay in Humanistic Anthropology.* Urbana, Ill.

Arnold, Matthew. 1865. *Essays in Criticism.* London.

Aschenbrenner, Karl. 1959. "Aesthetic Theory—Conflict and Conciliation." *Journal of Aesthetics and Art Criticism* 18:90–108.

Baumgarten, Alexander. 1735. *Philosophicae de Nonnullis ad Poema Pertinentibus.* Halle. Trans. Karl Aschenbrenner and W. B. Hoelther as *Reflections on Poetry.* Berkeley, Calif. 1954.

Barry, Herbert. 1957. "Relationships between Child Training and the Pictorial Arts." *Journal of Abnormal and Social Psychology* 54:380–83.

Barthes, Roland. 1967. *Elements of Semiology.* Trans. Annette Lavers and C. Smith. London.

——. 1972. *Mythologies.* Trans. Annette Lavers. New York.

Bell, Clive. 1914. *Art.* London.

Blackmur, Richard P. 1952. *Language as Gesture.* New York.

Boas, Franz. 1927. *Primitive Art.* Oslo.

Brenneis, Donald. 1987. "Performing Passions: Aesthetics and Politics in an Occasionally Egalitarian Society." *American Ethnologist* 14:236–50.

Bright, William. 1980. "Coyote's Journey." *American Indian Culture and Research Journal* 4:21–48.

Brooks, Cleanth. 1947. *The Well Wrought Urn.* New York.

Carlyle, Thomas. 1828. "The State of German Literature." In *Works,* ed. H. D. Trail. 30 vols. London, 1896–99.

Carroll, Noël. 1986. "Art and Interaction." *Journal of Aesthetics and Art Criticism* 44:57–68.

Child, Irvin L., and Leon Siroto. 1965. "BaKwele and American Aesthetic Evaluations Compared." *Ethnology* 4:349–60.

Clifford, James, and George E. Marcus, eds. 1986. *Writing Culture: The Poetics and Politics of Ethnography.* Berkeley and Los Angeles.

[251]

References

D'Azevedo, Warren L. 1958. "A Structural Approach to Esthetics: Toward a Definition of Art in Anthropology." *American Anthropologist* 60:702–14.

D'Azevedo, Warren L., ed. 1973. *The Traditional Artist in African Societies.* Bloomington, Ind.

Deetz, James. 1967. *Invitation to Archeology.* Garden City, N.Y.

Devereux, George, and Weston LaBarre. 1961. "Art and Mythology." In Bert Kaplan, ed. *Studying Personality Cross-Culturally.* Evanston, Ill.

Dickie, George. 1971. *Aesthetics: An Introduction.* New York.

Douglas, Mary. 1966. *Purity and Danger: An Analysis of Concepts of Pollution and Taboo.* New York.

——. 1970. *Natural Symbols: Explorations in Cosmology.* New York.

Duncan, Hugh D. 1969. *Symbols and Social Theory.* New York.

Dundes, Alan. 1964. *The Morphology of North American Indian Folktales.* Helsinki.

Durkheim, Emile. 1915. *The Elementary Forms of the Religious Life.* Trans. Joseph Swain. New York.

Eichenbaum, Boris. 1926. "The Theory of the 'Formal Method.'" In *Russian Formalist Criticism: Four Essays,* ed. and trans. Lee T. Lemon and Marion J. Reis. Lincoln, Neb. (1965).

Eldridge, Richard. 1987. "Problems and Prospects of Wittgensteinian Aesthetics." *Journal of Aesthetics and Art Criticism* 45:251–61.

Fischer, John. 1961. "Art Styles as Cultural Cognitive Maps." *American Anthropologist* 63:79–93.

Forrest, John. 1983. "Why Do Duck Decoys Have Eyes?" *North Carolina Folklore Journal* 31:23–30.

Fry, Roger. 1920. *Vision and Design.* London.

Geertz, Clifford. 1957. "Ritual and Social Change: A Javanese Example." *American Anthropologist* 59:991–1012.

Glassie, Henry. 1975. *Folk Housing in Middle Virginia.* Knoxville, Tenn.

Gluckman, Max. 1954. *Rituals of Rebellion in South-East Africa.* Manchester.

——. 1955. *Custom and Conflict in Africa.* Oxford.

——. 1962. "Les Rites de passage." In *Essays on the Ritual of Social Relations,* ed. Max Gluckman. New York.

Gluckman, Max, ed. 1963. *Order and Rebellion in Tribal Africa.* New York.

Hall, Carrie A., and Rose G. Kretsinger. 1935. *The Romance of the Patchwork Quilt in America.* New York.

Hockett, Charles. 1958. *A Course in Modern Linguistics.* New York.

Hutcheson, Francis. 1725. *Inquiry into the Original of Our Ideas of Beauty and Virtue.* London.

Hymes, Dell. 1976. "Louis Simpson's 'The Deserted Boy.'" *Poetics* 5:119–155.

——. 1977. "Discovering Oral Performance and Measured Verse in American Indian Narrative." *New Literary History* 8:431–457.

Jaynes, Julian. 1976. *The Origin of Consciousness in the Breakdown of the Bicameral Mind.* Boston.

Jopling, Carol F., ed. 1971. *Art and Aesthetics in Primitive Societies: A Critical Anthology.* New York.

Kaeppler, Adrienne. 1967. "The Structure of Tongan Dance." Ph.D. diss., University of Hawaii, Honolulu.

Kant, Immanuel. 1790. *Kritik der Urteilskraft*. Berlin and Liebau.

Kaplan, Abraham. 1954. "Referential Meaning in the Arts." *Journal of Aesthetics and Art Criticism* 12:457–74.

Kennick, William E. 1958. "Does Traditional Aesthetics Rest on a Mistake?" *Mind* 67:317–34.

Lawlor, M. 1955. "Cultural Influences on Preferences for Designs." *Journal of Abnormal and Social Psychology* 61:690–92.

Leach, Edmund. 1976. *Culture and Communication: The Logic by Which Symbols Are Connected*. Cambridge, England.

Lévi-Strauss, Claude. 1963. *Structural Anthropology*. Trans. Claire Jacobson and Brooke Grundfest Schoepf. New York.

——. 1965. "Le Triangle culinaire." *L'Arc* 26:19–29.

——. 1966. *The Savage Mind*. Chicago.

——. 1969. *The Raw and the Cooked*. Trans. J. and D. Weightman. London.

Lomax, Alan. 1968. *Folk Song Style and Culture*. Washington, D.C.

McElroy, W. A. 1952. "Aesthetic Appreciation in Aborigines of Arnhem Land: A Comparative Experimental Study." *Oceania* 23:81–94.

Malraux, André. 1967. *Museum without Walls*. Trans. Stuart Gilbert and Francis Price. New York.

Mandelbaum, Maurice. 1965. "Family Relationships and Generalizations concerning the Arts." *American Philosophical Quarterly* 2:219–228.

Maquet, Jacques. 1986. *The Aesthetic Experience: An Anthropologist Looks at the Visual Arts*. New Haven, Conn.

Mauss, Marcel. 1924. *The Gift: Forms and Functions of Exchange in Archaic Societies*. Trans. Ian Cunnison. New York.

Merriam, Alan P. 1964. *The Anthropology of Music*. Evanston, Ill.

Mills, George. 1957. "Art: An Introduction to Qualitative Anthropology." *Journal of Aesthetics and Art Criticism* 16:1–17.

Morris, Charles W. 1939. "Esthetics and the Theory of Signs." *Journal of Unified Science (Erkenntniss)* 8:1–3, 131–50.

Needham, Rodney, ed. 1973. *Right and Left: Essays on Dual Symbolic Classification*. Chicago.

Osborne, Harold. 1970. *The Art of Appreciation*. London.

Otten, Charlotte M., ed. 1971. *Anthropology and Art: Readings in Cross-Cultural Aesthetics*. Austin, Tex.

Parker, DeWitt H. 1926. *The Analysis of Art*. New Haven, Conn.

Parsons, Talcott. 1951. *The Social System*. Glencoe, Ill.

Passmore, J. A. 1951. "The Dreariness of Aesthetics." *Mind* 60:318–35.

Peacock, James. 1968. *Rites of Modernization: Symbolic and Social Aspects of Indonesian Proletarian Drama*. Chicago.

——. 1971. "The Southern Protestant Ethic Disease." In *The Not So Solid South*. Ed. J. Kenneth Morland. Athens, Ga.

——. 1975. *Consciousness and Change: Symbolic Anthropology in Evolutionary Perspective* New York.

References

Preziosi, Donald. 1979. *The Semiotics of the Built Environment: An Introduction to Architectonic Analysis*. Bloomington, Ind.

Price, Kingsley B. 1953. "Is a Work of Art a Symbol?" *Journal of Philosophy* 50:485–503.

Price, Sally. 1984. *Co-Wives and Calabashes*. Ann Arbor, Mich.

Price, Sally, and Richard Price. 1980. *Afro-American Arts of the Suriname Rain Forest*. Berkeley, Calif.

Ransom, John Crowe. 1941. *The New Criticism*. Norfolk, Conn.

Redfern, Betty. 1983. *Dance, Art and Aesthetics*. Cambridge, England.

Redfield, Robert. 1941. *The Folk Culture of Yucatan*. Chicago.

——. 1947. "The Folk Society." *American Journal of Sociology* 42:293–308.

——. 1956. *Peasant Society and Culture*. Chicago.

Sims, Walter H. 1956. *Baptist Hymnal*. Nashville, Tenn.

Sorokin, Pitirim. 1957. *Social and Cultural Dynamics*. Boston.

Sperber, Dan. 1975. *Rethinking Symbolism*. Trans. Alice Morton. Cambridge, England.

Tate, Allen. 1968. *Essays on Four Decades*. Chicago.

Tedlock, Dennis. 1971. "On the Translation of Style in Oral Narrative." *Journal of American Folklore* 84:114–33.

——. 1977. "Toward an Oral Poetics." *New Literary History* 8:507–19.

Tejera, Victorino. 1965. *Art and Human Intelligence*. New York.

Tönnies, Ferdinand. 1887. *Gemeinschaft und Gesellschaft*. Trans. Charles Loomis as *Fundamental Concepts of Sociology*. New York (1940).

Tracey, Hugh. 1954. "The Social Role of African Music." *African Affairs* 53:234–41.

Turner, Victor. 1957. *Schism and Continuity in an African Society: A Study of Ndembu Village Life*. Manchester.

——. 1969. *The Ritual Process: Structure and Anti-Structure*. Ithaca.

Urmson, J. O. 1957. "What Makes a Situation Aesthetic?" *Proceedings of the Aristotelian Society*. 31:75–92.

Van Gennep, Arnold. 1960. *The Rites of Passage*. Trans. Monika Vizedom and Gabrielle Caffee. London.

Vivas, Eliseo, and Murray Krieger, eds. 1953. *The Problems of Aesthetics*. New York.

Walsh, Harry M. 1971. *The Outlaw Gunner*. Cambridge, Md.

Weber, Max. 1958. *The Protestant Ethic and the Spirit of Capitalism*. Trans. Talcott Parsons. New York.

Weitz, Morris. 1950. *Philosophy of the Arts*. Cambridge, Mass.

——. 1956. "The Role of Theory in Aesthetics." *Journal of Aesthetics and Art Criticism* 15:27–35.

——. 1977. *The Opening Mind*. Chicago.

Whiting, John W. M., and Irvin L. Child. 1953. *Child Training and Personality*. New Haven, Conn.

Wittgenstein, Ludwig. 1953. *Philosophical Investigations*. Oxford.

Wordsworth, William. 1800. "Preface." In Samuel Taylor Coleridge and William Wordsworth. *Lyrical Ballads, with Other Poems*. 2d ed. 2 vols. London.

Ziff, Paul. 1984. *Antiaesthetics*. Dordrecht, The Netherlands.

Index

Aesthetic community, 217
Aesthetic forms, ix, 19–21, 26–33, 217–218. *See also* Formal analysis and *entries for individual forms*
Aesthetic-incorporative relations, 208–217
Aesthetics:
  in anthropological theory, 20, 24–25
  definitions, 20–21
  of men, 126–127, 170, 190–191, 193, 231–232
  in philosophical theory, 19–24, 33
  of women, 97, 126–127, 193, 202, 232
  See also Affect; Art; Critical judgment; Disinterested appreciation; Formal analysis; Multigenre analysis; Quantitative analysis; Sensory perception; Single-genre analysis; Symbolic analysis
Affect, 21–22, 188, 223, 229, 231–232
Alcohol, 72, 105, 125, 137–138, 157–159, 186, 188–190, 198, 215–216, 234
American Legion, 189–191, 198–199
Animals. *See* Natural environment
Anthropological method. *See* Aesthetics, in anthropological theory; Field methods
Architecture, 31
  church, 115–120, 218–219
  house, 46–58
Armstrong, Robert, 32
Art, 25–30, 96
Asbury Park, N.J., 250

Baltimore, 176, 180–181, 183–184, 196, 248
Baptism, 140–141, 147–149, 200–201, 203–205, 230

Barry, Herbert, 29
Baumgarten, Alexander, 22
Bible, 124–125, 132, 145. *See also* Biblical references
Bible class. *See* Church
Biblical references:
  Acts 4:32–35:11, 128; 6:1–8:3, 128; 8:27–40, 148; 9:26–31, 144, 244
  Amos 7:7–9, 238; 8:1–3, 238
  1 Cor. 11:23–26, 151
  2 Cor. 2:10–11, 240
  Eph. 6:10–16, 144–145
  Exod. 14:10–13, 144, 243; 32:1–6, 125
  Gen. 3:1–13, 125
  Isa. 11:6, 125
  Job 1:6–8, 240
  John 1:12, 237; 1:35–42, 235; 3:1–16, 144, 146; 6:5–13, 234; 12:1–8, 125
  1 Kings 14:1–7, 236; 17, 230
  Luke 4:1–4, 230; 5:4–9, 136; 9:10–17, 230; 12:22–31, 230
  Mark 6:30–44, 230
  Matt. 4:1–4, 230; 6:25–30, 136, 230; 14:13–21, 230; 16:13–20, 144
  Mic. 5:2, 136
  1 Pet. 2:8, 240
  Phil. 4:10, 144, 243
  Ps. 66:1–2, 157; 119:105, 128
Blinds, 160–164
Boas, Franz, 22, 26, 28
Boats:
  construction, 107–108, 186
  shad, 107
  skiffs, 2, 108–109
  yachts, 107
Bridge clubs, 37, 99

Library of Congress Cataloging-in-Publication Data

Forrest, John.
  Lord I'm coming home.

  (Anthropology of contemporary issues)
  Bibliography: p.
  Includes index.
  1. Ethnology—North Carolina. 2. Aesthetics—Social aspects—North Carolina. 3.
North Carolina—Social life and customs. I. Title. II. Series.
F265.A1F67 1988   301'.09756   88–47728
ISBN 0–8014–2146–2 (alk. paper)
ISBN 0–8014–9483–4 (pbk. : alk. paper)